Bhagavat Gita 101
Vibrant Vintage Verses

Bhagavat Gita 101
Vibrant Vintage Verses

HullasaBehera

BLACK EAGLE BOOKS
Dublin, USA | Bhubaneswar, India

 Black Eagle Books
USA address:
7464 Wisdom Lane
Dublin, OH 43016

India address:
E/312, Trident Galaxy, Kalinga Nagar,
Bhubaneswar-751003, Odisha, India

E-mail: info@blackeaglebooks.org
Website: www.blackeaglebooks.org

First International Edition Published by
Black Eagle Books, 2025

BHAGAVAT GITA 101
Vibrant Vintage Verses
by Hullasa Behera
3-D-3, Jeevanabima Nagar
Maitri Vihar, Bhubaneswar, Odisha,
India, Pin-751023

Copyright © **Hullasa Behera**

All rights reserved. No part of this publication may be reproduced, stored in a retrieval system, or transmitted, in any form or by any means, electronic, mechanical, photocopying, recording or otherwise without the prior permission of the publisher.

Cover & Interior Design: Ezy's Publication

ISBN- 978-1-64560-798-4 (Paperback)

Printed in the United States of America

Dedicated to
Ipsita Nayak, daughter-in-law &
Goutam Sankar Behera, eldest son
For their forever dedication
- Author

Acknowledgements

I do not know how much exactly I owe to whom in the preparation of this book but I certainly know that I owe a lot to a lot many sources, individuals who have rendered their aid and advice ungrudgingly, gladly. William Shakespeare said in his famous tragedy, Hamlet, "Neither a borrower nor a lender be..." But in writing a book, one would borrow and burgle. If one is fortunate enough, one would lend leniently and indiscriminately to a writer.

First of all, I express my incalculable indebtedness to search engines, websites, YouTube, WhatsApp and other digital devices that have enriched my knowledge and from which I have borrowed fearlessly, with full knowledge and intention or fortuitously. You may call it intellectual pickpocketing, not plagiarism; if you insist on calling it plagiarism, please call it playful or pious plagiarism.

I am grateful to Shri Pratap Chandra Sahu, State Programme Coordinator, Odisha, of Women and Child Development Department, Odisha, Bhubaneswar, for his assistance in typesetting and lay-outing in part.

I cordially thank my wife Associate Professor Dr Renubala Mahakud, retired, for her sincere criticism and guidance in the writing of the book.

My fabulous filial indebtedness is to my youngest son, Tirthankara Krushna, nicknamed Jisu, who assisted greatly in typesetting and computer nitty-gritty.

And my reverent thanks to the publisher BLACK EAGLE BOOKS for agreeing to laying their hands on the whitest of books, namely, Bhagavat Gita.

- Author

Publisher's Note

We, as publisher, are new to Hullasa Behera, the writer; though he is right there in the job or journey since 1980s. So, this could be called old wine in new bottle, or better, a good wine needs no bush. But this book has nothing to do with wine except for the solitary reference to it in The Pardoner's Tale by Geoffrey Chaucer to highlight lust, greed for a good amount of gold that sends the three evil, fake, false friends to hell. This exemplifies the versality and vibrancy of the author who can incorporate Valmiki, Vyas, Kalidas, Charak, Chaucer, Shakespeare, Carlyle, Kavir, Manikkvackar, Tolstoy, Tagore, Tilak, Vinoba, Jainism, Buddhism, Khandagiri, Udayagiri caves, Konark, Singhnath temple, Kharavela, Bhojaraja et al in the course of this Gita work, wonderfully blending, winding, binding the austere, august, abstract Gita text with contemporarily acceptable, agreeable technique, style, language, lucidity.

His acquaintance with and scholarship in Bhagavat Gita could be assessed from his reflection 26 years ago in his first book on Gita,

"I am born into a rich and pleasant tradition and environment of the Gita like millions of other Indians who have a rural India background by birth and bring-up. *********In leisure and serious studies, in rituals and festivals, in teaching the kid alphabets and listening to the wandering monk, what comes in handy and unfailingly is the Gita. It is the Gita, and the Gita alone, that matters to them; nothing more nothing less. The Gita guided them to realise the grandest and soundest truths of worldview and universe view. Like all other villagers, Digambara would go his fields on day-break only to return at night-fall. Domestic chores kept him confined to home till 10 PM. He would be free, after a modest dinner, for his daily ritual of Gita recital only after ten ****** Karttika, Laxmidhara, Daitary, Nidhi, Shesadeva and myself, all adolescents and high school students, were perhaps the right ones that he searched for. At the outset, he persuaded and pampered us to participate in the Gita readings and recitals. More out of respect for an elderly villager than out of any respect for Gita, we obliged him. He would read out aloud the slokas in Sanskrit and their Odia renderings in nine-lettered two-feet verse form. Half-asleep and half-awake, but totally oblivious of what he was reading or explaining, we would be reciting the Odia verse form. Perhaps our tender speech organ produced the requisite resonance and rhyme appropriate to the solemn Gita recital. He would be enthralled and elevated to a higher plane. He would cheer us up and read and re-read more excitedly, passionately. His emotions and intonations would drive sleep out of our tired eyes. We would sit erect and pay attention to his voice and gesticulations. Attentive and conscious, our recital in unison would be clearer and sweeter. The still and cool night air of the sleepy, dark village on the bank of Mahanadi would be echoing our sweet, solemn recital."

[Pages 6-8, 50 Flowers from Bhagavat Gita: A Solace Against Frightening Materialism, 1998: by the author]

Appeal and Apology

While writing a book on the venerable Bhagavat Gita that literally means the Celestial Lyric or God's Song, I am inclined and obliged to appeal to your good sense, sensibilities and sympathy to go through the book with interest and without bias. I am apologetic because the Gita is unique as a book, as a theme and any discussion or analysis thereon demands depth and wisdom that I definitely do not have. Yet, I have ventured upon this anthology to satisfy my outstanding urge to write my second treatise on the Bhagavat Gita and to satisfy, to some extent, your curiosity to read a book on Gita that is novel in treatment, style and technique, and reads like a novel; not a dry, dull, abstract, theological discourse as most books usually are.

I am apologetic for several omissions and commissions that may have crept in out of my ignorance, arrogance or inadvertence. Here I means me 85 per cent and the printer, the publisher 15 per cent. Then, why this adventure or misadventure? Because, our ancient adage saves authors, little-learned but enthusiastic like me for that matter, with a shield,

Bhimasyapi ranebhango munerapi matibhramah
Yadi shuddham ashuddham va mama dosha na vidyate.

Bhima, the most powerful Pandava, at times fails in

fighting; the contemplative sages also sometimes confuse; hence, my shortfalls and mistakes, if any, may be excused, and the piece be read and interpreted in the correct perspective. This simple saying stresses that the reader is, should be wiser than the author so that the forner can correct the inaccuracies and appreciate the interpretation, exposition of the author in proper perspective.

What exactly is Bhagavat Gita? Bhagawan Krishna delivered a long and learned speech to Arjuna, the ace, incomparable archer of the day, who, all of a sudden, shuddered to think that he would kill his kith and kin, elders and superiors for the superfluous gain of a lost kingdom. Krishna cleared his confusion, dispelled his doubts and instilled in him the primacy, priority, pivotality and philosophy of "present assignment" in particular and "duty" in general. Arjuna asked scores of questions, raised reasonable riddles and Krishna answered them intelligently, eminently, eloquently, elegantly, in an equanimous, tranquil manner. As such, Gita is the dialogue between Krishna and Arjuna. Krishna, some say, took 45 minutes to tell Gita. While 574 slokas are uttered by Krishna, Arjuna spoke 84 verses. That Gita is great is not said by Krishna, although He has said in chapter X, verse 37 that Vyasa, the Gita composer, is the primus inter pares sage.

Gita has been greatly glorified by a great many sages, scholars, critics, activists, reformers, researchers, teachers, preachers—Indian as well as foreign—from Shankaracharya, Ramanuja, Gnaneshwar, Aurobindo, Vivekananda to J K Krishnamurthy, Anni Besant, Max Muller, Edwin Arnold, S Radhakrishnan etc. It was Krishna's lullaby to Arjuna, not induce the latter to sleep but to incite, excite him to fight, to the call of duty, to awaken him to the importance, inevitability, inescapability of duty, one's duty. It chimes with popular Sanskrit moral,

Akrtuty naiva karttavyam pranatyagoapisamsisthe
Na cha krutyam parityajyameshah dharmah santanah.

A human should not do a forbidden act even for the sake of his/her life nor should skip, shrink from doing a prescribed duty even at the cost of his/her life. It is the eternal, Sanatana Dharma.

Dharma is socially, individually esteemed highly since ancient times. It is believed that Gita is the best script on Dharma. Eternal, Sanatana Dharma.

In the moralising message quoted above from Panchatantra, not dharma, but karttavya, duty or dos and don'ts, is emphasized. Gita speaks of the paramount importance of duty, karttavy. Not karttavya only but conduct, character of human is emphasised, eulogised, admired in Gita. Thus, Gita, is the compendium of karttavya and conduct.

Nevertheless, Gita is glorified, lauded as the sacred text of/on dharma. Not that Gita is alien to, antithetical, anathematic to or incompatible with dharma, though dharma is alluded to infrequently. When dharma is referred to, it is referred to glowingly, eloquently, importantly, intricately, as among others, in the verses reproduced below,

Sarvadharman parityajya mamekam sharanam vraj
Aham twam sarvapapebhyoh mokshayishyami ma shuch.
[18/66]
Give up all dharmas and surrender to Me, I shall save you from all papas, do not worry!
Shreyan swadharmo vigunah paradharmat swanusthitat
Swadharme nidhanam shreyah paradharmo bhayavahah.
[3/35]

Even if defective, it is worthwhile to stand firm in one's own dharma. It is better death in one's own dharma than opting out for other's dharma, because of the dreadful consequences of the paradigm shift.

Shreyan swadharmo vigunah paradharmat swanusthitat Swabhavaniyatam karma kurvannopnoti kilvisham. [18/47]

It is better being in, doing with one's own dharma despite defects, if any, than embracing other's dharma however well established. Because when you perform your duties according to your innate dictates, you acquire no fault, sin.

Balam valavatam chaham kamaragavivarjitam Dharmavirudho bhooteshu kamoasmi bharatarshabh.[7/11]

I am force of the forceful but devoid of desire and love, but I cause desire in the people opposed to dharma.

It is, therefore, natural that most ascetics, critics, scholars, fanatics call Gita a/the dharma grantha, the book of faith/religion. Gita encompasses crux of creeds and is a superior spiritual text that is meant to refine and purify manners, minds, mentality of men and women of all times, all places, all ages, all sexes, all colours, all creeds, all credentials, all characters. The emphasis on spiritualism in Gita is less than the stress on suitable socio-psychological earthly life. Gita is meant for men and women here and now more than for after-life, better future life. Gita stresses on duty; not abdication of duty, renunciation of duty, abhorring, abjuring worldly duties. Cool, comfortable, concentrative work characterises humans. As cognitive, conscious being unlike multitude other living things, humans have to discharge their duties with diligence and dignity.

Bal Gangadhar Tilak and Vinoba Bhave are two stalwarts of Indian freedom movement. Both were outstanding scholars of orientalism and oriental studies and scriptures. Both were ardent followers of Bhagavat Gita and both have written books on Gita. Tilak accords top priority to karma yoga and avers that karma yoga is superior to jnana yoga and bhakti yoga. Tilak was as revolutionary in political activities as in Gita interpretation. Vinoba, the man of God, dealt with Gita in the beaten-track manner without mannerism but with magnificent, mellifluent style, treatment and annotation. Light and lucid, his Gita analysis goes deep into the reader's heart, mind and consciousness. I have devoted some pages to these two to awaken interest of modern general readers in their Gita treatise. Mahatma Gandhi was all admiration for Gita. He, like Vinoba, compares Gita to mother. Gandhi's interpretation of verse 66, chapter 18 is enlightening. He said that one may read the first three chapters of Gita if one does not have enough time. If one cannot have time to read these three chapters, it is okay if he reads chapter III only.

As I am an ardent admirer of all these three as far as discussion on Bhagavat Gita is concerned, as I am myself convinced of karma as the cardinal principle of Bhagavat Gita, I place importance on verses of Gita that talk of karma, karttavya, duty. Choice of slokas is whimsical but not chaotic. I start with chapter 1, verse 1 to be followed by chapter 18, verse 78. The number of slokas chosen from different chapters are unequal. While 2 verses from chapter 10 make the minimal presence, chapter 1 fares no better with only 3 verses. Chapter 2 and 5 contribute 10 verses each to this compendium, while chapters 17 and 18 do with 12 verses each. Other chapters do not bother about their shares, though with 9 verses chapter 16 has a good score. As aforesaid, slokas do not come serially, but they are stitched like in a garland. This new fashion may frustrate the fastidious few but be likeable to the novice and the scholarly in accordance with the old adage, "Variety is the spice of life." Fanciful and fashionable that I have become, I have incorporated several folktales, tales, legends, lyrical poems, historical events to facilitate understanding and appreciation of the slokas better and quicker, to make the exposition appealing and earthly, to make the book read like a novel or short story collection despite retaining of Gita's originality, spirituality, rich epic and puranic quality.

Initially, I planned to discuss 75 verses of Bhagavat Gita in this book to commemorate the 75th Independence Day celebration, the Platinum Jubilee celebration of Indian Independence. But as I proceeded, things went haywire. Gita is live-wire. Once you touch it, you think it, you work it; you do not know the shock and awe that awaits you. When you want to write, when you are up and doing to write; you fumble, you stumble, you tumble. Ironically, once you just want to while away some indolent, indifferent moments by jotting down something on the desktop, you go on writing, you cannot stop writing. That is why and how I arrived at 101, while I planned to write on 75 verses. Not bad!

On intending to write on 75 verses of Bhagavat Gita, I have to read, reread, ruminate, rummage, search, research, write and rewrite for four years by fits and starts, occasionally with tough and tight sits and thoughts. Finally, I have finished the book with 101 verses. I have been enormously enriched by the intellectual, spiritual richness and resplendence, beauty and tranquillity of Bhagavat Gita.

Now, the book, this upahaara, this flower is on your hands. You may like it, love it and pocket it permanently or sniff at it, scoff at it, molest it and throw it—as you like, as you please. Both are equal and same for me, for I wrote with the motto, the message in mind,

"Karmanyevadhikaraste ma phalesu kadachana."
It applies to you equally well when you read.

In the end, my unending request is--: praise me profusely if the form, focus, fashion is in fettle; but blame me scantily, thriftly for my pitfalls, faux pas, faults.

May you be amply blessed;
May you simply bless me!

Hullasa Behera,
Author

Buddha Jayanti,
May 23, Bhubaneswar, Odisha, India

The Index

Serial Number	Contents	Page Number
	Preface	23
one	Whilst I sing, I am a King, Although a poor blind Boy	41
two	To tell the truth, Did Sanjay tell the truth?	45
Three	Did Gita go beyond Arjuna's intellectual antennae?	48
Four	Got rid of doubt-trap, stable and able, I shall abide by You!	52
Five	Arjuna saw the seesaw- own people arrayed against own people.	55
Six	courage, not cowardice; submission, not obstinance- Are friends guide and guru?	58
Seven	Are we born again and again ad infinitum?	60
Eight	No problem, you must die and must take rebirth!	63
Nine	Your song sweetened my ears- My declarations sweetened your ears- Is there anything more?	65
Ten	Ego? Go, go, go!	70
Eleven	Fault of fratricide, sin of amicicide	73
Twelve	Commit a sin to get rid of many a sin?	78
Thirteen	Pass or fail is equal As Yoga would tell.	92
Fourteen	Not the idle or inactive But the up and doing is yogi, is sannyasi.	96
Fifteen	What is in a name? That which we call a rose, By any other name would smell as sweet.	101

Sixteen	What is in a name? His Highness Shrimant Rajashri Shivaji VI Chhatrapati Maharaj Sahib Rao Bahadur Is incurably mad	109
Seventeen	Plague on you, rogue Rand and Ayerst!	116
Eighteen	Jnana- Yoga there is, yes; Bhakti-Yoga there is, yes. Who says not?But	122
Nineteen	Jail or hell, Vinoba, tell Gita, tell!	125
Twenty	Thou alone, Thou alone, Thou alone	130
Twenty-one	Pundit and prostitute- Father of sin: have you seen?	138
Twenty-two	Man is mortal- Pundit's goat is not!	148
Twenty-three	My witness? Yes, Raghunath ji!	158
Twenty-four	Mithyachara sa ucchyate…. You are not one certainly!	162
Twenty-five	What a shame to be a giver or doner!	166
Twenty-six	Father feasts on flesh of son, as he is Karna.	172
Twenty-seven	Vali and Vaman- Dwarf and demon- What's our lesson?	179
Twenty-eight	How much land does a man need?	187
Twenty-nine	All that glitters is not gold: Gilded tombs do worms enfold	192
Thirty	Nitai, who pulled up my ladder?	198
Thirty-one	O, come stealing jackfruit!	207
Thirty-two	O pundit! Why don't you give Me My coconut?	213
Thirty-three	Why God after all asks of or accepts paltry or pitiable articles from us?	217
Thirty-four	Upahaara and shraddha	219
Thirty-five	Flowers are your daughters, aren't they?	225

Thirty-six	They[gods] show more care for us than we do for ourselves	227
Thirty-seven	Live life king size	234
Thirty-eight	Buddham sharanam gachhami	237
Thirty-nine	Speech is silvern, silence is golden Apriyasya cha pathyasya vaktaa shrotaa cha durlabhah	241
Forty	The food that is good is Ayuhsattvalarogyas-ukhapritivivardhanh	245
Forty-one	He is the fire to consume your food	248
Forty-two	*Root bhook, Hit bhook, Mit bhook*	252
Forty-three	Yuktaharaviharasya yuktachestaya karmasu the golden mean	255
Forty-four	The more He eats, the hungrier He becomes!	258
Forty-five	Trividham narakyasyedam dwaram nashana-matmanah	264
Forty-six	Sadbhavapratipannanam vanchane kim vidgadhatam?	266
Forty-seven	Who else is there like me?	272
Forty-eight	If there is no God, who created the world?	275
Forty-nine	Who is God?	277
Fifty	Hell is empty and all the devils are here.	284
Fifty-one	Born you be must innumerable times.	283
Fifty-two	Lead kindly light amid the encircling gloom.	287
Fifty-three	Flight of the Light	290
Fifty-four	Where do you go when you go? Flower falls off: scent travels.	292
Fifty-five	Let us, then, be up and doing, With a heart for any fate;	295
Fifty-six	From death row to kingship- possible?	298
Fifty-seven	Everyone is conduit.	304
Fifty-eight	He is Kaala- how cruel?	305
Fifty-nine	Yasoda, Akura, Arjuna- how do they compare?	307
Sixty	Who is pious, who is paapi?	310

Sixty-one	Kaala- the killer of creatures.	315
Sixty-two	Do you act or made to act?	317
Sixty-three	Do sattvic win trophies?	320
Sixty-four	Uneasy lies the head that wears a crown	323
Sixty-five	Even in sports, you have sattvic, rajasic and tamasic?	327
Sixty-six	Good and bad: He is all	329
Sixty-seven	But friendship is a nobler thing- When I had money, money, O!	333
Sixty-eight	The Pardoner's Tale Go to hell! O they were friends all!	344
Sixty-nine	Pittuvani Ammayar and Vaigai flood- A Friend in need: the cool Coolie- Came all the way to Puri to be Witness.	347
Seventy	Kavir and Kamal, father and son- saint or thief?	356
Seventy-one	Saga and story of Konark- sacrificing son for clan. After you the deluge, Munja?	365
Seventy-two	Who does HE like? Who is not afraid of nor fearful.	384
Seventy-three	Shun all isms to be shorn of sins The path of surrender strewn with suffering. Set the mind and be Brahma!	389
Seventy-four	Who are ferried across the ocean of Death?	.399
Seventy-five	Does God give *papa* to people? No eulogy, No elegy. Let us close, happily, freely.	407

Number of the Sloka and of the Adhyaya written in Devanagari script

Sl No.	Number of Adhyaya	Number of Sloka
1	I	1, 38, 39
2	II	7, 27, 2, 3, 38, 47, 48, 13, 22, 12
3	III	24, 19, 6, 12
4	IV	5, 7, 8
5	V	2,7,8,9,10,11,14,15,23,28
6	VI	1,5,6,16,17,30
7	VII	10, 11,14,19
8	VIII	6,7,8,16
9	IX	18,26,34
10	X	34,36
11	XI	28,29,30,32,33
12	XII	5,13,15,16,6,7
13	XIII	22, 23
14	XIV	16,17,18
15	XV	8,9,14
16	XVI	7,8,13,14,15,16,18,19,21
17	XVII	4,4,6,8,9,10,14,15,16,20,21,22
18	XVIII	56,57,59,60,61,62,63,65,66,72,73,78

Preface

Another book on the famous and popular Bhagavat Gita could be least expected or welcome. So, the writer who has ventured on the voyage of navigating the vast, veritable Gita Ocean or perennial, clear, captivating stream of Bhagavat Gita needs must mention of his mind, motive and madness, as may seem to some, in undertaking the job, shouldn't he?

It is not long ago that the go of the world was lockdown; the world was agonised with the ogre of lock-down. It was individuals' luck down; it was mankind's luck down; it was enjoyment, entertainment, employment's luck down. It looked as if humanity's hopes and highness were locked down; as if human society's luck was locked down, was hibernated hopelessly. But everything was not locked down. If down, not out.

It was imperative that people would lock themselves in the safety and solitude of their homes, and hum day and night upon the humdrum of the recent past, the dread and danger of the Covid -19 scare, the good old days, sweet memories, sensitive and sensational happenings, old friends, old films, old music, old classics. People were persuaded and pressured to talk and chat with kids, colleagues, classmates, clubgoers. People reverted to the three Rs, i.e., Reading, Writing and 'Rithmetic.

I sailed in the same boat as the many millions of Indians were doing. I was a member of the mindboggling multitude of men and women sailing in a big, beautiful ship that might sink any time impacted by the uncertain climate in her uncharted course. Covid-19 caused colossal terror and trepidations in the placid ambience of pre-pandemic days of the world. O to the bedevilling, woebegone Covid days! How I wish the days never came!

The days, nonetheless, came. The covid-19 days came. Terrible psychic terror struck me as it did many others everywhere in the world.

II

I tried as much as I could to spend the punitive time with a positive perspective despite the horror of Covid- 19 cloud hovering overhead. I abided by the Corona- specific advisory minutely and mindfully. As I was not deeply disturbed by distressing news about Covid spread and prevalence, so was I immune to the innumerable rumours on enhancing immunity by doing such and such things. I was hopeful that sooner or later scientists and medicos would find a solution to the horrendous human health hazard called Corona. Yet, days and nights were unbearably long and lingering.

Painfully unbearable was the eerie silence in the small but beautiful Samanta Chandra Sekhara College, Puri, campus colony where I stayed then. Children did not come out to go to school or to play. I was deprived of the pleasure of cutting a joke with them or of teasing them to bouts of laughter. Neighbours, especially women, kept indoors infallibly. My plight of not teasing nor talking to them progressed pitiably. Neighbourhood children, women and adults as well avoided me like hell. Should they see me, they slithered silently, as if we are rank strangers! Or as if I was spying on them on behalf of an enemy country! Should I try to talk to them over mobile phone, I could not, because they were talking to their relatives, friends far off and near, most of the time.

I talked to my friends, relatives, ex-colleagues, ex-classmates as much as I could. The talking and chatting was depressing and discouraging since everyone sang the same ballad about Corona. Nonetheless, the exchange of ideas and apprehensions was reliving. Jokes and nonsense in conversation with friends was a whiff of fresh air in the demoralising despondent atmosphere.

That was not enough to consume the unending time available. I read some books, especially classics as much as I can lay my hands on. The vast volumes did not hold me hostage that much as they did decades ago. The culprit was the advancing age and the cataract-removed waning eyesight. Watching TV every now and then to be apprised of current status of Corona pandemic; the plight and problems of migrant labourers, of Indian students and travellers abroad, due to sudden and almost wholesale lockdown; and the measures taken by the government etc. consumed some time. Films in Hindi and Odia, serialised stories and saga shows kept me engaged well and for a good deal of time.

III

Nonetheless, time hanged like an autumnal cloud that did not disperse nor burst in showers, but forced one to keep indoors, involuntarily, indignantly. It was time to do something; not to waste time but to utilise time, to employ time to harvest golden crops on barren land.

Writing attracted me from boyhood, studentship, though that is the general hobby or pleasurable pastime of most adolescents and students sixty years or so ago. Later on, I have bitterly failed to follow writing as a pastime or career. Nevertheless, I laid my hands on writing in the thick and thin of my Odisha Administrative Service career. The first Odia novel titled "Palabhuta" [Scarecrow] was published in 1987 by Books and Books, Cuttack. Thereafter, I penned and published books, including one on Bhagavat Gita, namely, **50 Flowers from Bhagavat Gita: A Solace against Frightening Materialism**, published by Pustaka Mahal, Delhi, in 1998. Even then, during the cursing Corona course, penning a book did not please or pamper me to ease the itching and pinching unease. The time was terrible, atrociously agonising, arbitrarily allotted to our lot or awarded as sentence by an injudicious judgement. I was no exception, even though I maintained marvellous cool and composure, and persuaded and prevailed upon friends and acquaintances to keep cool and keep up spirits because the cause of the worldwide curse in the guise of Covid-19 would be cleared in the course of time; not in decades and years but in days and months.

Like many casual, cosmetic counsellors, I was utterly bitter within contrary to the counsels I rendered and could find no way to come out of the turbulent whirlpool in my mind, moods and manners. It was excruciating, and inescapable, lasting ad infinitum, it appeared.

But. Bad times bless us, to us, all of us. In ignorance

or negligence, we may disregard or dismiss such blessing. "Uneasy lies the head that wears a crown**'" said Shakespeare. You can rewrite it "Uneasy lies the head that wears a frown". Only because we fume and frown during the bad times, we do not count the blessings adversity hides behind the smokescreen of unease, obstruction, disadvantage. The savant looks around and within from the adversarial vantage with vivacious visage. During such Covid reign of terror and trepidation, once it dawned upon me that I was in a very same vexatious vortex as was Surendra some six decades ago. He came out, why not I?

IV

Surendra Chaudhury hails from Tunapura, a riverbank village on the north bank of Mahanadi, about 3 KMs downstream Singhanatha temple on the beautiful, small, riparian island opposite Gopinathapur on north bank and Baideswara on south bank. Lord **Singhanatha** is an ancient phallic idol of lord **Shiva** seated pretty in the small, sandy island shadowed by a dwarfish, pyramidic hill of black and grey, hard, sedimentary rocks on west and south, well-knit and neatly protecting the island from Mahanadi flood ravages year after year.

The small stone temple, marvel of a monument, is exuberantly crafted with exquisite stone carvings of puranic stories and saga, erotic sceneries and exciting drawings, musical instruments and dancers and danseuses, warriors and wrestlers, trees and creepers, snakes and sambars, langurs and lions, chariots and horses, and images of gods and goddesses...In her remarkable book, Stone Temples of India, author Vidya Ahuja, speaks of the temple being an eighth century structure. And the oldest stone temple of Bharata.

Mahanadi has dried up. Almost dead nowadays. But it was one of the most prominent and turbulent rivers of Bharata, causing irreparable loss to agriculture, horticulture, livestock; mud, wooden and thatched structures, household articles and agricultural implements in the riverside villages when in high floods. And floods came year after year; once, twice, three times or more a year. Year after year, the riparian villagers, almost all peasants and tillers of fertile and fallow soil, nominal, marginal and small farmers, raised kharif crops in chime with the onset of monsoon. The paddy stalks grew well as much due to the fertile, alluvial soil as to the laborious toil of the tillers, the sons of the soil.

But…. Floods come in Mahanadi and the stalks sulking underwater for 1,2,3,4,5,6,7…days die lamentable death. Then usually, floods go. Farmers rush afield in mud and slough, patchy water pools and shallow potholes, to see the devastation and to sigh! The multi-purpose river valley project at Hirakuda in Sambalpur district of Odisha with the globally longest earthen dyke constructed in early 1950s eased the recurring ruinous spates of Mahanadi. Of late, dozens of dams on Mahanadi and her tributaries upstream Hirakuda in Chhattisgarh have made floods in Odisha few and far between.

That year, there was incessant rains for about a week in the Mahanadi catchment areas upstream and downstream. Then rains stopped, say abruptly, and pre-autumn sunny season seemed to have arrived. Rains stopped but Mahanadi swelled. Swelled initially slowly and steadily. Then, as usual, rapidly and raucously. The muddy, greyish purple flood water gushed day and night with large and small dead and live trees, branches, bushes, leaves, fronds, flowers mostly dried and dead, on her burgling, ballooning, burgeoning breast. Once a while, a dead or live deer or jackal, goat or buffalo, snake or lizard, a cot or a mat, rags or rotten crops, broken utensils or new articles be seen floating on the fleeting flood.

Floods have subsided. Things went on as usual, notwithstanding foamy, light grey water with strong current running day and night with a murmuring melody of its own. Who has the time or ears to hear the sweet song of full-bodied, partly-subsided flooded water of Mahanadi? The villagers bathed in the mish mash muddy water. Womenfolk forked that bloody muddy water to fill the brass, aluminium or earthen pitchers to cater to the drinking water needs at home.

Maidens swam and played hide and seek under water, and giggled despite watchful, reproachful eyes of elders, men and women. While taking their leisurely, pleasurable bath, the peasant lasses were immerged in plentiful mirth, forgetting for the present the deprivation they are drowned in their homes back home.

Boys and students have their fun and fantasy to the fullest measure. The school-going higher-class students like Surendra count the flood water bath as a memorable moment, mirthful event. The muddy bloody flood water with strong currents and dangerous eddies, foam bubbles and under water quicksand, are attractions of a unique kind to riparian adolescents and teens to show their fortitude and finesse in swimming, playing wild water sport, and cutting rustic vulgar jokes. Swimming skill and stamina manifests their manliness. The more able-bodied and daring the youth, the more adept he is in swimming against current to the applaud and astonishment of his peers and the sight-seers.

Surendra stood out as a swimmer of the first water. Well-built and agile that he is, he surpasses his classmates and playmates in extra- curricular activities, though a so-so student in classwork and curriculum. That year, to that flood-subsided river, he jumped like a frog jumps to the pond or well. Though he was late for school, though his schoolmates had left the bathing ghat some time ago, and though he muttered to himself indistinctly that he was late and needed to finish bathing in a hurry, he did not. In fact, he could not. In fact, none of his age and agility, athletic spirit and sporting vivacity, could have done otherwise.

As his wont, he dived well into the river to get rid of the filthy, foully muddy, almost stagnant water on the shore up the spur. The riverbank upside the eroding shoreline serves like a diving board. Teens and adolescents, school-going or cattle-tending, make it a point to dive into the stream from the bank- diving- board. The old and the elder lot don't derive the diving pleasure that the younger male lot do. They use the bathing ghat adjacent to the spur upstream or the placid backwater downstream to be on the safe side.

The longer you are off the shore, the more you plunge in, play with, and swim in comparatively clearer water, if not crystalline clear water. Most of his bathing mates do so very often and normally. What matters is the distance off the coast. Further out in the stream, stronger is the current you are supposed to wrestle with. While the older people avoid the mid-stream clearer water as a rule as their age does not permit, most chicken-hearted, drowning-phobic youngsters don't venture in there. It is kind of "Fools rush in where angels fear to tread" for them.

As a swift and stubborn swimmer and as adept and excellent in breaststroke, butterfly, backstroke etc, and as a savant grade diver, Surendra avoids bathing in the filthy, stagnant water up or down the spur. Since in a hurry, he needed to have taken bath in the onshore standing water and come back. But attraction of the clear current a little off the coast was irresistible to him. He swam some strokes to reach the comely, clear water. One or two dives under the unclear water added to the appeal of the clear current ahead. Oblivious of school time, unmindful of being almost alone then, and being drawn by the deceptive undercurrent, he found after some time that he is at the tip of the spur. And to his wonder and worry, he found further that the current at the submerged tip was ferociously stronger than he could ever imagine in his wildest dream.

Born and brought up on the banks of Mahanadi, the river is not new or enervating to him. Fifteen metres from his home flows Mahanadi from time immemorial. When he was fifteen weeks old and was crying aloud as infants invariably do, women and men strolling on the Mahanadi bank would descend on his home to caress, cajole and fondle him. Mainly teen-age girls were all glee to see him crying with a high-sounding pitch. Elder women chided his mother for dereliction in motherly duties. When fifteen months old, he was carried on shoulders or in armpit by his father, elder sisters or cousins to the Mahanadi bund to pacify him, stop him from crying. And then, once on the bund, he stopped crying abruptly. None knew the reason nor he was ever able to decipher the mystery of the Mahanadi bank bund that so miraculously mollified a crying child. Perhaps the riparian zephyr accompanied with the sweet murmur of the river under the vast blue sky calmed and cooled the crying child with a sweetening sensation. The slightly green bund running like a thin green band from west to east in a landmark landscape aroused celestial sobering in the child's limbs and limerick. Even when Mahanadi was in spate and the river roared like a lion, the child taken to the river bund stopped crying instantly, maybe out of fear of the unknown. Surendra, as a child, was witness to seasons and time passing fast on Mahanadi. He did not know the nuances of seasons and suffering but he invariably viewed the versatility of Mahanadi because he was as close to Mahanadi as he was close to his father, mother, siblings, friends. So, when grown up, Surendra has come across severe floods, fierce currents, ferocious undercurrents …but the strong current that he was encircled today was unknown, unseen before!

V

Before long, he saw him in a frightening gorge in the backwater down the spur. And the gorge at the confluence of current and standing water was mother of a monstrous eddy. Since the backwater water gorge was stirred by the strong current, Surendra was caught in the violent whirlpool. He saw to his dismay that he could scarcely swim out of it. He could not wriggle out despite his best efforts to swim off, to swim away, to swim ashore. The strokes and techniques he learnt and adopted adeptly before were of no use; rather poured cold water on his vigorous endeavours. The more he exerted to pull out of the whirlpool, the more was he repulsed into the watery maelstrom. When he rose up to skip out of the spiral gorge, he was pushed per force down to the dark deep. When he dived to escape under water, he was flung up like a splint or sprinkle; then, of course, he fell into the same pit, the same spot. The whole thing happened to be a quizzical trick of the water goddess or the river ogre. The cross current commotion was inescapable and intimidating. He was exhausted with strokes and dives, faultless and fine though, finally futile. He was breathless out of fatigue and frustration. Nevertheless, he was not drowned. He kept himself afloat in the eddy, hoping that he would edge out somehow.

Soon there was an uproar. The few bathers who were around and happened to see his mishap made light of the matter at the outset. They guessed that he had leapt into the gorge on his own accord to show his showmanship and would soon be out of the whirlpool as of fun. Later on, and, especially to the elders, it appeared that he was caught in a vicious, violent crosscurrent of which escape was foreclosed. It was kind of a small fly stuck in a sticky spider web, the end of which is premature death. The elders who are habitually flood- water- swimmers and crosscurrent-escapers were worried but not out of their wits. At other time, they would have first scolded him roundly for his indiscreet daredevilry. They would have made fun of his mindless show of swimming manliness. But they abstained from nasty comments and unnecessary post mortem remarks. Just school-going and mostly illiterate most of the village folk know how to deal with a fellow being in distress and danger. The first credo is to ignore the victim's fault, fancy or frivolity. The second is to instil hope and availability of help in his mind, his demeanour.

Though there was a small crowd of able-bodied, all-swimmers, mainly-men on the ridge of the spur, and a bit larger crowd on the riverbank upstream and downstream the spur, there was little noise but widespread whispers on how all that happened. Inaudibly but invariably, every onlooker prayed "May Sura come out safe and unhurt!" The leading men advised him in loud and clear voice from almost on the tip of the spur not to lose heart nor be frightened.

"Do not fear, Sura! Nothing will happen! We are here, here for you, aren't we?", they said softly and reassuringly.

"Don't swallow water that forcibly goes down your ovula, your throat! Whenever draughts of water enforces entry through your forcibly opened mouth, gurgle it out as quickly as possible!"—was the kind, consoling counsel.

Surendra tried to abide by these well-known sermons but draughts of water from the rising and encircling waves round the vortex forced through his mouth opened by exhaustion and panting. Good doers and do-gooders that they traditionally were, the elderly males threw sarees, dhotis, and ropes from the spur with one end with the thrower and the other on water. He was instructed to stick tightly to the floating end so that he could be forked out of the swirling water. The ropes, sarees, dhotis flung were either too short to reach near the whirlpool or weaker and slender enough to remain afloat for minutes. Fatigued and frightened, Surendra could not stretch his hand long enough to catch the floating/sinking end of the rescue rope/saree.

VI

The rescuers realised soon that short-length, little things would not do because the aquatic vortex was deep and the current strong. Short, small articles like saree/dhoti/ rope would be of no help, no use.

What then? Will he be left in the lurch? Will he die a desperate death? No, no, no! All possible risks be taken, ways be explored to save him! He cannot die before our eyes. He must be snatched from death's jaw. In the war between good and evil forces, good has always won, why not we? Surendra is son of the soil, a good soul. He must win the war with the watery grave, mustn't he?

Someone in the crowd who has observed the futile rescue attempts from the beginning shouted, "Ho, why this hula baloo for nothing?"

There was silence. And the crowd looked askance at the elderly soul who may perhaps put forth some plausible, sensible rescue suggestion.

Clearing his throat, he uttered a little louder, "A long and strong thing like a pole could be the rescue instrument, understand!"

"A log!", quipped someone.

"Heh, Heh ....", giggled several souls in unison even in such a tragic situation. They wondered at the speaker's tom foolery at suggesting a heavy material like wood log to wriggle out a drowning man stuck in a spooky aquatic crevice.

The first speaker was empathetic to the fool-like speaker and explained sensibly, "Logs are heavy, heavier than water whatever may be their girth or length. They sink and he who sticks to them will invariably sink with them. Something strong but light...."

With a sense of de ja' 'vu, one shouted, "Bamboo!"

"That's absolutely right. A strong and long, dry, bamboo pole could be his saviour."

"Yes uncle, yes, that certainly will."

Another joined in to announce, "There is a huge heap of dried, long, strong bamboo poles in Sura's backyard."

It was common knowledge that Surendra's father, a well to do and literate farmer, has grown a good crop of bamboo famed for long, light and strong poles. In fact, the heap of bamboo poles was cut, trimmed and dried, and was ready for transportation to Titagarh Paper Mills at Choudwar, near Cuttack.

No sooner was the suggestion okayed than two/three youths rushed, picked two/three long/light/strong bamboo poles, and arrived on the spur ridge. The longest, strongest and lightest of the lot was chosen. A tall and strong, middle-aged, muscular man held one end tight-hand and set the pole on water afloat, directing the other end towards Sura. Sura who was head and shoulder in swirling water, and was pale and bluish with continual thrashing of the gushing waves was on the verge of collapse. The bamboo pole was the last straw on the camel's back. Should he fail in catching the end of the floating pole, that would be end of the matter, the end of his strife, the end of his life. He was hopeful that the bamboo pole would bamboozle his imminent end, must save his life.

The pole deftly directed towards Sura did not disappoint the couple of rescuers. It floated on the small waves and surfs, mild current and standing water to the brink of the whirlpool. As was instructed and advised, Sura mustered the last morsel of his vanishing strength. He watched the pole afloat around the vortex's tangent. Still inside the swirling water, he stretched one hand out, and caught hold of the pole.

Immediately and instinctively, he extended the other tired hand. And gripped the pole end in the fist, and fast. The eddy did not let him go. He did not let the bamboo pole go. By now, the bystanders who so far let hope go, hopped with hope. They initially doubted whether there would be a slip between Sura and the pole. Now that he had caught hold of the pole, he is saved from the yawning jaw of the watery doom. The two/ three men who held the spur-side end of the pole tightly pulled up their muscular might mightily so that by no means it gave them a slip, went off their grip. As if their collective strength straightened the floating and oscillating pole, it stayed put afloat, fixed; as if its two ends held tight by two sturdy sumo wrestlers. Initially slowly and then forcefully, the spur- top rescuers dragged their end of the pole. Surendra clung to his side end with all his strength. The rescuers dragged the pole without late or lapse. Surendra, floating passively, was drawn ashore like a large, lifeless fish.

There was a sigh of relief and a high of the success. Some wanted to press his belly to belch out drunken water. But Surendra smiled feebly and forbade them from so doing. Unuttered, he indicated that he fought a lot to adhere to the fundamentals of drowning i.e., not to gulp water while drowning. Soon things were normal. Surendra went home in his wet shorts and curly hairs, his bare body glistening with water drops reflecting clear morning sun ray.

He came out of the killing, curling water vortex.

I can also come out of the cursing Corona times by churning the perennial, positive current of hope, harmony and high-thinking of Bhagavat Gita.

VII

The other thing that weighed in my mind was the Platinum Jubilee Celebration of Indian Independence, the great festival of our motherland. Azadi ka Amrit Mahotsav, the magnificently styled celebration, excites and enthuses every Indian, all countrymen and women, notwithstanding the outstanding diversity in nativity, ethnicity, lingua franca, religion, culture, heritage, region, food, fashion, dress, decorum et al. I desired to celebrate the Azadi ka Amrit Mahotsav, utilise the Amrit Kala in style, in a memorable manner. What can I do? What can I do at a time I am hundred per cent indoors, immobile, incommunicado?

I am lucky that I am alive to be part of the two Jubilees jamboree, am I not? So you are, aren't you? So are all of them who have lived long enough to have observed the observance of the Golden Jubilee festivities of Indian Independence in 1997 and that of the Platinum Jubilee Celebration observed now in a grander, greater, more glorious manner.

I did something 25 years ago when we observed Golden Jubilee of Indian Independence. I wrote a book on Bhagavat Gita, captioned, **50 Flowers from Bhagavat Gita: A Solace Against Frightening Materialism.** Something similar did not seem out of place. 25 years ago, we observed the golden jubilee of India's independence. Now 25 years after, we celebrate platinum jubilee of Indian freedom, Azadi. In my humble but hopeful manner, it would be great and glorious to dive into Bhagavat Gita depth, to have a comely and cool bath before the upcoming cold death [of mine, of course].

You may be curious or questioning about Bhagavat Gita discoursecompatibility with Azadi ka Amrit Mahotsav spirit. Try to find out the answer in the following pages.

Suffice it to say that Bhagavat Gita is not a poem of spiritualism, righteousness or duty here in the world now that has a bearing on life hereafter but also the magnificent magnum opus of freedom, independence, emancipation, liberation of the individual, of the Indians, of all others, who read and brood over the Bhagavat Gita.

ONE

**Whilst thus I sing, I am a King,
Although a poor blind Boy**

*dhṛitarāśhtra uvācha
dharma-kṣhetre kuru-kṣhetre samavetā yuyutsavaḥ
māmakāḥ pāṇḍavāśhchaiva kimakurvata sañjaya [1.1]*

O Sanjaya! Tell me what my sons and the sons of Pandu assembled to fight in the pious battlefield of Kurukshetra did.

Though not serially nor due to its importance, we may start with the 1st verse of 1st chapter of the Bhagavat Gita.

Up to 11th verse of Chapter II, Gita -Acharyas do not consider the preceding slokas Gita proper. 1st Chapter, Arjun Vishad Yoga, consisting of 46 slokas, could be called the preface, prologue or preamble of the Bhagavat Gita. Without this chapter, the beginners, the novice readers, cannot plunge into the essentials and intricacies of Gita. It is not unnecessary nor sheer waste of time for scholars or spirituals to deal with and debate Arjun Vishad Yoga [AVY]. The AVY starts the "Krishna Arjun Sambada" [KAS], the Krishna-Arjun dialogue. It is the cause celebre of Bhagavat Gita. It is worthwhile to note that Krishna would not have opened His mouth during the course of the Kurukshetra war, had not Arjun been drowned in deep, disastrous despondency. Of course, Krishna, the unarmed charioteer of Arjun, pledged not to participate in the fighting, but not committed to keeping quiet.

Part and parcel of the battle and a leading player of the prominent battle for that matter, He could not leave the battle unfinished or the Pandavas mid-stream their suffering. As Krishna spoke on to ameliorate Arjun's despondency, the Gita *Amrit* flowed.

Those writers or preachers who hint upon or halt for some time on Arjun Vishad Yoga scarcely discuss the 1st verse. The reason is not far to seek. The 1st sloka is spoken by Dhritarashtra, the reigning and ruling emperor of Hastina, who descends from the great Kuru and heads the Kauravas. The one and only verse uttered by him in the great and glorious Gita is a simple, innocent query of Sanjay as to what was happening in the sacred Kurukshetra where the bellicose sons of Pandu and his assembled to fight.

Thereafter the Gita narrative starts. Sanjay names the great warriors and fighters on both sides. The battle proper is to begin. But, all of a sudden, the arch archer of the field, Arjun, descends into inexplicable despondency.

Dhritarashtra speaks only one and the initial sloka of Gita. Since he is the monarch of all he surveyed, since he is the scion of the illustrious Shantanu, he is supposed to outweigh other characters of Gita. But that is not the case. None considers him anything more than a nuisance, a non-existent character, a nonentity. The reason? He is the villain, the arch villain of the piece. It is argued that Duryodhana could be excused for his omissions and commissions, but not Dhritarashtra. Their argument is that son's sins are sown in the field of father's indulgence, insensitivity, irresponsibility, immorality. They quote the old adage, "Spare the rod, spoil the child." The inexcusable, unmonarchical, excessive partiality of Dhritarashtra for all the wrongs of Duryodhana that exceedingly wronged the just, decent, obedient Pandavas was extremely, enormously costly not only for the Kauravas, but also for the Pandavas, and also for the whole Bharat Varsha as well.

In that view, Dhritarashtra is the arch villain of Mahabharata, if Duryodhana is the villain. Duryodhana could be forgiven for his faults but Dhritarashtra could not be excused for his blunders. If Duryodhana is the sinner, Dhritarashtra is the Satan. Even then, Dhritarashtra is not unpardonable because he is born blind. Because he has not seen light since he alighted upon the earth. He who has groped in the dark whole of his life, how can he be expected to distinguish between light and darkness? Between what is wrong and what is right, between what is just and what is unjust, between what is moral and what is immoral?

Maybe he is the Mahabharata villain. Since he is the monarch, since he is assisted and advised by a galaxy of intellectual giants, maybe the plea of physical blindness does not stand him in good stead.

But Gita is different. Structurally a tiny part of the Mahabharata epic, it has assumed epic proportions for its distinct features and fame. A few know or bother to know that Gita originates in the Mahabharata epic. In fact, in the 10th Chapter of Gita itself, it is shown that the entire Mahabharata and millions and millions of verses and Vedas originate in the Gita, or more precisely in the Gita Purusha, isn't it?

So, Dhritarashtra as in Gita needs be given some thought, some consideration. Why did he keep mum after the only question he asked? Did he keep quiet because he could not make head or tail of what Sanjay narrated so nicely of the super sensible "sambada" of Krishna and Arjuna? Or, alternatively, is it he alone who was imbibed with the Gita jnana more clearly than Arjuna or Sanjay? You can hazard a guess but must not leave Dhritarashtra in the lurch while going through Gita.

The very 1st sloka of Gita is, therefore, significant and suffused with sense. You do not have to skip it, ditch it; rather, think it, think over it.

TWO

To tell the truth
Did Sanjay tell the truth?

*yatra yogeśhvaraḥ kṛiṣhṇo yatra pārtho dhanur-dharaḥ
tatra śhrīr vijayo bhūtir dhruvā nītir matir mama [18.78]*

Sanjay says more to himself than to Dhritarashtra that where there is the Lord of Yoga, Krishna, where there is the supreme archer, Partha, I do not have an iota of doubt in my mind that there are blessings, victory and riches galore.

After the first verse, let us jump to the last verse, the 700th verse, the verse that could be called the conclusion. It is important because it is spoken by Sanjay on his own. And he jumps to the conclusion that the Pandavas must win the war, though a single arrow had not been shot nor a single blow been struck. In fact, Sanjay spoke of the last five verses of his own volition. He was authorised to see the battle field details minute by minute minutely and relay the same to Dhritarashtra, the blind monarch, who did not accept the distant-detail-vision virtue proffered by Vyas, the former's father. In this single act, Dhritarashtra showed his magnanimity, his generosity for his confidante, counsel and escort. Sanjay should have stopped when the Krishna-

Arjuna sambada stopped. These five verses were beyond his brief. The last one is absolutely unacceptable when spoken by him.

The last verse as uttered by Sanjaya emphasising Pandavas' victory at the end of the war is factually true. Unarmed Krishna, the fountain of yoga, the source of all yoga siddhi, is the most influencer of the war, is the most impactor of the combat. He is the tide-turner, the direction-diverter. With rapt attention, Sanjaya saw online the on-field dialogue of Krishna- Arjuna duo. And he observed keenly how a dismally disheartened Arjuna cast off his sentimentality for grandsire Bhishma, guru Drona Acharya, Kula guru Kripacharya, even the ever-hostile Kaurava brothers. Arjun, the archer as meticulous as Bhishma, Drona, Karna and Ashwatthama, if not more, was marvellously motivated by Krishna. Once motivated, empowered, inspired, Arjuna is incomparable as an archer, a warrior, a winner. When Krishna and Arjuna take the same side, the outcome of the war favours the Pandavas. Then do come glory and great wealth to the Pandavas.

That is right. Uttered elsewhere by somebody else, Sanjaya's sum-up of Gita is prophetic, praiseworthy. But here, at the end of Gita, to say, to conclude, that the Pandavas must win is not winsome. It defeats the object of Gita. It militates against the spirit of Gita. It combats the cream of Gita. Gita is not meant to help you get this or that. Gita is not intended to ensure victory, success, resources, renown. Those who admire and adore Krishna are not entitled to win, success, wealth aplomb. Those who become as submissive and surrendered to Krishna as was Arjuna in Gita do not endear themselves to Krishna, the Cosmic

Soul, the Supreme Spirit. The essence and intricacy of Gita is beyond earthly botheration of winning or losing, glory or ignominy, beauty or ugliness, opulence or destitution. Don't forget this unforgettable lesson while perusing, pursuing Gita, the Geet, the lyric, composed and sung by the Lord!

THREE

Did Gita go beyond Arjuna's intellectual antennae?

*kachchid etach chhrutaṁ pārtha tvayaikāgreṇa chetasā
kachchid ajñāna-sammohaḥ pranaṣhṭas te dhanañjaya*
[18.72]

O Partha! Did you heed to what I said with undivided attention? O Partha! Did you eliminate entirely the ignorance and attachment by imbuing with the wisdom therefrom?

Sloka 72nd of chapter 18, the 694th sloka of Bhagavat Gita deserves no discussion in an ordinary, traditional sense. But I deal with it for two reasons; one there is still dearth of Gita literature and the present treatise needs therefore not be given a short shrift; two, if Krishna could not be sure that Arjuna assimilated Gita spirit, how can we mere mundane human beings boast of grasping Gita jnana? Or how can one claim that this or that discourse disseminates quintessence of Bhagavat Gita completely? Or who can assure that there is no need of further dissertation on Gita? If Arjuna was asked to answer whether he comprehended Gita, who else would not be questioned on their grasping Gita? In fact, those who speak of, boast of, grasping Bhagavat Gita have mostly, at best, groped in the dark, haven't they?

What Arjuna says in the following sloka is a different matter. What you have to ponder is how difficult or delicate Bhagavat Gita is so that Krishna was not sure of Arjuna assimilating the fundamentals thereof, what to speak of the finer points. By now 694 slokas had been spoken, i.e., 99.86% of the Gita. Yet, Krishna doubted whether Arjuna heard Him attentively and understood the Gita essentials, my God!

Arjuna is not stupid nor senile. He is sentient and competent to comprehend the sententious and sermonic oration of Krishna in the Kurukshetra war zone. That Arjuna was disarrayed transitorily when the Kaurava army was arrayed against the Pandava fighters did not deprive him of his formidable faculty. Then, why did Krishna utter so? Why did Krishna question Arjuna's attentivity and mental ability to course through the quintessence of Bhagavat Gita?

As the teacher asks the student, as the guru asks the disciple, at the end of his lesson, so did Krishna ask Arjuna at the end of His sermon if Arjuna was enlightened. Krishna never doubted Arjuna's cognitive calibre or competency. He had seen numerous times how Arjuna coped with copious constraints with his mental and intellectual ingenuity. But Gita was a different cup of tea. It requires the listener's learning and yearning. Gita is not for earning knowledge. It requires one's undivided attention, single-minded attention, wholehearted attention. Complete concentration, comprehensive concentration. Conspicuous contemplation, copious concentration. Krishna asks this specifically. We who ever read or speak about Gita do so scarcely with *"ekagrena chettasa"* as spoken of here, do we?

Arjuna was insanely desperate when he asked Krishna

of what he should do, why he should do. He committed carte blanche to do what Krishna would direct or dictate. Why should he be unmindful? How could he be inattentive? He can't. He wasn't. In fact, he was so out of his wits that he would abide by any foolish or childish advice by Krishna. The point lies there. A desperate person is attentive. He can't afford to doubt or divert or hesitate. Insofar as we are caught in a dilemma, we cannot imbibe Gita jnana, because we cannot be mindful, can we?

Of course, some people were famed for their concentration. Take the case of Swami Vivekananda. Even when he was the mischievous, nuisance Narendra Nath Dutt, he was renowned for his conspicuous concentration and sustaining memory as far as reading class books and classics were concerned.

The second point is still more significant. Krishna asked whether Arjuna got rid of the *Moha* that arose out of his *Ajnana*. As a matter of fact, the great Bhagavat Gita starts here and ends here. And we mortals muse where we are. Whether we should end reading Gita here or ruminate Gita again from here. It is all the more quizzical when we look at the words "*Sammoha*" and "*Pranasta*" occurring in this verse. Moha could be manageable, manoeuvrable, but Sammoha is not, cannot be. To surmount Sammoha, one needs must be enlightened, illuminated in entirety. Elimination or destruction of Ajnana, Moha, could be momentary, transitory until the enlightenment is enduring and eternal. When ignorance is entirely erased, eradicated, inescapably uprooted, it is Pranasta as occurs here.

Hence, the verse is very important as it speaks of Arjuna's unsurmountable ignorance being entirely eliminated by what Krishna annotated of the eternal truths of enlightenment. As for us, the four foremost things of Gita are,[1] to be extremely attentive while going through Gita, [2] to realise that Moha and Ignorance are one and the same thing, not two sides of the same coin, [3] Moha is massive, mirage-like that needs must be destroyed totally and once for all, [4] all that the Gita is about in the preceding 693 slokas is comprehensive destruction of Moha by enlightenment.

How easy or difficult it is to comprehend the crux of the matter is the thing. Yet, when one claims his erudition in Gita, he needs must show that his "Sammoha" is "Pranasta". He had hundred per cent ridden of ignorance and attachment. One needs must not show so; it must have been sown in his interior, his inner, his soul. When the inner, the anterior, the "In" is enlightened, illuminated, the outer, the exterior shines and shimmers like soft sun ray or salubrious scent that attracts and delights, pleases and placates.

FOUR

Got rid of doubt-trap, stable and able,
I shall abide by You!

It is puzzling that Krishna queried of Kaunteya about the latter's contemplation and comprehensive eradication of Moha. What Partha replied is pertinent for we people,
arjuna uvācha
naṣhṭo mohaḥ smṛitir labdhā tvat-prasādān mayāchyuta
sthito 'smi gata-sandehaḥ kariṣhye vachanaṁ tava [18.73]

O Achyuta! My lust was lost; I retrieved my lost memory by Your mercy; my doubt is cleared; I shall certainly abide by what You say as I am unwavering, unshaken, not indecisive anymore.

Arjuna is an exemplary, ideal pupil to absorb the guru's axioms and advice out and out. He emphasised with all humility that his Moha is destruct. Equally important point that Arjuna made is that he revived, retrieved his memory [that was lost, eclipsed or obscured]. And these extraordinary events happened due to enormous compassion of Krishna. As he regained his memory or consciousness and did destroy his Moha due to Madhava's mercy, his doubt was gone and he stood stable and firm [as a man, as a warrior, as Arjuna, as before]. Now that he was devoid of doubt and dithering, regained his consciousness, smashed and shattered the satanic Moha, emerged from the ignominious, abhorrent, erratic eclipse of Ajnana, he must act according to Krishna's counsel and command.

If sloka 694[72/18] is the penultimate sloka of Gita, 695[73/18] is the conclusion, closure. Krishna casually and/or quizzically queried whether Arjuna listened to Gita contemplatively and could weed out his Moha by the enlightening instructions. Arjuna replied humbly but clearly that [1] his doubt and dilemma evaporated,[2] that he retrieved his memory/consciousness, [3] that his Moha was destroyed,[4] that he was transformed or was his original, usual self of Arjuna, the ace archer, the trump card of Pandava camp,[5] that his transformation/ transcension was the grace, bliss of Krishna,[6] now he was at the disposal of Krishna to discharge his duties as directed.

The question-answer of Krishna-Arjuna, the ultimate Krishna-Arjuna sambada is extremely important because it pushes you back, back to the beginning.

With some semblance of discipleship, we readers should try to decipher the seemingly simple but, in essence, intricate credo as cited herein. Firstly, we should get rid of doubt, dilemma in the most of cases to the best possible extent. In other words, we must look forward, walk forward, act forward. Though there is no need to be in a hurry, much less in a dead hurry, there is no need to tarry. Delay and dithering must not wither our fair-weather forward-looking foliage, flower. This obviously obviates our negative, weak, wicked attitude. Stability and felicity solidify our existence, our essence. Of destruction of Moha and retrieval of primeval, primordial consciousness, we may discuss later, if space permits.

kachchid etach chhrutaṁ pārtha tvayaikāgreṇa chetasā
kachchid ajñāna-sammohaḥ pranaṣhṭas te dhanañjaya
[18.72]

FIVE

Arjuna saw the seesaw
own people arrayed against own people

When, in conclusion, Krishna queried of Arjuna's single-minded contemplation to assimilate truth and thereby destroy Moha, should we not bother where Krishna spoke of Arjuna's Ignorance and consequential Moha for the first time? Or where for the first time was Arjuna's Ajnana and Moha evident?

As the fighters have assembled with their weapons and wizardry, as the battle beagle blew, everyone expected the other party's chief commander's clarion call to "attack" to dart his arrow or smash his mace. Abruptly, Arjuna requested Krishna to drive his chariot straight to the median whence he could see his foes with whom he would fight to the finish. This may have been a sincere, innocent query out of simple empathy. Most of the warriors were unknown to Arjuna personally. And most of the enemy warriors who faced Arjuna in the combat could scarcely return unscathed. Most of them would not return to the enemy camp from where they had started in the morning as the evening would be their last evening on earth, under the sun. This could be great heroic conduct, neither Ignorance nor Moha.

Krishna kept the chariot on the centre of battle ground. Arjuna saw from his chariot pedestal, armed and warrior-attired Bhishma, Drona, Kripacharya, Duryodhana, his brothers et al. What did he see? He saw a sea of seamless warriors related to him. He looked back at his army. Who were there? They were all as related to Duryodhana as Duryodhana's fighters were related to him. Arjuna saw the seesaw of own people arrayed against own people, not enemies against enemies. Arjuna reasoned how Duryodhana's brother-in-law Jayadratha could be his enemy or his father-in-law Drupada be Duryodhana's. No way. He shuddered to think how Duryodhana could smash Abhimanyu with his mace or how he could dart his arrow at Laxman Kumar, Duryodhana's son's chest. It is simply inhuman, incomprehensible, irresponsible, reproachable, mused Arjuna in silence and suffocation. Maybe the milk of human kindness overflooded his heart like never before.

Was it unbecoming of Arjuna? Yes, it was unbecoming of Arjuna alighted on Kurukshetra to kill the Kauravas who have crossed all limits of injustice and unrighteousness. Yes, it was unbecoming of Arjuna to count his relatives in the battle of justice and piety. Nonetheless, Arjuna is Ajuna; *"Arjuna's tula nasti Keshavasya's nachopamaa."* There is none like Arjuna; none can compare with Keshava. Arjuna is as kind as conquistador. He is as super marksman as superbly human. To him, the battle field of fratricide was a vicious device or suicidal design. He argued that he could not commit the sin of killing his kith and kin to pay Duryodhana in his own coin, who had perpetrated perpetual injustices and wrongs on the Pandavas. He justified his stand by stating that Duryodhana committed the vices and injustices out of ignorance, hence excusable. But his killing of Kauravas would be with knowledge, hence inexcusable.

In spite of the forceful reasoning, Arjuna could not convince himself. He felt out of place, like a fish out of water. When all and sundry around were readying their weapons to fight to the finish, the ace warrior there, Arjuna, was inexplicably emotional, cheap-sentimental. Here does Ignorance take over his reason. Here does Moha overshadow his sense of justice and piety.

SIX

Courage, not cowardice; submission not obstinance Are friends guide and guru?

kārpaṇya-doṣhopahata-svabhāvaḥ
pṛichchhāmi tvāṁ dharma-sammūḍha-chetāḥ
yach-chhreyaḥ syānniśhchitaṁ brūhi tanme
śhiṣhyaste 'haṁ śhādhi māṁ tvāṁ prapannam [2.7]

Arjuna confesses that he had descended to uncharitable, uncharacteristic weakness and wobbliness of his character out of [1] fear of killing so many kith and kin [2] his greed for the kingdom [3] his knowledge that consequences of the war would woefully corrupt the Kuru clan. But he was unsure of the injunctions of piety and spirituality in the instant case. And found himself in a dire dilemma. How to escape between the two horns of the dilemma? That was Arjuna's problem. That is our problem. That is universal, eternal problem. Since Krishna always guided him to his good, he submitted to Krishna to escort and advise as a guru does to the disciple.

As such, the query by Krishna in verse 72/18 is the consequence of sloka 7/2. Arjuna submitted to Krishna as a disciple to the guru to clear his doubt and dilemma on fighting and slaughtering his kith and kin including the ones like Bhishma, Drona, Kripacharya etc who bestowed bountiful love and well-wishes on the Pandavas in general and him in particular. Ajnana and Moha emasculates the immaculate archer and warrior Arjuna! So does Anjana and Moha emasculate us!

SEVEN

Are we born again and again ad infinitum?

If this is about Moha and Ajnana of Arjuna that was destroyed with Krishna's counsel, what about revival of his lost memory/consciousness? When for the first time Arjuna is alluded to have lost his memory/consciousness?

When Krishna began Chapter 4 by eulogising yoga/jnana yoga and why Arjuna is ignorant of it, He said, first of all He preached the precious precept to Sun who instilled the same in his son Manu/ Vaivasvata Manu who imparted the same to his illustrious son Ikshvaku. From Sun to succeeding sons and to philosopher kings and scholars passed on the stream of jnana yoga. But somewhere somehow the clear stream of jnana yoga got lost in the desert sand of intended or unintended corruption/commotion. So much so that the great jnana of jnana yoga is extinct in the society at present [1,2/4]. As a result of which, Krishna implied, a worthy warrior and erudite like Arjuna faces infamous dilemma between pious, glorious duty and weakness for wicked kindred.

That may be true. True because Krishna says so and Arjuna could not dispute that on the basis of any reason or authority at his command. Maybe true because of Krishna's preceding sermons that distinguished the mortal body and the immortal being, that made light of death and shed light on the inescapabilty of death, that delineated the indestructibility and undeniability of Soul. He also enlightened exhaustively the need for and indispensability of duty, karma, without caring for consequences.

But Arjuna was astonished how the contemporary Krishna communicated the cream of jnana to SUN who precedes Krishna by innumerable eons. Arjuna wondered how this young mortal Krishna instilled jnana yoga in Sun who shines in the firmament for eons and eons and is worshipped over centuries and centuries as the dispeller of darkness, depravity and destitution? So, Arjuna asked how that could be? He retorted that Krishna existed then, right then, but Sun is seamlessly extant from time immemorial. How the later in time preach his predecessor in time?

śhrī bhagavān uvācha
bahūni me vyatītāni janmāni tava chārjuna
tānyaham veda sarvāṇi na tvam vettha parantapa [4.5]

O Arjuna! I have lived innumerable lives and so have you. While I remember those prodigious past lives, you do not.

This is where Krishna spoke of Arjuna's memory loss, consciousness disruption.

Krishna commented coolly that not only himself but also Arjuna had lived innumerable lives. The difference was that He remembered, was aware of all His past lives, but Arjuna was not. Arjuna could not remember, recall of his past lives, his spiritual history. In fact, Arjuna cannot. It is the irony. It is quizzical, perplexing. Arjuna and Krishna appeared and were active in the same time span, in the same landmass. In archery or weaponry, in erudition or emotion, in intellect or empathy, both stand the same footing, though Krishna could be more fortunate or furnished, endowed with more faculty or finesse. As far as consciousness is concerned, how could Krishna be fathomlessly superior to Arjuna?

Even the second foot of this verse has no answer. It spells out why the Cosmic Soul Krishna comes in mere mortal frame, form. In verses 7 and 8 of this chapter is elaborated the critical time and conditions of Krishna's earth advent. On Arjuna's awareness disruption, nothing is there. But in verse 73/18, Arjuna affirms that he has revived, recovered or retrieved his awareness. We may understand that awakening is awareness. Arjuna awakened to his awareness.

EIGHT

No problem, you must die and you must take birth!

Here we see an inkling of the truism that life and death follow each other incessantly, unbreakably because,

jātasya hi dhruvo mṛityur dhruvaṁ janma mṛitasya cha tasmād aparihārye 'rthe na tvaṁ śhochitum arhasi [2.27]

The born must die, must be burnt out. He that dies must be born. Thus, you must not mourn for the inevitable. This is the truth, eternal, universal truth. But it is not easy to comprehend or apprehend, not even by the likes of Arjuna. Hence, Krishna counsels in the second foot that Arjuna needs must not mourn the demise of Bhishma, Dronacharya, Kripacharya etc because they must be born again. Arjuna cannot annihilate them once for all. Read with sloka 27/2, sloka 5/4 confirms that death is as temporary as life, that for one life there is one death and for one death there is one life. That life and death are a plain hide and seek game in the material and spiritual plane in a conjoined configuration. The appreciation of this is Jnana; the absence of this understanding is Ajnana. Arjuna cried over the imminent death of his kith and kin due to his Ajnana but stopped sobbing after he heard Gita and entered into the kingdom of Jnana. He declared this himself in verse 73/18.

Hence, we had many lives hereto before and must have innumerable lives hereto after. Let us not cry over departure of dear ones from this life to another! That is the go of the world, that is the way of life. Life is stronger than the bond between father and children, husband and wife, teacher and student, friend and friend. So much so that it snaps the bondage at will. Filial or fraternity, conjugal or friendship bonds are never so strong as to stop, prevent or pre-empt life from jumping the fence of bondage.

Try not to forget but to ruminate each death around you in this perspective!

NINE

Your song sweetened my ears
My declaration sweetened yours
Is there anything more?

If Krishna queried of Arjuna whether he heard Gita with rapt attention and completely culled his Anjana and Moha [72/18], previously, just previously, he spoke coolly,

iti te jñānam ākhyātaṁ guhyād guhyataraṁ mayā
vimṛiśhyaitad aśheṣheṇa yathechchhasi tathā kuru [18.63]

This is the secret of secrets as annotated to you by Me in the clearest language. It is now up to you deliberate and decide to act as the way you please.

By now, the Krishna-Arjuna dialogue is 685 verses long. Krishna had been enunciating eternal and universal truths on life, death, duty. And the visible link of body, and virtual link of soul, with life-death-life-death... chain, partly visible, partly invisible circle. It looks simply simple, sufficiently simple. On the contrary, it is extremely intricate, quizzical, complex, critical. Enigmatic or intriguing, isn't it? The underlying wisdom is how it happens, who reins in the circular or chainlike motion, momentum.

In the instant verse, Krishna clears the case by saying Jnana as expounded supra is secret. Secret of secrets, the topmost secret. Krishna was, so to say, partisan, biased towards Arjuna to divulge, decode the secretive wisdom of ages, of sages. Yet he is not sure Arjuna understood the Gita Jnana, the Bhagavat secrets. He is equally unsure of Arjuna's intention of accepting the advice and acting thereupon. All the same, as an enlightened entity, as the embodiment of secrets and sermons, Krishna does not thrust upon Arjuna the Gita Jnana. He rather speaks of Arjuna's option, alternative, to discard, reject the sagacious injunctions as per his will and volition.

This verse is very important. It highlights one's will and willingness to act according to the advice in Gita. Most people most often read, reread Gita regularly, ritually. Some of us have got the great Gita by rote. Some can recite the Bhagavat Gita from A to Z, not a single sloka excepted from the total 700. That is great fun. Great achievement. Great credit. They no doubt cling to, stick to the Gita as they cling to, clutch to their apparel. To some extent, they are attached to the Bhagavat Gita. But most of them cannot apply Gita principles in life, in daily life, in the earthly life. It is not that they do not; it is that they cannot. That is the crux of Gita. You can't master Bhagavat Gita as you can master quantum physics or palaeontology, logarithm or logic, Kalidas' classics or Carnatic classical music, Odishi dance or dentistry, paediatrics or Picasso painting.

O Mister! Don't mind mastering Gita verse by verse, chapter by chapter in toto or in parts! Go to the meaning, go the beginning! Don't master the paraphernalia. Be mindful of and apply mind to Gita! Gita is not music, sweet music;

not even lyric or song, even though Gita is a book of *geet* *[song, lyric]*. In English, the Bhagavat Gita is The Celestial Song or the Divine Song or The Song of God. Despite that, Gita is not to be read, heard or remembered as a song. The sense underlying, the spirit overflowing and the essence inundating the Gita is important, essential.

A story, in this regard, is worthy of reproduction.

Once a renowned and popular singer happened to be in the royal court. Praised profusely by most of the dominant courtiers, the king directed the singer to sing. He sang and, at the end, the king announced a pearl chain as prize. Excited, the singer sang the second lyric and the king announced the bonanza of a thousand gold coins. Elated still more, the singer sang the third song and, in a matter-of-fact manner, the king declared the grant of a rich revenue estate upon the singer. Courtiers and commoners as present there applauded hysterically as much for the singer's sadhana as for the sweet songs. They were equally hysterical at the munificence of the usually reticent, close-fisted king.

Assembly over, the singer looked hither and thither for his gifts and grants. But as the king retreated to his interior chambers, so dispersed the counsellors and onlookers. The singer stood alone wondering. Soon enough, he thought gifts and grants could be handed over immediately or after some time as the king desired. And it is everybody's knowledge that kings are whimsical and unquestionable. Despite their whimsical attitude, kings adhere to their orders and declarations and execute them sooner or later.

The singer went home empty-handed but happy-hearted with the honour and the promised largesse. His wife saw him happy as never before. Joining the hubby's happiness, she first of all served him with romantic chitchat and sumptuous lunch, and then enquired of his unusual joyous mood. Being informed of the royal court incident, she jumped in delight and thanked God profusely that though late, their miserable life was transformed to a life of plethora and pleasure, luxury and leisure.

The couple spent the night delightfully with full fond hope that the king's promises would translate into material language the next day. The sun rose on the eastern horizon soon after the pleasant dawn. The singer who usually takes bath in the river ghat at dawn and worships the Sun with his sweet lyrical oblation did so that morning with more excitement and more devotion. He was obliged to the gods in general and the Sun god in particular for the announced royal largesse. His wife at home was quicker in her domestic chores and lovelier to the neighbourhood ladies and lasses. The day progressed to nightfall and late night. The expectant couple had dinner with no less joy and went to bed, comforting themselves that the king was awfully busy to comply with his command respecting them. But the third day passed in vain. And so did pass the 4th, 5th, 6th day without a gift or a word from the king.

After detailed deliberations, the singer left for the royal palace to ascertain the certainty or otherwise of the king's declared donations. The singer was escorted to the court with all courtesy and seated suitably in a chair. The king went on with his normal business except for nodding his head to the singer's respectful salutation. The singer sat still, watched court proceedings silently. The council session ended and the courtiers departed. The king was about to leave for his inner chambers when he looked at the singer and queried what his case was.

The singer narrated the incident in the royal assembly about a week ago when the king was kind to declare the bountiful gifts to him. The king laughed and lampooned, "So you are here to obtain those gifts!" The singer was dumbfounded to respond. Still more hilariously the king laughed and concluded, "Your songs were sweet to my ears then. So, I declared some gifts to sweeten your ears. As your songs pleased my ears, so should the announcement would have pleased your ears. The matter ends then and there."

Gita is not meant to sweeten your ears or the hearers' ears. It ought to permeate your senses, sweet heart and soul to change you, chastise you, baptise you.

TEN

Ego?
Go, go, go!

The Bhagavat Gita, the great epic, the great lyric, the great epistle of peace, spirituality, happiness is, in fact, the clarion call to war, fight, duty in the ascending order. We are forced to discharge our duty. If and when we say I won't do this, it proves to be blatant lie because we are compelled to perform or perish. The short, transient "No" becomes a big "Yes" soon. The temporary announcement or inaction simply exemplifies enormous ego. And "Ego", as you know, has no other go than to go the way it has come. So, the cool consequence is you "Do" what you said "Not to Do" just seconds or minutes or hours or days or weeks or months... before. The verses cited hereunder emphasize so.

yad ahankāram āśhritya na yotsya iti manyase
mithyaiṣha vyavasāyas te prakṛitis tvāṁ niyokṣhyati [18.59]
swbhāva-jena kaunteya nibaddhaḥ svena karmaṇā
kartuṁ nechchhasi yan mohāt karishyasy avaśho 'pi tat
[18.60]

O Arjuna! If out of ego, you think "I shall not fight", you become bitterly, utterly untrue as your nature will drag you to this battle. O Kounteya! What you wish not to do out of transitory temptation, you will discharge that assignment per force under the impact of your nature which must lead you to your duty without letting you have any other option, alternative.

Krishna exhorts Arjuna from the beginning to jump head on into the battle. He pleads that there is no time, it is not the time, it is not the place to say "No" to the imminent, inevitable war. He has persuaded Partha to arise and awake to the call of duty for avoidance of duty, keeping duty in abeyance, for the present or under any pretext, is palpably deplorable.

Krishna expounds if you refrain from fighting, if you absent yourself from fighting by the force of your ego, whatever you say or do for the time being is despicably false. Because sooner or later, you would be compelled to join the fighting under duress your nature. In other words, Krishna stresses that we perform our duties perforce. Temporarily, we may say NO to certain duty at some point of time, but we discharge the same duty after some time. How is it? Why is it?

When we feel, when we think "I am the doer, I am the actor", it is obvious we can say NO to a particular act at a particular time. This happens because our EGO overtakes our NATURE. We do things naturally, by the dictate and demand of our nature. Our nature directs or demands us to act. As is nature, so is the order of nature is invisible, but inevitable. Arjuna is a valiant, just fighter. His presence in the battlefield was due to his nature. If he would not be Arjuna, who would require him on the Kurukshetra field? As much as the Pandavas suffered, so much, or even more, did Kunti suffer, didn't she? Why was not she there in the battle ground? Because it was not in her nature to participate in war.

Arjuna, at the outset of the war, said NO. Said NO because he felt he is the doer. He can do and undo things. He can make or mar this massive war. He was part and parcel of Pandava quintet. He suffered the injustices heaped on the Pandavas as much as Bhima or Nakula, or even more.

Then why did he say NO to war? Because he was clouded, captivated, overcast with EGO. That part of him, that point of time in his life, was against his NATURE, not in keeping with his nature. Naturally, it was unnatural. Of course, the curse of ego-domination was short and temporary. This phase, this point was fallacious, fallow, hollow.

Nature ousts, drives out ego sooner or later. In Kurukshetra, Arjuna's nature, real nature or pure nature, as you may like to say, emerged soon or invaded soon so that Arjuna rose and fought, and fought to the finish fabulously, fantastically.

In sloka 60/18, it is supplemented that ego-invasion or ego-subjugation is momentary. And ego-driven transitory refusal to act would soon vanish. Then nature-driven Arjuna would fight as there is no other go, there is no alternative.

Was it not so? How soon did Arjuna rise, cast off his despondency and fight we all know, don't we?

ELEVEN

Fault of fratricide, sin of amicicide

In chapter 18, verses 59 and 60, Krishna concludes that Arjuna would perforce fight under the pressure of his compulsive nature. Why did he take so long to tell Arjuna fight he MUST, though he might wail the loss or might will to abjure bloodbath? No, Krishna said so soon after Arjuna swooned, though in different language. It is right in the beginning of Dwitiya Adhyay,

śhrī bhagavān uvācha
kutastvā kaśhmalamidaṁ viṣhame samupasthitam
anārya-juṣhṭamaswargyam akīrti-karam arjuna [2.2]

klaibyaṁ mā sma gamaḥ pārtha naitat tvayyupapadyate
kṣhudraṁ hṛidaya-daurbalyaṁ tyaktvottiṣhṭha parantapa
[2.3]

O Arjuna! How did you slide, slip into such abyss of dismal debasement? How did you land in this debilitating dilemma that is at once unholy, unethical and behoving the base and beastly?

In slokas 28 to 46 of chapter I, Arjuna cries out his heart. Overwhelmed with imminent death of Bhishma, Dronacharya, Kripacharya, Duryodhana, Dushasana and other relatives and kins, he found no utility in the fratricidal fight. He pleaded that Duryodhana should not be paid in his own coin, must not be meted with "tit for tat" treatment. He excused Duryodhana's frailties and faults owing to the latter's ignorance. He asserted that the Pandavas are not, nor can be, ignoramuses like the Kauravas in general and Duryodhana in particular. So, they should not tread the improper, impious path trodden by Duryodhana so far. He almost confronted Krishna with the moral question,

yady apy ete na paśhyanti lobhopahata-chetasaḥ
kula-kṣhaya-kṛitaṁ doṣhaṁ mitra-drohe cha pātakam
[1.38]

kathaṁ na jñeyam asmābhiḥ pāpād asmān nivartitum
kula-kṣhaya-kṛitaṁ doṣhaṁ prapaśhyadbhir janārdana
[1.39]

If Duryodhana and company of Shakuni, Karna, Dushasana etc find no fault in this ferocious fratricidal feud that would diminish the kula and would kill friends owing to their grave craving for the empire, how can we aware of the sins and evils of the devilish consequences of this war be engaged in it? asked Arjuna.

Reduced to rule, it means acts of sin engineered by ignorance should not be retaliated, even if the sinner, the doer's motive of greed is not pardonable or negligible. Krishna replied to this in subtle, serene sermon. In fact, Krishna's reply to this question is the Gita per se.

But the immediate answer to Arjuna's dilemma, question or overwhelming attachment to warriors in Kaurava army as in slokas 2/2 and 3/2 is insensitive, incongruous, especially when the answerer is Krishna. Krishna chides Arjuna in no uncertain terms. The former wonders how the latter slid so low in the ladder of loathsome attachment, Moha; how unholy, lowly, lumberjack and lobworm-like has the learned, luminescent, lustrous Arjuna become! The reproachful reprimand by Krishna that landed upon Arjuna at a time when he was at his wits end is certainly unworthy and unwitty. But the foulest abuses flew from the ever-smiling lips of the ever compassionate, ever conscious Krishna.

Why? Why did He heap the choicest expletives on His dearest and surest friend and follower Arjuna? Did Krishna go mad to burst out venom on His fan and faithful who simply spelt out his intriguing emotional problem?

Surely not. Then, why?

Because Krishna loves the call of duty more than He loves Arjuna. Because Krishna fancies the natural order, the order of nature more than He fancies Arjuna. Because Krishna hates idle excuses and wish-washy, sentimental weakness more than He loves Arjuna. Krishna cannot except anyone who refrains from beholden duty, not even Arjuna.

Krishna is a hard- bargaining, wheel dealer honcho when it comes to duty, because none can do without duty, activity, not even Krishna.

Do you doubt?

Krishna has clarified fairly,

Name parthasti kartavyam trishu lokeshu kinchan ...
[22/3]

O Partha! I have no duty to discharge in this three-tier universe since nothing obtaining in these three worlds is unavailable to Me, yet I am dedicated to duty.

That he performs his duty per force nature is referred to earlier in this Adhyaya and explained clearer,

Na hi kaschit kshanamapi jatu tisthatyakarmakrut .... [5/3]

Ho Arjuna! None born on this earth, in this universe can live for a moment without doing anything. On the contrary, everybody is up and doing every now and then everywhere due to the inherent nature of the being.

It is therefore inferred that birth is activity; death is inactivity. Life is action; death is inaction. So long you are alive, you are doing something. When you say, "I shall do this", you are overtaken by your ego. When you say, "I shall not do this", you are fabulously false.

Your duty?

Not dictated by ego nor defined by falsity. It is destined, defined, demarcated, delineated. By whom?

The nature that inheres you.

You are wrong, awfully wrong, when you say, "I shall do". You are wrong, woefully wrong, when you say, "I shall not do".

You "just do".

When you realise, when you really feel, when you just think that "you just do"; then you are right, hundred per cent right. Don't fright if others shout. Don't delight if others applaud and incite. You just do- -nothing more, nothing less, nor anything beyond that, beneath that. In "you just do" mentioned first time in the first sentence of this paragraph, "you" should be "You" to be grammatically correct, because in the paragraph/sentence within quotation mark, the first letter shall be in capital. But I have deliberately written "you just do" to emphasize that "you" is always "small", not great, large, significant. On the contrary, "you" are insignificant, negligible, unsubstantial, ignorable.

"Just do" is just and must; magnificently just and mightily must.

This obviously is what Krishna reproached Arjuna for in verses 2/2 and 3/2 with expletives like "*anaryajusta, akirttikara, kliva, kshudra durvala hrudaya,*" etc. Of all, Krishna was aware of Arjuna's aristocratic, dignified pedigree and personality, his aspiration and ambition to fame, his audacity, high-mindedness and lionheartedness; yet He heaped upon him intolerable insults and unbearable offences.

You cannot say "no" to "act".

If and when you say "no", ignominy, infamy, insult and injury to your reputation and respect awaits aplenty.

TWELVE

Commit a sin to get rid of many a sin?

Duty day and night, in sunshine and rain, at home and abroad, in the pits of a mine and on the summit of the Everest, is the essence of your existence, your being. None is exempt, excepted from action. However high and mighty, however full and fulfilled, however unearthly and ethereal, one has to act and act. If even the all-powerful and fully-fulfilled refrain from action, all go haywire, topsy turvy,

utsīdeyur ime lokā na kuryāṁ karma ched aham sankarasya cha kartā syām upahanyām imāḥ prajāḥ [3.24]

Krishna says, O Arjuna! If I don't work, the world would be chaotic and confounded. The world would be ruined ruthlessly and I would be solely responsible for the anarchical, chaotic world affairs. The degenerative, destructive character of the people would be due to My inaction. As a result, there would be untimely end of all people and the fault would lie on My door.

Undoubtedly, Krishna is the highest of the high, mightiest of the mighty, most right of the right and best of the best power, potential and intent to Arjuna [to you and me as well, and to the whole humanity for that matter]. Hence, Krishna emphasises the extent and import of His action, Arjuna cannot question or take it casually. Nor can you or me, can we? Can anyone anywhere anytime for that matter take it casually that His inaction would deprave and corrupt human character, cause chaos and commotion, destroy the society and extinguish the universe impromptu and untimely?

Of the inherent, coherent urge in us to act as spoken of supra, this verse is supplementary, explanatory. It implies none can be spared or exempted from duty, not even the Highest, Supreme Spirit. In this seen world everyone acts irrespective of the fact we see or do not, know or do not, feel or do not. That holds true to the unlimited, unfathomed, invisible universe as well. Action, activity, to act, acts as the guiding principle of creation, the birth of creatures and manifestation of the Cosmic Spirit.

Action may or may not be palpable but inaction is and will be and must be palpable. Inaction is utterly and obviously culpable because inaction causes intolerable, unmentionable consequences. Why Krishna forces Arjuna to fight a war the latter does not wish or want? Simply because the inaction unwittingly and unknowingly corrupts and depraves the Kuru empire, its subjects and subjects of the dominions allied to or under subjugation of the empire. When you and me fail to perform our duties, we commit the same blunder, unforgivable, inexcusable offence.

Why waste time in performing perforce instead of acting at the first instance?

You are free to do your duty at the first instance with a moment's reflection that this my performance seems to be unpleasant or unwelcome or to delay doing the same thing.

The difference is that in the first case you show your sense of being what you are. In the case of delay or dithering, the world around you, sees your foolishness, ignorance and egotism, since you would do the same the very same way you disliked or denounced.

It is obviously a big problem to do, discharge unpleasant, unsavoury job. It was the same sensible, stupendous problem with Arjuna. Discharging unpalatable duty, doing indignant job. Krishna solved the problem, the dilemma for Arjuna and for us as well, did not He? He solved it for all, for all time to come, for all homes and habitations.

How?

When He said Sukheduhkhe same krutwa labhaalabhou jayaajaou

Tato yuddhaya yujyasva naivam papamavapyasi [2/38]

O Arjuna! You just take pain and pleasure, loss and gain, defeat and victory as the same thing and enter the war without fear of sin [in the manslaughter of innumerable fighters and quite a lot of kindred].

Men and women everywhere, always delay, dither, waver in doing the job at hand as they are afraid of evident or invisible sin inhering the job. There is the problem. The invigilator in the examination hall should immediately catch hold the examinee indulging in malpractice, shouldn't he? If he dithers on the ground that the examinee is extremely poor, that he has failed the exam umpteen times, that he might commit suicide by crushing under a moving train if he fails this time etc, what will happen?

Did or didn't the invigilator commit a sin?

If he abetted the malpractice, he committed sin, didn't he? If he caught hold of the copying examinee and, as a consequence the examinee failing the test committed suicide; did he commit the sin of abetting suicide?

Arjuna was kind of invigilator and the Kaurava army as a whole was kind of copying examinees. That the Kauravas would be killed wholesale by the ruthless arrow of the third Pandava was not sinful in itself. On the Kurukshetra, Arjuna had no excuse to say "no" to the upcoming devastating battle, did he?

Manslaughter, that too mostly his loving kins, siblings and superior elders, bewildered and baffled Arjuna, the valiant warrior and the heart-of-gold person at the same time. Manslaughter is massively immoral and impious; one can ardently argue. But there are exceptions, aren't there?

The story or joke hereunder underlies an exception.

A devilish dacoit and highway robber was feared far and wide for his mindless murder of men, women and children for measly money or grams of gold. He murdered humans more for the heck of it than for the woeful wealth or paltry pelf. You can liken him to dreadful Angulimala of Buddhist literature. He killed and killed people indiscriminately and impulsively. Looting and blood- chilling killing was his calling and he did a sterling job of that. The victims of his vicious vandalism reached 108. He had count of his kills for he derived schanfreude satisfaction after his cruel killing or the woeful bewailing of the victims. There was no stop or sufficiency to his murders, meditated and meticulously executed. His cruellest killing could not be called homicide by any stretch of imagination or reasoning.

But a day dawned when he suddenly shivered at

the thought of the hundred plus gruesome killings he had committed for petty pennies or jots of jewellery. Quite culpable slaughter of innocuous and armless, harmless and honest travellers that he committed coolly, casually and callously daily disturbed him disastrously. He ran out of his den in search of solace and soothing sermons for his remorseful soul. In the beginning, people ran away from his sight despite his gentlemanly attire, temperate ambling and decent demeanour. Old fears of him did not die soon or sensibly. By degrees, he could be courted by the common folk. So much so that when he uttered his pitiable predicament, people began believing him.

But who can find a remedy for his reckless manslaughters, reeking life? Who can suggest him a way for appropriate atonement? His sea-change character and characteristics left the hearers in no doubt that he had regretted his past deeds [misdeeds] melancholically, not mischievously. But everyone was afraid the stupendous vice of murders he had committed overwhelmingly outweighs his sincere, sensible remorse. His regret was great but failed short of his venomous, virulent vices. He sought refuse in the suffusive scholarship of pundits, profuse wisdom of priests and pujakas, soothing sermons of saints and sages as he could meet. And he met many of them through his long repentant journey. He wore rags and bore the brunt of taunts, teases, criticisms, and sarcastic, sadistic, bitter, vulgar jokes; all on his hateful, sinful past and the present futile hunt for redemption and salvation.

Unmindful of obstacles and the frustrating quest, he went on and on, physically lean and thin but mentally determined and drawn.

His quest and jest did not go in vain. He finally met a sadhu on a roadside ashram in an isolated landscape. The sadhu donning orange robe, long matted hairlocks with face full of twitching moustache and dense, black beard smoked Ganja with the chela in tow. The chela was young, wore white but untidy koupin, had unshaven face but smiling, satisfying countenance. The twosome was, as usual, casual about the visitor. But started abruptly at the ghostly look of the untimely, unwelcome guest. As is their wont, the chela took the lead to ask,

Chela—Who are you, Mister! What do you look for here? Shelter? No shelter here for sure! There is no bread nor bed for uninvited guests, that too at this time of the day.

The dacoit kept his cool. He looked intently at the saintly sadhu who has stopped smoking by then, looked at the visitor as casually as curiously, maybe kindly.

Sadhu— [to chela] Why shout for nothing! You have learnt nothing in life, what to speak of a whit of good behaviour! [to the dacoit] How come you are here and alone, that too at a time when the congregation chanting bhajan is gone home for dinner and slumber!

The dacoit was well comforted by the soft, sweetened words of the sadhu and sat down on the ground as indicated by the sadhu, and then spoke lowly but clearly.

Dacoit – Maharaj! I was a dreadful dacoit just days ago, nay, months ago. I robbed pedestrians, bullock-cart-mounted gentry, even horse-riding small heroes with my sharp sword and shinning spears. I was strong and stout enough to pound half a dozen youths at a time with my piercing punches. Hard-hearted and hard-hitting that I was, I was able to bitterly knock down better looking and amply armed men in the highway encounters. Of course, I pounced upon the pack from behind bushes or trees when I saw them armed and admittedly prepared. I did not rob only unsuspecting travellers but butchered them brutally. I did not kill the victims on their resistance nor on suspicion that they might divulge my gory story to the public in general and the police in particular. They were so frightened after the vandalism that the man would not even speak out the gory story to his wife! Nevertheless, I killed for the sake of killing, for skilling and upscaling the craft and acumen of killing. I murdered men and women without mercy or motive only to derive sadistic, horrific, satanic pleasure! And committed homicide without scruple or conscience day after day for years. The victims of my brutish sport, vicious hobby increased day by day... one, two, three, four, five...ten, twenty, thirty......The poor victims lost their livelihoods, lives. And I counted their fallen heads 1,2,3,4,5...till it touched 108.

Heaving a heavy sigh, the dacoit continued,

Dacoit—O divine soul! I don't know why but abruptly I was awakened to the devilry of my despicable, demonic, horrible deeds. I wondered was I the very same abhorrent, deviant dragon that sucked human blood relentlessly, playfully! I pondered over from my schooltime purana-hearing that doers of smaller, far smaller sins were hell-bound even after heartfelt regret and repentance; what stinging, stinking, singeing hell awaits me!

I wept and wept inconsolably and uncontrollably, though there was none to comfort or console me. It's said somewhere in another context, "Men must work and women must weep." Hence, I refrained from the unmanly wailing and came out seeking counsel and comfort from pundits, priests, professors and pious, piteous souls like you. I met a many of them who were scared listening to my satanic tale and scarcely said anything worthwhile or practicable to please or pacify my scarred soul. Most of them disposed of me quickly, casually; several of them callously, comically; some even disdainfully, dishonestly, deceptively. In most cases, I could see through their tricks and was hopelessly unhappy, unnerved, so much so that I could have done away with them, had I been a ghost of my former self!

Maharaj! I am terribly troubled and intolerably tormented by the guilt and sin of my commissions. My ardent and arduous quest to find a guru who can shower benedictions on my sins and my sinning soul seems to have ended in vain. Will you show, suggest a redeeming, resuscitative way out so that I live the present, relive the rest of my life a humble, honest, honourable life in harmony with nature and the society? I shall be a resurgent human on and from the death and ashes of my renegade persona.

The guru and chela kept quite quiet, not knowing how to respond to the tortuous soul of the stupendous sinner who had, no doubt, been transformed to an untarnished saint by then.

The tormented dacoit added,

Dacoit- Great Guru! I shall undertake all austerities, all penance, all repentance that may be required of me to cleanse my soul of the soil, filth, dart that had accrued to due to dozens and dozens of homicides committed cruelly and constantly. Please show the redemptive path, the path of righteousness and piety so that I escape from eternal, torturous, damn hell to which I must be condemned and consigned!

The dacoit hung his head low over his drooped shoulders like a ninety-year-old, emaciated haggard, and sat benign speechless, without bothering what the duo does or says.

The guru and chela were utterly aghast and bitterly tripped and tossed for the first time in their ashram life. They failed to suggest a spiritual or temporal means to this meanest of the mean soul who was presently, profusely well-meaning. They sat silent for some time, communicated between them in silence but in signs and symbols, and then,

Guru—Beta! Don't lose heart! You have committed condemnable, cruel acts too often, consciously and carefree, oblivious of the abominable outcome. Yet, you have repented a lot. I don't know whether your repentance suffices your vices. But I hope and believe your quest for peace and salvation would be complete if you tour the teeming tirthas of the country.

The dacoit raised his head, his face radiant with intense hope. He quipped,

"Yes Maharaj! I shall do that certainly and seamlessly. But how and when can I know that my tirth tours have paid dividend, my sins and guilts have been cleansed, cured? When can I feel being like clarified butter turning ghee out of the abyss of dismal damnation?"

Guru and chela were outwitted for some moments. But as if prepared, the chela said,

Chela- Maharaj! He is right. Why should he tread trodden and untrodden paths to tens of thousands of tirthas of this vast land if he cannot be absolved of his gargantuan guilt and seamless sin? Better he shall....

Guru –Take the black umbrella in the corner and dip

the same in the tirtha-jala of seas and rivers, ponds and lakes. When the black flag changes colour, turns white, and flutters bright; you should know that your sins and vices have been washed clean as trash and waste drained in municipal gutter is pure and potable water by a treatment plant.

The chela was loud and clear in emphasizing, explaining what guru said.

It was okay dickey for the dacoit. Distance or dangers enroute were no deterrent or debilitating to the incorrigible, un-corrosive dacoit of the recent past. He set out on his strenuous tirtha tramp. While bidding good bye to the benevolent guru, he was all obsequious. From the bottom of his heart, he hoped high and honest that this last guru is really a saint, seer and saviour extraordinaire.

He went on and on day and night in sun and rain, scarcely minding his physical wants or the external impediments. He walked fast, almost running, though his emaciated physical frame aroused pity in co-travellers, companion tourists. Some of them offered him lift in their bullock-carts, horse coaches or donkey-backs. But he declined those graceful offers with grateful gesture, telling them that the devotee must endure afflictions on pilgrimage to arouse God's mercy.

He visited all and sundry shrines and temples, went into the sanctum sanctorum, prayed piteously, made possible oblations, and took prasad happily. He paid his pilgrimage to Kali, Kamakhya, Kedarnath, Badrinath, Vaidyanatha, Puri Lokanath, Somnath, Viswanath, Sankatamochanan, Ajodhya, Mathura, Vrindavan, Prayag, Gaya, Mahakala, Omkareshwar, Rameswaram, Tirupati, Anant Padmanabh, Minakshi, Mallikarjun, Kanchi, Chidambaram,

Chamundeshwari, Jagannath, Samaleswari, Vaishnodevi, Dwarika, Pushkar, Trimbakeshwar, Kapilash Chandrasekhar and so on. He had tirth bath in Ganga, Godavari, Sindhu, Kaveri, Saraswati, Jamuna, Krishna, Mahanadi, Narmada, Brahmaputra etc.

Conscious of the sage's instructions, he cautiously dipped the black flag with fabulous hope and unfaltering belief that the black would shine white this time. Lo! Nothing of the sort happened. He construed he was still short of purity and piety. Though disheartened for a while, he steeled his resolve and started the pious pilgrimage again. Fractured in faith, though for a few minutes, he was not frustrated for long. He was convinced the guru was absolutely right and he would one day be absolved of all his heinous acts and sins when the black flag fluttered white! He did not stop nor lost hope, and went on his austere quest, disregard of the adage, "Black will take no other hue." His pilgrimage was over; he paid his obeisance in all the shrines and sanctum sanctorum of the deities worshipped as possible as ever. He missed no munificent or mysterious-power-wielding deity nor did he ever fail to plunge the black flag in any sanctimonious pond, lake, river or sea. In spite of all his labour and love, the black flag did not whiten! The impossible did not happen. He was finally frustrated and fatigue-bitten.

More and more frequently now, the proverb rang in his ears, "*Angara shata dhouten malinatva na jayate*," [the black charcoal won't whiten even after hundreds and hundreds of washes]. The charcoal can't be whitewashed nor can the black flag be whitened. He thought, he ruminated— What went wrong? Where was he wrong? Was I not penitent enough? Was my penance, repentance not enough? Did I forge, falter in my faith, my conviction, my devotion? No. Never! Not at all! Was I ever wavering, faltering, frittering, failing in my faith? No, No, No!

Then what is "Yes"! The "Yes" is that the guru and chela made a fool of me, made a full, final, fantastic fool of me! A dreaded devil, a heinous criminal, a stubborn sinner like me must be condemned and consigned to the cruel, consuming hell for eons and eons till it is empty of all sinners. When the whole hell would be entirely emptied by the merciful amnesty decreed by the omnipotent, omniscient, omnipresent GOD, I alone be exempted! I must not be eligible even for a short parole from hell, what to speak of reprieve or remission. GOD would simply say, "I don't have the inherent jurisdiction to grant a short parole to this heinous human!"

Finally, fully frustrated and flattened, he reverted to his old bad days. He was anguished and angered with the guru chela duo who plainly deceived him to pursue an irrational impossibility for the fun of it. They are small, lazy leeches, earning their bread by the compassion and charity of the rural multitude who wish to fruitfully utilise their solitude after a hard day's labour by reciting the name of and listening to the saga of God in the secluded ashram premises. They are a stain, a stigma on the good name of God, godly people and goodly souls who usually practise rectitude in ashrams and hermitages. Their enigmatic looks, chattering, gesticulations and gossips concerning me demonstrated their demonic demeanour. As they say, "He that is down needs fear no fall" applied to me, appealed to me, as I was fallen, fell and earnestly yearned to get rid of my barbaric commissions, unpardonable sins by any means with all afflictions, all pains associated with the pious, piteous gains. Should have the duo dealt with my plight, my pitiable state so uncritically, so sarcastically, so jocularly? I think not. The farcical, frivolous, fraudulent duo be dealt with deservedly; be done away with my indefatigable blood-hungry sword and spear that have spilled blood and broken bones of many a simple, noble, innocuous soul. Have I ever butchered crafty cons like the guru and chela? Never.

How can I encounter such crooked hooks who are spooked of their shadow and shy off ditches, dacoits and dangers kilometres off? They talk plentifully and faultlessly on immortality of the soul and the destructible, perishable body. When it comes to their own case, they act diametrically opposite by clinging to their mortal body as fast, frantically and frenetically as the lowliest of the low, most fallen might ever do.

Fie on the duo! Fie on the flimsy, fraudulent, farcical cockroaches, bugs, pigs!

The devil incarnate dacoit rushed back to the ashram with lightning speed, so to say, and reached the ashram like a Pacific typhoon or Atlantic hurricane. The guru and chela after their sumptuous lunch were smoking Ganja in a pacific ambience. No sooner did they see the old, bloody dacoit than the chillum fell fragmented, shredded to pieces.

Their peace being gone, they shuddered at the ghostly sight of the ghastly dacoit. Nonetheless, they resumed their cool cunningly, and asked,

"How do you do, fella!".

"Fine! Cried the dacoit." And beheaded the two in chime with his loud "Fine". The just severed heads fell on the ground amidst a pool of scarlet blood. The dusty, dry ashram floor was all red, all blood. The dacoit looked at his blood-stained sharp spears for a moment and at the black flag the next moment.

Lo and behold, the black flag leaning on ashram wall had a dramatic chromatic transformation! It fluttered finely white!

The two homicides aggregated his man slaughter to 110. And his quest for remission, reprieve, absolution of his vices, sins ended in vain, did his?

THIRTEEN

**Pass or fail is equal
As Yoga would tell**

You have to act, do your job under duress. It is inherent and inborn impulsion, compulsion to act, to act non-stop, to act day and night, to act irrespective of your being hale and hearty or unwell and rusty. It is ok; it is alright.

But how can a human perform a task without bothering about the consequences, without thinking on the sequence? It is a pertinent point. Humans can act blindly or blindfold. Your assignment arises out of a target and aims at a goal. How can you detach gain or loss, pleasure or pain from your action?

Other creatures may act aimlessly, impromptu, impulsively. Why should humans? They are rational and responsible unlike millions and millions of other creatures ranging from unicellular worm to one-horn rhinoceros, from hippopotamus to whale, from sparrow to eagles, from tigers to starfishes, from amoeba to orangutan. They act according to inherent, inborn compulsion, instinct. They do not care for success or failure, though failure forces frustration and success happiness in them.

They kind of follow sloka 38, chapter 2.

sukha-duḥkhe same kṛitvā lābhālābhau jayājayau
tato yuddhāya yujyasva naivaṁ pāpam avāpsyasi [2.38]

O Partha! Count pain and pleasure, gains and loss, victory and vanquishment like one, as the same, and fight. Then you would not be smeared with sin, speak of sin, think of sin [not sin in the traditional sense but also /and dilemma, doubt, dithering that arise in the mind when one acts].

Unlike them, humans can refrain from working, say no to doing despite the appreciation or deprecation that accrues to such resistance. Humans must act as blindfold as other creatures because they have the "right" to do their duty. And real accountability, rationality lies in doing your duty as a "right",

karmaṇy-evādhikāras te mā phaleṣhu kadāchana
mā karma-phala-hetur bhūr mā te saṅgo 'stvakarmaṇi
[2.47]
yoga-sthaḥ kuru karmāṇi saṅgaṁ tyaktvā dhanañjaya
siddhy-asiddhyoḥ samo bhūtvā samatvaṁ yoga uchyate
[2.48]

O Dhananjay! You have the right to act, but not to the consequences thereof. Never mind the karma phal. But that does not mean you should not mind doing evil action, find excuses in indulging in devilish dos. You are great, noble [as a human] and must not be marked with akarma.

O Dhananjaya! Discharge your duty, perform your job without caring for outcomes. You do your karma in yoga, disregarding, detached from, consequences. And what is YOGA? To count success and failure as equal, to weigh success and failure in the same scale is YOGA.

Here Arjuna finds his answer. Here you find your answer, don't you? You act , you must act, you should act, you need to act, you will act, you shall act because nature compels ultimately you to act, though out of false, faulty, flimsy, filibusterous egoyou might say no at the outset[59/2]; you act, you must act because of the impulsion by your nature though you initially say no to act out of lust or attachment[60/2]; you act, must act, needs must act because whoever is born here on earth[inclusive of other creatures] shall act and cannot stay for a minute without acting because of the abiding, binding inherent nature.

Is it all? No, the significant facet of your working lies in your" right", in your "right to work", not in your whim or caprice, egotism or conceit to say "I shall not work". Your "right to act" is right; your assertion or arrogance "I shall not act" is not right. It is absolutely, obviously, overtly and indefensibly wrong,

But there is a rider, an overriding rider for that matter. And what is that?

You must work unmindful, oblivious of the result, the consequence, the effects. How strange? I work but not think of the effects that affect one or many instantly or later, directly or remotely. Right, you have the right to karma, not to Karmaphala.How?

Karma is essential, inescapable to you, your nature, your existence; not Karmaphala.

Doing away with, doing without Karmaphala may sound hollow and hysterical; ideal, not illustrative. No, it is real, not illusory; abiding, not advisory. Actually, Karmaphala follows Karma as day follows night or summer follows spring.

But what you have not to follow is Karmaphala in shape of success or failure, in the form of loss or gain accruing to your Karma, occurring in your Karma. You have to "see" both, the two opposites as "equal". Equality of success and failure is yogic. Since you are or shall or must be a YOGI, your problem is over.

FOURTEEN

Not the idle or inactive
But the up and doing is yogi, is sannyasi

Are you a Yogi? Difficult to answer impromptu or immediately, after thorough thought or lightly.

Since, right now, you are reciting Gita, you are a Yogi with all certainty, aren't you? Quizzical but crystal clear that all Gita readers are indubitably Yogis. How? Each chapter of Bhagavat Gita ends with,

"Iti Shreemahabharate Shatasahahasryam Samhitayam Vaiyasikyam Bhismaparvani Shreemadbhavadgitasupanishatsu BrahmaVidyam YogaShastre Shreekrushnarjunasambade ---Yoga namoh ---Adhyayah". *[the blanks could be filled up like , say Karma and Tritiya respectively]*

Gita is part of Mahabharat which is a Samhita of one hundred thousand verses; Gita is out of Bhishma Parva; is an Upanishad; a study of Brahma Vidya; Yoga Shastra [the scripture of Yoga]; in the dialectics of Kirshna-Arjuna duo. The insightful ending of each chapter thus ends all controversy about Gita's independence and interdependence with Mahabharata. All the 18 chapters eulogise, in the end, the Yoga Shastra facet of Bhagavat Gita. It is not facetious and fictious; it is fact and fundamental. Gita is Brahma Vidya and Yoga Shastra. So, when engrossed in reading, reciting Gita, you are a Yogi must, aren't you?

But those who do not read or brood over Gita are no less Yogi. They are the Yogi of sloka 48, chapter 2. And they are the superior, serene Yogis, because they act without anxiety or apprehension about the result. They care the Karma, not the Karmaphala. And they see good and bad Karmaphala as equal. So, the two tests of a Yogi are [1] engaging in Karma and [2] considering the positive or negative, good or bad implications as equal.

Unmindful and unworried of Karmaphala but active Karmi is not only Yogi but also Sannyasi.

śhrī bhagavān uvācha
anāśhritaḥ karma-phalaṁ kāryaṁ karma karoti yaḥ
sa sannyāsī cha yogī cha na niragnir na chākriyaḥ [6.1]

O Arjuna! He who is active without consideration of consequences of actions is a Yogi, is a Sannyasi; not the one who is inactive or refrains from action including sacrificial fire ritual.

We generally believe life is short and salvation from the worrisome, wearisome earthly life is extremely difficult, nay, next to impossible. Salvation is our short-term goal as humans are endowed with the intricate cognitive skill to discern and discriminate. Once you waste this iridescent, intelligent earthly life, you do not know what kind of life, what form of life you are destined to, you are entitled to, have in the next life, do you?

It is therefore imperative to disengage from all earthly

activities and be a Vairagi, a Yogi. So, thousands and thousands of humans renounce the world, wife and children, friends and festivities, to wander half-naked, half-starved, homeless, hopeless, hoping that austerities and acuities in concentration on God would get rid of painful future births. Or there would be no more births, at least those of worms, insects, bats, centipedes and the like. Or if the next birth comes perforce, it should be that of a sage who is showered with obsequiousness ubiquitously or that of a benevolent, just emperor whose deeds and demeanour shall be remembered for eons. In all these cases, it is as good as moksha, though not better.

Vairagya characterised as above, is no vairagya. Vairagya is devoid of *raga*. Vi + raga makes vairagya etymologically. And it is that that way really. Raga is attachment, love, attraction, fascination, friendship, infatuation and so on; so many things that emerge from in human heart and mind. When you shun the excesses, the extremities, the acuities, the abnormalities, the absurdities, the immoralities, the indecencies, the inadvisability, the unethicality, the inappropriateness etc, you shun raga. Then you are bereft of raga. And the state or condition is vairagya. Vairagya is not outwardly, exteriorised, extrinsic, ostentatious, superfluous. On the contrary, it is intrinsic, inwardly, interiorised, substantial, inside. You do not have to hide vairagya; it is your hideout. Vairagya plays hide and seek with you. If you catch it this moment; it slips the next. You miss it, if you are too careful; you miss it, if you are careless. My God! What a paradox this vairagya involves!

You should have all, friends and family, intense activity and immediate and mediate necessity. But a vairagi you are for sure. The world is the veritable, vast ocean with gulf and gorges that may drown and devour you. But you have to cross it. Do not be cross with the ocean; be in crush upon the ocean. Learn how to swim, then jump head on, and thereafter swim, without caring whether you reach ashore or be drowned and gone to the deepest bottom of the unfathomed ocean.

It is cowardice and unbefitting of human to run away from the beach like a frightened bitch or sit down like an intensely introvert intellectual to meditate and contemplate how to swim across the ocean before and without stepping into the shallowest shore!

It is only action that matters. Action is innocence; inaction is ignorance. Action is bliss; inaction is despondence, melancholy, cadaveric uselessness. Learned and wise, sage and serene, sadhu and yogi and sannyasi act, act and act and act.

The lazy, the lethargic, the idle, the waste, the bare and barren, the parasite and the pest, the stupid and the stub, the stagnant and the rust, the benumbed and the beast, avoid work, give up work, ditch and dither work.

You work, you are a Yogi. You work, you are a Sannyasi. There is no Yogi without Karma; there is no Sanyasi sans Karma. Mind your Karma and you are Yogi, you are Sannyasi.

The only proviso is never mind about Karma Phala.

It is to be borne in mind that Kaunteya queried in verse 1, chapter 5, about which between Karma Yoga and Karma Sannyasa is preferable. Krishna replied,

śrī bhagavān uvācha
sannyāsaḥ karma-yogaś cha niḥshreyasa-karāvubhau
tayos tu karma-sannyāsāt karma-yogo viśhiṣhyate [5.2]

O Arjuna! Sannyasa and Karma Yoga both are incontrovertibly beneficial and best. But, when distinguished between the two, Karma Yoga is better than Karma Sannyasa.

Hence, karma yogi is better than karma sannyasi; karma is preferrable to sannyasa.

Sannyasa does not outweigh karma, whereas karma edges ahead sannyasa. It is the popular precept and it is the concise concept. From time immemorial to the present times, humans have been working hard and hour by hour. They have, of course, often cursed themselves and praised a sannyasi's life out of disgust or desperation. But, given the choice, they would not opt the sannyasi life, because a Karmi is better than a Sannyasi.

Most of us most often mind this and mind our job. But some of us, including intellectual luminaries and luminous spirituals like Lokmanya Bal Gangadhara Tilak, eulogised and practised this principal principle piously and palpably.

FIFTEEN

**What is in a name? That which we call a rose,
By any other name would smell as sweet.**

Lokmanya Bal Gangadhar Tilak was a great Indian freedom-fighter, revolutionary and modern thinker, social reformer, patriot, teacher, writer, journalist, Jan Sevak, pleader and proficient orator, to mention a few. And after all, a pensive and persuasive spiritual thinker, propagator, promoter and writer of exceptional calibre and exponential erudition. He was born on July 23, 1856 in Chikhali village of Ratnagiri district of Maharashtra to Gangadhar Tilak and Parvati Bai Gangadhar. His father was a teacher, grammarian and Sanskrit scholar as well. His village nestled in the western ghats on Arabian coast was ideal for thinking and imagination. Since he was born into the famed Maratha Chitpavan Brahmin family and since his father was an eminent Sanskrit pundit, he leaned towards ancient Indian texts, though he was a magnificent mathematician and illustrious lawyer, eminent organiser and outstanding orator, powerful politician and fabulous freedom fighter with scanty time for intellectual inquiry and insight. Straightforward and truthful was what Keshav Gangadhar Tilak was from his childhood and all through. When he was 16 years old and before a few months to his father's death, he married to Tapi Bai or Nee Bal who was renamed Satyabhama Bai as a Marathi matrimonial tradition.

A married bachelor and burdened with household chores and liabilities, he might have refrained from studies to studiously follow the Brahminic chore, had he not been Keshav Gangadhar Tilak. But he was what he was, Keshav Gangadhar Tilak, KGT, for short. Wait, wait a minute! History knows him; you and I know him; the then whole India knew him; most part of the world knew him as Bal Gangadhar Tilak, BGT, for short.

How was Keshav Gangadhar rechristened Bal Gangadhar and Keshav Gangadhar was buried in deep dark chamber of oblivion? The former name became more and more notable and popular in the annals of India, while, inversely, the latter sank deep and deep into history's dungeon, history's Lethe.

It is interesting to note that the intellectual giant of the then India was not even an average student. He was detained for a year in class IX as much because of mental immaturity as of physical deficiency. He was lean and thin, and short, far short of his classmates in physical features. The classmates and schoolmates, and playmates as well made sarcastic, snide remarks of "Bal", meaning child, infant, of him. Made notoriously, the adjective became noun and became notable as "Bal". He grew physically and mentally strong and stout soon and made most of the ignoble adjective "Bal" by making it an endearing, enduring particular noun, a nationally nostalgic name.

In addition to that, it is noteworthy that Keshav had the second family name Balwant, the shortened version of which is "Bal". Instead of Keshav, Bal became the popular family and elders' address, which was not only shorter but also softer, sweeter. Nicknames scarcely make a name or earn fame, what to speak of occupying a page or chapter in history. It is different here because the person is precocious and precious and, obviously, different, no, radically different.

William Shakespeare, the peerless English playwright, more fondly referred to as the Bard, says in his popular play "Romeo and Juliet" [Act I, Scene II]

> Juliet –O Romeo, Romeo! Art though Romeo?
> Deny thy father, and refuse thy name;
> Or, if thou wilt not, be by sworn my love,
> And I'll no longer be a Capulet.
> Romeo[aside].
> Shall I hear more, or shall I speak at this?
> Juliet.
> 'Tis but thy name that is my enemy; --
> Thou art thyself though, not a Montague.
> What's Montague? it is not head, nor foot,
> Nor arm, nor face, nor any other part
> Belonging to a man. O, be some other name!
> What's in a name? that which we call a rose
> By any other name would smell as sweet;

The neighbours, Capulet and Montague, were sworn enemies. But Juliet, the Capulet clan maiden, was madly in love with the boy next door, Romeo, belonging to the Montague dynasty. The stern wall separated the lovers physically. So, they made nocturnal sneaking conversation with Juliet looking from her upstairs bedroom window and

Romeo perched upon her orchard garden wall. The famous balcony scene of the romantic tragedy, Romeo and Juliet, beautifully berates the worth or utility of a name.

Frustrated by her father's firm resolve not to have any truck with the inimical Montague, Juliet speaks out that except for the "name" Montague, Romeo has nothing adversarial about him as far as the Capulet clan is concerned. She wonders the "name" is not the head, face, arm, foot or any other limb of a man but the aggregate of these limbs that identifies a man.

The identifying mark is the "name" and the "name" makes or mars the man. She ponders that Romeo ceases being father's enemy as soon as he shuns Montague, the "name". And Romeo is exactly the same in, with any other "name"; with all other "names". It is not the "name" but the man that counts. Likened to the rose, one does not flatten his/her nose with the flower's fragrance, should rose be named jasmine, gold mohur, *Kadamba,* lotus, lily or the like. The simple logic is that the fragrance, not the name, makes rose a rose; the lovely, sweet, soft flower; the queen of flowers.

In case of Bal Gangadhar Tilak, Shakespeare is absolutely right in writing, "What is in a name? that which we call a rose by any other name would smell as sweet". He would have been as patriotic, nationalist, reformist, educationist, journalist, public speaker, pleader, thinker, writer et al, had he been Keshav Gangadhar Tilak or even Balwant Gangadhar Tilak.

The only loss would have been in the chiming of "Lal-Bal-Pal". It must have sounded unpleasant or discordant to say, "Lal-Keshav-Pal". Who knows how the triple stalwarts, the patriotic triumvirate, the nationalist trinity, the rationalist trident, the revolutionary tripod, Lala Lajpat Rai, Bal Gangadhar Tilak and Bipin Chandra Pal would have been called in short, in fondness, if Bal Gangadhar had been Keshav or Balwant Gangadhar? From Punjab to Maharashtra to Bengal, the stream of Independence movement gained momentum by convergence, confluence this *Triveni*. This nationalist, patriotic, revolutionary and reformative Triveni is as historic in annals of modern India as the Prayag Raj confluence of Ganga, Yamuna and Saraswati is holy since time immemorial.

His chequered career as an activist was sparkled with splendour and colour. Nationalist and patriotic par excellence, he passed his Matriculation, BA, LLB in 1873, 1876 and 1879 respectively even after marriage and with the household burden, because of his firm conviction that modern education and higher intellectual interest was indispensable to national endeavours and enterprises, emancipation from foreign yoke and obsolete orthodoxy and from illiteracy with multiple attendant evils. And the youthful Tilak believed:Individual education and illumination were not the end in themselves but the means of a higher, nobler end, i.e., reformation of the society and freedom of the country from alien imperial subjugation. And Bal Gangadhar was never selfish nor subjective. His Sanskrit learning and Indological inclinations sparked the flames of *"Paropakaraya swargaya papaya parapidana*m": Service to others paves the path to heaven, while harming and tormenting others leads to sin, the shortcut to hell.

Towards such end, spread of modern, motivating education among the masses was crucial and the correct path. As a beginning, he founded an English School in Pune on the first day of the Gregorian calendar of 1880. During those times, it was tribulations galore for a 24-year-old Maratha brahmin youth to jump head-on into the impure ocean of propagation of English education in the ancient holy soil of India. But Bal Gangadhar is Bal Gangadhar whose enthusiasm and inspiration was like the unstoppable bluish emerald waves of the Arabian sea which dash against the rough and rude rocks and ridges of the western ghats, and being broken, pull back to rise and rush against the incorrigible shore again and again.

The single project was not enough for BGT. He founded in Pune with faithful and fine friends, Gopal Ganapati Agarkar and Vishnu Shastri Chiplunkar, Kesari, a daily newspaper in Marathi on January 4, 1881, owned and managed by the Kesari Maratha Trust. Agarkar edited the daily till 1887 when he left to publish his own paper named Sudharak, meaning rescuer or reformer. BGT took over editor's onerous responsibility on Agarkar's departure. When BGT was behind the bars in 1897 and 1908, erudite and all-weather associate Narasimha Chintamani Karlekar was entrusted with the editorial assignment. Mahratta, the English weekly, was published from Mumbai on January 2, 1881, just 2 days before Kesari's appearance. The galaxy of the greats like Vishnu Shastri Chiplunkar, Mahadev Ballal Namjoshi, Vaman Rao Apte and Gopal Ganapati Agarkar gave the invaluable company to BGT.

In the beginning, BGT was enthusiastic on expanding modern education base by founding English medium schools. A gold medallist graduate in Mathematics and Sanskrit, he taught maths in the school he founded. Success in the education expansion arena, inspired him to found the Deccan Education Society on October 24, 1884 in Pune, which established Fergusson College to cater to pre-university learning. A giant in maths, Tilak took maths classes in the said college. Teaching and journalism were two wings, two weapons of BGT's ambitious objective to uplift Indians in general and Marathas in particular who seemed to be servile and selfish in the slothful slumber of British subjugation which appeared to last into eternity. Initially, education and journalism weighed equal in GBT's mind but soon he leaned upon the journalistic joyride with more fancy and fervour. Besides, he was as much unhappy with the subservient Indian ruled as much discontented with the British rulers who needed must address to the appalling condition of the subjects, but did not bother or care.

To awaken Indians, he thought of extending education network and modern education for that matter on the one hand; while he embarked upon his writing flair and journalistic josh to draw apathetic British establishment's attention to the pathetic economic and abject social conditions of the masses on the other. It was no secret to Indian intellectuals of the day like GBT and his comrades that the British empire fleeced the Indian soil to line the former's coffers and drain out the latter's treasures. Floods, famines, epidemics, disappearance of indigenous sources of livelihood triggering unemployment, soaring prices of imported goods and services, high taxes on indigent farmhands and exploitation of benevolent landlords and businessmen were go of the British rule those days. BGT felt, and rightly so, that most often and in most cases the people's problems and the appeals of the masses did not reach the ears of the local, provincial or central administrative authorities, what to speak of the imperial biggies in London. Though the ruling elite often turned blind eye to the vagaries and adversities of the masses and though oftener the mass petitions and people's representations fell flat on British rulers' deaf ears; yet, Tilak reasoned, more and more public petitions and collective grievances be aired to rear the strong but silent, indirect, voice of resistance. Newspapers and weeklies were newer but stronger mediums of communication and public platforms to arouse sleepy Indians against insipid Britons.

Hence, he bade farewell to academia and indulged in the turbulent and troublesome pursuit of reporting, editing, public-speaking and opinion-making.

SIXTEEN

What is in a name?
His Highness Shrimant Rajashri Shivaji VI Chhatrapati Maharaj Sahib Rao Bahadur
Is incurably mad

Even when he was thick with education expansion and curricula modernisation, he was engrossed in and intoxicated with anti-British and pro-Indian exhaustive reports and incisive editorials. His fight against intrusive imperialism started early in his journalistic jingling, resulting in his 4 months imprisonment in 1882 when he was in the right side of 30.

And the notorious defamation case was the Mahadeo Barve of Kolhapur case. It is really surprising that a youth of just 28 mustered enough strength of will and audacity to blow the banalities and brutalities of the British ambushing the Dalhousie Lapse Doctrine in one way or another, even after a quarter century of the 1857 War of Indian Freedom.

Then what is the un-brave Barve case?

The widow of Rajaram II of Kolhapur adopted Shrimant Narayana Rao Dinkar Rao Bhonsle who ascended the throne in 1871 when only 8 years old. Shrimant Narayan Rao Dinkar Rao Bhonsle became His Highness Shrimant

Rajashri Shivaji VI Chhatrapati Maharaj Sahib Rao Bahadur, Raja of Kolhapur. On January 1, 1877, he was saluted as His Highness Shrimant Rajashri Sir Shivaji VI Chhatrapati Maharaj Sahib Rao Bahadur, Raja of Kolhapur, on being knighted.The British protected him and appointed Mahadeo Barve to take care of the young Raja Sir Shivaji VI said to be suffering from incurable insanity.

The youthful Raja in his early teen was awarded coveted British titles like Knight Commander of the Star of India [KCSI] and the Empress of India Medal in 1877 when just 14. But when he was 19 and was manly enough to look after his monarchy, he could be lunatic, that too incurably. Was it an irony of fate or somebody's infatuation for his fortunes?

It was incredible, even to the goofy gullible. The British rulers were what they were famous or infamous for. The British diagnostics and doctors who diagnosed Sir Shivaji VI might have been mightily pressurised by the foreign rulers and bribed by the native Mahadeo Barve to declare a mild, temporary mental instability as a dreadful, dangerous insanity that would be deadly injurious to his subjects' and his interest. The machination was meticulous when the pro-British papers like Times of India and Bombay [now Mumbai] Gazette gurgled the news and praised imperial action as any gutter press does.

The Indian owned media of the day like Indu Prakash, Kesari and Mahratta disbelieved the Barve-manipulated make-believe story as medical machination at the behest of British rulers to benefit Mahadeo Barve, the kingdom-protector and de facto ruler. Kesari editor Agarkar and Mahratta editor Tilak tore away the British story that the

Chhatrapati was unhealable of the alleged dementia and derangement. On the contrary, they hammered that there was abundant evidence in the form of letters to editor from Kolhapur and nearby areas that Barve hatched the plot to hold his highness Sir Shivaji VI hostage and exercise absolute power of Kolhapur state. Apart from instructing his subordinates in person, he wrote confidential and conspiratorial letters to them to slow-poison and segregate the Raja.

Barve did not take the young hotheads, lying low. He filed defamation suit against Agarkar and Tilak, editors of Kesari and Mahratta respectively. Though the trial was farcical of the first order and though the prosecution could not prove defamatory accusation satisfactorily, still the duo was held guilty and sentenced to 4 months imprisonment each on July 16, 1882. The Chhatrapati was shifted to Ahmednagar under Mahadeo Barve's protection where he breathed his last on December 25, 1883, while Tilak and Agarkar languished in Dongri Jail of Bombay[Mumbai]. The declared death of heirless His Highness Sir Shivaji VI in an intriguing brawl with his bodyguards deepened the suspicion of Mahadeo's treachery and British tom foolery. Unfortunately, Sir Shivaji VI's successor Shahu was antagonistic to the nationalist Tilak. It is another story how quickly British bureaucracy penetrated into Indian psyche alongside intruding Indian geography.

It is important to bear in mind that when Tilak was imprisoned for the first time for the fault of defaming fraudster and falsehood fabricator, Mahadeo Barve, India heard her first nationalistic, patriotic lyric of significant note during the British regime. And the composer was the famous novelist, essayist and administrator Bankim Chandra Chattopadhyay [1838-1894 AD] who served as Deputy Magistrate of Jajpur in Odisha, then part of the vast Bengal-Bihar province. The headquarter town Jajpur situated on the right bank of Baitarani, famous for the seat of Biraja, a well-known Shakti incarnate. The town is named after Jajati Keshari [922-955 AD], son of Janmejaya I[882-922 AD] famous emperor of the Somavamshi dynasty[9th to 12th Century AD]. Jajati I first ruled from Vinitapur, modern Binika in Suvarnapur district of Odisha.

The national song sung by Bankim in his famous novel, Anand Math, in the mouth of a host of ochre-colour-clad recluses of Bengal, starting with "Vande mataram*****" was the patriotic cry, freedom struggle slogan. Nowadays, it is recited respectfully and ritually on Independence Day, Republic Day celebrations throughout India with evocative enthusiasm. The song assumed epic importance when Rabindranath Tagore, the Bengali literature stalwart, sang it in Indian National Congress Session of 1896. The Partition of Bengal in 1905 heightened the patriotic appeal of the song so much so that it was the freedom struggle mantra of the Indian masses.

As a matter of fact, the freedom movement classic, Anand Math, rests on the monk mutiny or sannyasi rebellion occurring between 1770-1777 AD under the leadership of Pandit Bhabani Charan Pathak. The locale is Jalpaiguri forests of Murshidabad and Baikunthanath Pur. The all-renouncing recluses nestled in the deep forests in peace with nature and themselves, reading Upanishads and Bhagavat Gita, spending time in meditation and contemplation, and discussing and discoursing with stray travellers and interested disciples, rose in revolt, in performance of their duty to the motherland Bharat in accordance with Bhagavat Gita spirit, after Clive conquered Bengal for East India Company, entitling the Company to collect land revenue. This was followed by the Buxar Battle of 1764 when East India Company commander, Hector Munro, humbled the combined combatants of Mughal Emperor Shah Alam II, Banaras Raja Balwant Singh, Awadh Nawab Shuja-ud-Daula and Bengal Nawab Mir Quasim. The Company win founded the Company rule and perpetrated the arbitrary and atrocious company administration. To compound people's misery, Bengal was struck by famine in 1770 when 10 million people from Ganga, Hooghly, Padma river basins perished. These events in quick succession set the sannyasis in rebellious motion. They targeted company carts carrying cash chests enroute and earned notoriety as thugs, plunderers, looters, though they distributed the booty among the needy. Nevertheless, the Indian morality did not stand behind them and they were discredited and denounced. With difficulty but determination, company army and police raided their hideout and hanged 50 sannyasis out a total 150. Fiction or fact, whatever that may be, Anand Math is a classic par excellence; Bankim Chandra Chatterjee is a litterateur of the tallest tier; and "Vande mataram***" is a patriotic mantra, nationalistic hymn for eternity.

The famous [or infamous] Barve defamation case or the Kolhapur Parikrama [Affairs] case as it is known locally and historically did not douse inspirited Bal Gangadhar Tilak, the fireball, the firebrand fighter and the inextinguishable flame of nationalism, patriotism.

The trial proceedings and the tribulations faced by

the accused twosome as reported exhaustively in Kesari and Mahratta and selected vernacular media made Bal Gangadhar Tilak trustworthy and true hero of Indian Independence struggle. Mahatma Gandhi later paid his homage to this rebel, this revolutionary, this fighter, calling him, "The Maker of Morden India". The British writer, diplomat, scholar, contemporaneous with Tilak, Sir Valentine Chirol [1852-1929], called him, "The Father of the Indian Unrest". The colonial masters realised that the appellation was apt and accurate and Tilak was a dry fish bone in the imperial throat that could not be swallowed nor spewed out. In fact, the British masters found ill omens of the 1857 Indian Freedom War in that youth who was born a year before the great unrest of 1857. So did see Indian intellectuals and patriots.

This imprisonment, though due to allegedly personal culpability, paved the way for his preparation for future imprisonment for patriotic and nationalistic cause. In the 1880-1890 decade, Tilak travelled on two routes simultaneously, i.e., spreading education and informing fellow countrymen, mainly Maharashtrians, through inciting reports and incisive editorials in vernacular and English press.

Day by day, the latter overtook the former as he found journalism and other writing more efficacious and widespread mode of outreaching and influencing the masses. British rule was, no doubt, ruthless in regard to welfare and development of Indians. The British officers and clerics had a brutish aversion for the natives when the latter were writhing and struggling in starvation, epidemics and superstition. They lay the fault on the natives' doors to wash their hands clean. The subjects had no other option than to subjugate themselves to the cruelties of nature on the one hand and the maladministration and maladroit handling of the matter by the top and petty British bureaucrats on the other.

But Tilak would not have any of it nor would he take it lying low.

SEVENTEEN

Plague on you, rogue Rand and Ayerst!

In 1896, Mumbai was panicked by bubonic plague. Soon did it spread to Pune accompanied by frightening famine that devastated most of the deccan plateau. By January 1, 1897, Pune was a precarious town perspiring by plague epidemic and singeing with fierce famine. The British rulers alarmed by the trepidations of the epidemic unleashed a reign of terror on the already terrorised poor natives. They blamed their poverty, illiteracy, superstition, unhygienic living conditions to the uncontrollable spread of plague. Though the local population seething with poverty and illiteracy was partly to blame for the bubonic plague spread, the plague was imported from Europe in British ships.

Indians almost aliens to bubonic plague must have failed to fathom its gravity and grave-like dimensions. Illiteracy and superstitious beliefs and sorrowful indigence may have enhanced the plague speed, accelerated the plague spread. The British rulers as much afraid of the frightful plague as of the native discontentment that may cause another revolt of the 1857 kind pressed into action. As far as Pune is concerned, they constituted a Special Plague Committee headed by Walter Charles Rand, an Imperial Civil Service officer, who was assisted by Lieutenant Ayerst as military escort. Rand deployed 800 army and police personnel to ensure, among others, that the town of Pune was cut off to outsiders and contained within with the inhabitants. The townsfolk barred from moving out were isolated and frisked from the plague infected people, and sent to tents and hospitals to quarantine the infected from the healthy ones. But the well-meant move was implemented ill-minded, ill-planned, and indecently, insensitively some of the time. The authorities dragged the infectious people and the suspects like dogs and donkeys. They searched homes and dwelling units roguishly and recklessly, and stripped and chased the menfolk, even women, inside their homes or outside in full public view. They vandalised hearths and homes, huts and hamlets, and disparaged and desecrated idols and symbols of deities and saints, gods and gurus that the natives revered and worshipped, even the abjectly poor and acutely illiterate, outcastes or ostracised, with deep devotion. The administrative torture outweighed the plague pathos.

There was outcry not so much against this outlandish epidemic as against the atrocious administrative measures by the outlandish rulers. Tilak who dominated the editorial desks of the two newspapers Kesari and Mahratta incited the natives to resist and revolt against the arbitrary, autocratic British officers. His powerful exhorts with quotes and exposition from Bhagavat Gita justifying assassination of assassins aroused tremendous temper in the masses. His inciteful, spiteful writings provoked Indians to deal with, even do away with disdainful Britons.

Under such a surcharged atmosphere, the unsuspecting

Rand and Ayerst were targeted by the Chapekar brothers. On 22.6.1897, Walter Charles Rand and his military escort, lieutenant Ayerst, were on their way to Government House for wholehearted enjoyment of fun and feast on the occasion of Diamond Jubilee celebration of reign of Queen Victoria. Damodar Hari Chapekar, Balakrishna Hari Chapekar and Vasudev Hari Chapekar had the scent of Rand's arrival at the party. The nocturnal creatures that the British and the Europeans were, they started arriving at the venue after full sunset. Walter Charles Rand and his escort, lieutenant Ayerst, aboard two coaches arrived at the Government House between 7 and 7.30 PM. Damodar, the elder brother and leader of the alien-shooting mission, with his two brothers, well- armed and appropriately ambushed, lay in wait near a yellow building on Ganeshkhind Road close to the venue. The three brothers had a pistol, a sword and a spear each so that one weapon failing or missing the target, the target would be hit with the next. And Walter Charles Rand must see his Indian, English and earthly end. And the boastful British bureaucrats would beware of dreadful Indian revenge.

    The Chapekar brothers hailed from a small hamlet nearby Chinchwad close to Pune. The plague prevention steps by the British bureaucracy were intended to save the European and British population from the cruel clutches of the endangering epidemic. Pune housed a cantonment and was home to the serving and touring Europeans consisting mostly of Britishers due to its spacious landscape and amiable climate. They did not mind welfare of the natives nor did mingle with the local masses. The plague prevention operation was discriminatory and derogatory to the Hindu culture, customs and practices. The good and modern measures like inoculation, quarantine, purification of waterbodies and streets, disposal of infected corpses separately and at safe distance from homes and hamlets were imposed and enforced insensitively. The orthodox Hindus who honoured their traditions and customs at the cost of their life and livelihood did not submit to the government instructions and injunctions. Agarkar and Tilak, the towering journalists wielding immense influence on the Maratha masses on the strength of their being editors of Kesari ad Mahratta respectively, indoctrinated youths like Chapekar brothers to revolt against and avenge upon British vandalism and venality. Chaperkar brothers had a chequered past.

Their grandfather Vinayak Chapekar headed a large joint family which was pretty well off. In 1869 when Damodar Hari Chapekar was born [25.6.1869], his fortune was in lakhs of Rupees, indisputably an astronomical amount in those days. But bad days followed as his independent attitude led him to resign from government service. He tried his hand in business but flopped. Independent-minded and self-respect-resplendent, a nineteenth century Maharashtrian that he was, he was bound to fail in business. Notwithstanding his waning wealth, Vinayak set off on pilgrimage to Kashi, the seat of Viswanath. The arduous journey cost Damodar's elder sister's life enroute Gwalior. Yet, things improved a bit, which was obviously attributed to grace of Kashi Viswanath. But Damodar believed that his grandfather reaped divine dividend of holy Gangasnana in Kashi. After the pilgrimage, Vinayak sent his son Hari to a secondary school. And then employed a pundit to impart

Sanskrit lessons so that Hari could be a kirtanakar. He also ensured that his other sons played musical instruments in the kirtan troupe. During those days, bhakti movement motivated people to lead peaceful and blissful life by chanting names and singing psalms of Rama, Krishna, Hari etc. Hari Chapekar's troupe did initially well but faced the music as Hari's brothers did not bother that the troupe and the artistes should prosper. Though kirtan troupes earned respect and money, there were many to whom it was a mean calling. Some people believed that kirtan as a full-time, all-season job did not behove caste Hindus or aristocratic people. The disapproval and disdain shown by villagers and relatives disheartened Hari Chaperkar. Even Vinayak Chaperkar headed northwards to Maratha capitals of Indore and Dhar to earn a decent livelihood with his language and literary skills and calibre. A skilled classical scriptwriter, he did well to live well. But that was temporary wellbeing. Lady luck did not smile upon him. He died on the bank of Kshipra or Shipra at a location 26 KMs off Indore. His sons, daughters-in-law and grandchildren could not see him on deathbed or bier, what to speak of performing obsequies.

Hari did not perform obsequies for want of travelling expenses from Nagpur where he resided then. Though his obsequious respect to his father was fast and unfaltering, other brothers and sisters suffering from abject poverty showed the same abhorrent behaviour. The deprivations of the family were so acute that Hari's wife died alone in his absence. Hari could not be beside his parents' deathbeds or funeral pyres. Other brothers bunked parental care and funeral rites solely because of the stifling poverty. They are claimed to be brahmin or high caste Hindus but people humbled them, snubbed them seamlessly because they failed to fire their parental pyres. Hari was horribly harassed for not being beside his wife's dying bed. Nonetheless, Hari harnessed his kirtan troupe days to his advantage. His socialisation with princes and landlords was beneficial to his learning, especially Sanskrit. That helped him to compose Satyanarayan Katha, a translation and annotation of Skanda Purana.

Tilak was, to a great extent, the cause of the assassination by Chapekar brothers. He did not divulge the names and details of the Rand assassination accomplices. Nonetheless, he stood trial for incitement to murder and was imprisoned for 18 months. When he came out of the jail in Mumbai after expiry of imprisonment, he was a greater, taller, more popular people's leader. His nationalist stature was great. He pronounced his classical statement in Maratha, "Swaraj is my birthright and I shall have it."

EIGHTEEN

Jnana-Yoga there is, yes;
Bhakti-Yoga there is, yes. Who says not?
But

Tilaka's enlargement from prison enlarged his popularity and political maturity. He was hellbent on ousting British regime and its atrocities on the Indians. He realised soon enough that the British empire was unjust and discriminatory to Indians in the administration of justice. From his own experience, he was sure that he was convicted and awarded 18 months' imprisonment on insufficient and indirect evidence because of his being Indian. The case against him would have run different course, had he been a European or British. Even with scant information in this regard, he regarded that the pan Indian panorama in this regard was no different. Just then, he came across the Muzaffarpur Conspiracy case.

Khudiram Bose and Praful Chaki, two young Bengali revolutionaries, were involved in the murder bid of Douglas Chelmsford, the hard-hearted British District Judge of Muzaffarpur on April 30, 1908. Though they threw bombs on two innocent British women by mistake, Khudiram Bose was arrested on May 1 and Prafulla Chaki shot himself dead on the 2nd May. The Calcutta[now Kolkata] police raided the residence of Aurobindo Ghosh and the garden house of his brother Barindra Kumar Ghosh. Arrest and trial of young Khudiram, and raid and arrest of Aurobindo, his brother and others, were hot news of the day. All over India, there was great support and appreciation for the nationalist revolutionaries. Aurobindo and his followers were charged with waging war against the British empire. Tilak jumped the bandwagon of national support for the revolutionaries. He wrote in the Keshari that the British should free Khudiram, Aurobindo et al and quit the country. He was charged with sedition and sentenced to six years imprisonment in Mandalay, Burma.

During the Burmese incarceration, he was transformed to a different person. He wrote the magnum opus, Gita Rahasya or Karma Yoga Shastra, in Marathi, which was published in 1915. He propounded that Gita preaches nishkama karma, selfless action or action disregard of result; not karma sannyasa, renunciation of action. He wrote the book in pencil in the precincts of the Mandalay prison over a period of six years from 1908 t0 1914. On his interpretation of Gita, he once said that Gita is as many creeds to as many interpreters. To him, Gita speaks of Karma Yoga, the Yoga of Action, sincere, selfless action without expectation of outcome; action not meant to benefit one exclusively. He emphasised that Jnana Yoga or Bhakti Yoga is subservient to Karma Yoga, not the other way.

He harped on action when he unequivocally says, " The conclusion I have come to is that the Gita advocates the performance of action in this world even after the actor has achieved the highest union with the Supreme Deity by Jnana

[Knowledge] or Bhakti [Devotion]." He goes on, "Jnana -Yoga there is, yes. Bhakti- Yoga there is, yes. Who says not? But they are both subservient to Karma- Yoga preached in the Gita. [In preface to Gita Rahasya]"

As clear and convincing in his political and social ideology, so clear is he here in emphasising the supremacy of Karma over contending Bhakti and Jnana as the quintessence of Gita. Among others, he harps on verse 19, chapter 3,

tasmād asaktaḥ satataṁ kāryaṁ karma samāchara
asakto hyācharan karma param āpnoti pūruṣhaḥ [3.19]

Ho Arjuna! Act, act always, incessantly, ceaselessly on what you are supposed to do: Do without expecting any outcome, considering the consequence. When you act without expectation of outcome, you achieve the best result, the topmost outcome. In fact, persons who act always without anticipating any return achieve the highest success, the highest accomplishment that humans are ever entitled to.

NINETEEN

Jail or hell
Vinoba, tell Gita, tell!

When deliberating upon action, predominance of action as enunciated in the venerable Bhagavat Gita, one has not to miss the theory of Gita essence introduced by Vinoba Bhave, the veteran freedom-fighter, Gandhian, saint and man of God [in the words of Jayprakash Narayan] of Paunar Ashram, Wardha, Maharashtra.

Born on September 17, 1895, he was 39 years younger than Bal Gangadhar Tilak; 26 years younger than Mahatma Gandhi. Even though an ardent believer in and follower of Mahatma Gandhi, he could be more likened to Tilak. Both were Maratha Brahmins and both were revolutionaries; both were erudite and evocative; both were well versed in Indian scriptures and epics. Both were not disenchanted with Indian ethics and morals under influence or delusion of western, especially British education and etiquette. On the contrary, they eulogised and glorified ancient and prevalent customs and systems. While Tilak talked of and practiced violent means to achieve his ends, Vinoba Bhave was conscious of the means employed. For instance, he was against the education system of the day. To express his displeasure with the education system, he quit university education midway. He remained an undergraduate but his academic excellence exceeded that of most of the formally, institutionally educated scholars and researchers of the time. In mastery of languages, knowledge of epistemology, he commanded respect of contemporary freedom fighters and formal scholars. He who gave up British education system must be against the British rule but he admired and adopted the Gandhian precept of non-violence to resist British rule.

1930s was the era of non-cooperation against British Empire. Vinoba participated in the mass non-cooperation movement and was jailed. While in Dhule jail in Maharashtra from January 18 to July 14, 1932, he utilised his time in reading and writing as Tilak did in his Mandalay imprisonment years. But Vinoba did something worthier. From the first Sunday evening on January 21, he gave a talk to the inmates on the great Gita.

It is indubitable that most Indians, mostly freedom-fighters, were avid readers of Bhagavat Gita. The inmates invariably read and discussed the glorious Gita. Even criminal inmates heard Gita discussion with rapt attention, being drawn by the eternal truths of life told in the mellifluous, lucid style of Vinoba who was a Gita scholar of repute. The proposal on his talk on Gita every Sunday evening was not unacceptable to the jail authorities. On the contrary, they enjoyed the weekly discourse which was not imperious nor anti-imperial.

Vinoba was not theoretical as far as Gita reading and recitation is concerned. He desired to speak on Gita as his duty during confinement. He was not conscious of its outcome as his actions always and everywhere were dedicated to the Lord. He did not mean his talk on Gita as teaching or preaching but just a talk with fellow inmates, friends in the fenced, walled cage-house. But once Bhave talked, it made all the difference. The jail staff were drawn to the weekly discourse, first out of curiosity and later under kind of compulsion. The inmates inhaled a whiff of fresh air in the language used by the youth on such thoughtful shastra as Gita. They were accustomed to preachers using high-sounding, pompous language placing Gita contents out of commonfolk's cognitive or emotive reach. On the contrary, Vinoba made Gita plain and commonplace, not diminishing the depth and dimensions of the divine song called Gita. This was possible because Vinoba, the youth, was old and wise, insightful and faithful, with his extraordinary intellect.

On the quality and content of the Talks on Gita by Vinoba Bhave, in the preface to the English edition said Jayaprakash Narayan, "Vinoba is not a politician, not a social reformer, nor a revolutionary. He is first and last a man of God. Service of man to him nothing but an effort to unite with God. He endeavours every second to blot himself out, to make himself empty so that God may fill him up and make him His instrument."

On Gita, Vinoba says,

"The bond between Gita and me transcends reason. I have received more nourishment from the Gita than my body has from my mother's milk. There is little place for ratiocination in a relationship of loving tenderness. Moving beyond the intellect, I therefore soar high in the vast expanse of the Gita on the twin wings of faith and experimentation. Most of the times I live in the ambience of the Gita. The Gita is my life-breadth. I am as it were afloat on the surface of this nectar when I am talking about the Gita and when alone, I dive deep into this ocean and rest there. Henceforth, every Sunday, I shall be giving a talk on the teaching of the Gita who is verily our mother."

On the contents and cream of the Gita, he says, "Almost every idea and thought necessary for the blossoming of life can be found in the Gita. That is why the wise have called it the encyclopaedia of dharma."

On his own case Vinoba has held the Gita as his mother of intellectual nourishment, improvement. In addressing the prison inmates, he calls the Gita "verily our mother". Hence, Vinoba could be a nationalist of a different kind whose symbol and strength was the Gita. The reason is not far to seek. According to him, the Gita has "almost every idea and thought" for the blossoming of life. He follows Gita steadfastly, even fastidiously, with the belief that Gita followers must find solution to every problem, can ascend high peaks of growth and fulfilment. When all men and women of the nation take the Gita notion sincerely, societally, the nation's problem would be solved. In course of his Gita discourse, Vinoba exhorted the inmates that the country would be freed of British subjugation sooner or later but surely.

An eminent scriptural scholar and linguistic light, Vinoba could have made his Gita talks spiritual lessons to the inmates who were mature adults addicted to selfless work. For instance, there was P S Sane, fondly called Sane Guruji, who shone on his own light, on his own right as a scholar, writer, social worker and freedom fighter, who took shorthand notes of the Talk with a view to publishing the same later on for wider appreciation and enlightenment.

But Vinoba, the man of God, meant nothing more than discussing Gita with the fellow Indians to imbibe a sense of selfless service. Besides, the prison time for him was time for reading, reciting, ruminating scriptures in general and the Gita in particular. His weekly talks were meant in essence to weaken inmates' wickedness by enkindling the noble and scriptural thoughts of ancient India. Yet, his erudition sparkles his lectures in clear evidence of his learning and leaning towards higher aspects of the Gita.

TWENTY

Thou alone, Thou alone, Thou alone

His talks were unconventional, being delivered in the closed compound of the Dhule Jail, unlike conventional place of shrines, monasteries, ashramas or townhalls. His treatment became unconventional perhaps out of the presumption that the suffering or struggling souls of the jail would better be benefitted by an unconventional but not unintelligible treat of the venerable scripture called Gita. More compelling reason could be Vinoba's gigantic intellect and colossal comprehension of the Gita. Hence, he conveniently rechristened the 18 chapters of the Gita. This was deliberate but not didactic.

The first chapter, generally styled "Arjuna Vishad Yoga or Sainya-Darshana Yoga" was called "Vishad Yoga". He pleads that vishad [depression or demoralisation] was not exclusive to Arjuna. That cannot be contended, countered by anybody, any living being. Some time or other, the most successful, the most cheerful, the most blissful, is subject to the vicissitude of vishad. In that context, he has stressed that the Gita could have been uttered, if not to Arjuna, then to someone else. Yes, Gita could have flown from the flowery lips of Kirshna on the very same Kurukshetra battlefield to

Yudhishthira, Bhishma, Drona etc, even to Duryodhana, Karna, Shakuni or even to Kunti, Gandhari, Draupadi. As all of them would have experienced the same dilemma, the same moral crises as Arjuna. The Gita could have been told by Krishna as a must; Arjuna's embarrassing emotion was an alibi. Gita was told by Krishna because the time came to tell the world about truth and illusion, right and wrong, justice and injustice.

Vinoba is in no doubt that "Vishad Yoga" would be more appropriately universal, not particular to Arjuna. "Arjuna Vishad Yoga" would exclude the entire humanity from attaching any importance to chapter 1 that is the basis, the foundation of the great Bhagavat Gita. Appositely, he calls the XVIII chapter the "Prasad Yoga", prasad being the opposite of vishad.

He does not stop there. He calls the second Adhyaya, generally called "Samkhya Yoga" as "The Teaching in Brief—Self-knowledge and Equanimity". The traditional headings given to each chapter and the headings given by Acharya Vinoba Bhave is given in the following table:

Adhyaya	Traditional Heading	Heading by Vinoba Bhave
1st	Arjuna Vishad Yoga	Vishad Yoga
2nd	Samkhya Yoga	The Teaching in Brief—Self-knowledge and Equanimity
3rd	Karma Yoga	Yoga of Selfless and Desireless Action
4th	Jnana Yoga	Vikarma: The Key to Karma Yoga
5th	Karma Sannyasa Yoga	Two-fold State of Akarma: Yoga and Sannyasa
6th	Atmasamyama Yoga	Control of The Mind

7th	Jnanavijnana Yoga	Prapatti or Surrender to God
8th	Akshara Brahma Yoga	Sadhana for Happy Ending of Life: The Yoga of Constancy
9th	Rajavidyarajaguhya Yoga	The Sovereign Science of Service to Humanity: Yoga of Surrender
10th	Vibhuti Yoga	Contemplation of God's Manifestations
11th	Vishwaroopadarshana Yoga	Vision of the Cosmic Form of God
12th	Bhakti Yoga	Saguna and Nirguna Bhakti
13th	Kshetrakshetrajnavibhaga Yoga	Distinction Between Self and the Not-self
14th	Gunatrayavibhaga Yoga	The Gunas: Developing Them and Going Beyond Them
15th	Purushottam Yoga	The Integral Yoga: Seeing the Lord Everywhere
16th	Daivasurasampadvibhaga Yoga	Conflict Between the Divine and Demonical Tendencies
17th	Shraddhatrayavibhaga Yoga	Programme for the Seeker
18th	Moksha Sannyasa Yoga	Conclusion: Renunciation of the Fruit of Actions Leads to the Grace of the Lord ---- Prasad Yoga

While Acharya Bhave has given new headings to all the 18 adhyayas of the age-old Bhagavat Gita, he had subdivided the chapters into----sections. Despites the adhyaya-wise division of the Gita, the sections, the subdivisions, are continuous and number 108 consisting of 432 paragraphs. In order to further elaborate and clarify, he had inserted 540 aphorisms.

It will be of immense value to have a bird's view of the sections/subdivisions of his talks on Gita. The chapters/sections may be noted as follows--

Chapter heading	Section heading
1 Introduction: Arjuna's Despondency	1 At The Heart Of The Mahabharata 2 Arjuna's Standpoint And Its Relation With The Genesis Of The Gita 3 The Purpose Of The Gita: To Dispel Anti-Swadharma Delusion 4 Honesty And Straightforwardness Make One Worthy Of The Gita's Message
2 The Teaching In Brief: Self-Knowledge And Equanimity	5 Gita's Terminology 6 Performance of Swadharma Through The Body 7 Awareness Of The Self That Transcends The Body 8 The Way To Harmonise The Two Principles: Renunciation Of The Fruits of Actions 9 Renunciation Of The Fruit Of Action: Two Examples 10 The Ideal Teacher
3 Karmayoga [Yoga Of Selfless Selfless And Desireless Action]	11 Renunciation: The Fruit Leads To Infinite Gains 12 Various Gains From Karmayoga 13 Obstacles In The Way Of Karmayoga
4 Vikarma: The Key To Karmayoga	14 Karma Needs Vikarma To Complete It 15 Karma+Vikarma=Akarma 16 Art Of Akarma Should Be Learnt From The Saints
5 Two-Fold State Of Akarma: Yoga And Sannyasa	17 Outward Action: A Mirror Of The Mind 18 The Nature Of The State Of Akarma 19 Yoga: One Aspect Of Akarma 20 Sannyasa: The Other Aspect Of Akarma 21 To Compare The Two Is Beyond The Power Of The Words 22 Two Analogies: Geometry And Mimamsa 23 The Sannyasi And The Yogi Are One Like Shuka and Janak 24 Still Yoga Is Better Than Sannyasa

6 Control Of The Mind	25 Aspiration For Redemption Of The Self 26 One-Pointedness Of Mind 27 How To Attain One-Pointedness Of Mind 28 Moderation And Regulation In Life 29 Equanimity And Evenness In Outlook 30 A Child As Preceptor 31 Abhyasa [Constant Practice], Vairagya [Non-Attachment] And Faith
7 Prapatti Or Surrender	32 The Magnificent Vision Of Bhakti 33 Bhakti Results In Pure And Unalloyed Bliss 34 Bhakti For Gains Too Has Value 35 Desireless Bhakti: Its Varieties And Fulfilment
8 Sadhana For A Happy Ending Of Life: The Yoga Of Constancy	36 Accumulation Of Good Samskaras 37 Living With The Awareness Of Death 38 "Ever Absorbed In That" 39 "Day And Night, The Fight Goes On" 40 Uttarayana And Dakshinayan
9 The Sovereign Science Of Service To Humanity: Yoga Of Surrender	41 Knowledge Through Direct Experience 42 The Easy Way 43 No Problem Of Eligibility 44 Dedication Of The Fruit Of Actions to the Lord 45 Dedicate All The Activities 46 The Whole Life Can Be Infused With God 47 The Lord's Name Destroys The Sins 48 Not What But How You Offer Is Important
10 The Contemplation Of God's Manifestations	49 The First Half Of The Gita: A Retrospect 50 An Easy Way To Learn To See God 51 God In Human Form 52 God In Creation 53 God In Animals 54 Seeing God In Villains Too

11 Vision Of The Cosmic Form Of God	55 Arjuna's Eagerness To Behold The Cosmic Form Of God 56 Full Vision Even In A Small Form 57 Vision Of The Cosmic Form Is Difficult To Bear 58 The Quintessence Of The Gita
12 Saguna And Nirguna Bhakti	59 From One-Pointedness To Totality 60 The Saguna And The Nirguna Devotee 61 Saguna Is Easy And Safe 62 Without Nirguna, Saguna Is Defective 63 Complementarity Between Saguna And Nirguna; Examples From The Ramayana 64 Complementarity Between Saguna And Nirguna: Examples From Krishna's Life 65 Saguna And Nirguna Are One: My Own Experience 66 Saguna And Nirguna Are Only Apparently Different: To Become A True Devotee Is What Matters
13 Distinction Between The Self And The Not-Self	67 Distinction Between The Body And The Self Helps Karmayoga 68 The Basic Foundation Of betterment 69 Attachment To The Body Wastes Life 70 "You Are That" 71 An End To The Power Of The Tyrants 72 Faith In The Power Of The Supreme Soul 73 Progressive Realisation Of The Supreme Soul 74 Basic Means For Knowledge

14 The Gunas: Developing Them And Going Beyond Them	75 Analysis Of Prakriti 76 Bodily Labour: Cure For Tamas 77 Another Cure For Tamas: to Conquer Sleep 78 Cure For Rajas: Living Within The Bounds Of Swadharma How To Determine One's Swadharma 80 Sattva And The Method To Deal With It 81 The Concluding Point: Self-Realisation And Refuse In Bhakti
15 The Integral Yoga: Seeing The Lord Everywhere	82 The Way Of Bhakti Is Not Different From The Way Of Efforts 83 Bhakti Makes The Effort Easier 84 The Triad Of Service 85 Bhakti Means Service Without Any Sense Of "I" 86 The Mark Of Jnana: Seeing The Purusha Everywhere 87 The Essence Of All The Vedas In The Palm Of My Hand
16 Conflict Between The Divine And The Demonical Tendencies	88 Divine Qualities: The Harbinger Of Purushottamayoga 89 The Forces Of Light And Darkness 90 Four Stages In The Development Of Non-Violence 91 A Great Experiment In Non-Violence: Giving Up Flesh eating 92 The Three Asuric Ambitions: Power, Culture And Wealth 93 Self-Restraint: The Scientific Way To Get Rid Of Desire, Anger And Greed
17 Programme Of The Seeker	94 Disciplined Life Makes Mind Relaxed And Free 95 Triple Endeavour For The Purpose 96 Making Sadhana Sattvik 97 Purity In Food 98 The Gita's Scheme For Harmonious Living 99 The Mantra Of Dedication 100 The Name Of The Lord Effaces Sins

| 18 Conclusion: Renunciation Of The Fruit Of Actions Leads To The Grace Of God | 101 Arjuna's Last Question
102 Renunciation Of The Fruit: The Universal Test
103 The Right Way To Extricate 0neself From Activity
104 An Insight Into Swadharma
105 The Full Meaning Of The Renunciation Of Fruit
106 Fulfilment Is Nothing But The Culmination Of Sadhana
107 The Triple State Of The Realised One
108 "Though Alone.... Thou Alone" |

TWENTY-ONE

Pundit and prostitute
Father of sin: have you seen?

    The division of the Gita into new chapter headings heads to simplification of the overtly complex contents. The 6 explanatory sections on an average for each chapter are indicative of discussion of the Gita. The section headings are not only lucid but also intelligible. The last section, for example, with the heading, "Thou Alone.... Thou Alone" is enthralling.
    Most of us who read Gita stop at once at,
sarva-dharmān parityajya mām ekaṁ śharaṇaṁ vraja
ahaṁ tvāṁ sarva-pāpebhyo mokṣhayiṣhyāmi mā śhuchaḥ
[18.66]
    Arjuna is addressed with assuaging, assuring message, "O Arjuna! Give up all religions, rituals, practices and paraphernalia, ideas and ideals, isms and egoisms, and take asylum in Me, shelter in Me, refuse in Me. I shall save you, protect you from all your sins, shortfalls; I shall exonerate you, set you free from all your latches and lapses, failures and fratricides. Never bother about them."
    In this verse appears the term "sin" which is held in high importance by one and all. It is actually important and

evocative. Indian masses of not- so- distant past were deeply concerned with the word "sin". Even nowadays, people in their sixties and seventies, are well-guarded against the guidelines of "sin". Their offspring excepting a few are influenced immensely by home and elders not to commit "sin", at least knowingly. What exactly is "sin"? We have been taught of "sin" in our schooldays and at home in our childhood. The elders around spoke soundly of "sin" softly and sincerely. At times, their dialogue and debate about "sin" spoke of their socio-cultural scholarship.

Plainly speaking, "sin" is committed when and if you tell a lie not for joke, thieve somebody's property of whatsoever little value, do something indecent and inappropriate socially, culturally. "Sin" stems from joking, mimicking and lampooning a weak, helpless, diseased or disabled. "Sin" accrues to not giving alms to beggar but beating or illtreating him. "Sin" springs from disregarding elders, teachers, parents, pundits, priests, gurus, kings, gods and God. The list could be long. All improper, illegal, illogical, immoral, unethical things could be sin jolly well. All violations, transgressions, deviations, deprivations, tampering, trampling, torturing, tormenting, trepidations, terrorisms are sin sufficient.

"Sin" makes us shiver for the sheer reason that we commit sins intentionally and unintentionally, with knowledge and without knowledge. Day and night, in season and out of season, we are susceptible to committing sins. Sinful thought is as bad as sinful deed, even worse. Suffice it to say that "sin", "sinful", "sinner", "sinning" is pervasively used and alluded to without a clear, cogent, compressive meaning of those terms.

A story in this context is worth quoting.

During those days in ancient times Kashi and Avanti were cities of learning and wisdom, housing hundreds of honourable gurus. Men of means sent their wards to learn lessons of spiritualism and philosophy, religion and worthy living. A not-so-well-off nor so-well-learnt man was aware of the glorious impact of gurus in Kashi and Avanti. So, he sent his son to Kashi, who stayed put in a gurukul for full twelve years as was the practice. On return, the father was full of joy at the first sight of the son but was doubtful, after a while, if his ward did really learn the lessons. He initiated the conversation,

Father –Did you learn your lessons right?

Son – Yes, I did. There is no doubt about it.

Father – Should I ask you a question?

Son- Yes, why not? You can ask any thing you may like to test my scholarship.

Father—Then the question: Who is the father of "sin"?

"Father of sin"? the son mumbled. He fumbled and brooded as much and as long as he could but could make no head or tail of the question. He had come across abundant occasions in the gurukul when the guru and the disciple pals talked indiscriminately of "sin". So did he. But none ever talked of "father of sin". The dad took the dude's ignorance importantly and said, "Now go away into the wide world in search of the answer. Never be back without the answer."

The son had never seen his father so stern. He did not show airs of a fake pundit or an appearance arrogance before his father. And the father, never counted for his erudition, did show off intricate ingenuity in asking a hair-splitting question. Without argument or alibi, the son left home to seek the answer. He met a number of pundits and professors to whom he put the question politely. But he got no answer. They beat about the bush or show off their airs by saying the query was bogus and bizarre. He met peasants and merchants, saints and school-pupils and put the query to them. They honestly and humbly replied "no" straightforward, instead of begging the question or attempting at a roundabout reply.

Day after day, the youth was on the move for the innocent but intriguing answer. His food and drink, rest and ease, or lack of those, were beyond description. He did not mind the troubles and tortures he encountered on the quest but was hopeful and confident that he must answer his father sooner or later. One day after a long and arduous journey without a morsel of food or a drop of water, he happened to be at the doorsteps of someone, almost collapsing. A well-clad, well- off lady came out to whom the youth articulated for a pale of water. The woman obliged. The youth looked at her in the darkness of sunset and uttered, "You saved my life, Vaishnavi!"

"Not Vaishnavi but a *veshya*, a *veshya*",
the woman quipped casually.

"Veshya! A veshya! and I drank water from her. Fie on me! Fie! Fie!" the youth shouted even with his parched lips and desiccated throat. Hamstrung with hunger, he could not holler louder or longer but buzzed for some time that he committed an unpardonable sin by drinking water from a fell, a fallen creature. The prostitute had seen unseeable scenes like this quite often earlier and had quietened the mentally-ill earls quickly but quietly with her manners and demeanour. This brat was unbearable, not unbeatable. The braggart youth rose and mumbled, "O, what a satanic sin!

Drank water from a harlot's pitcher and at her place. Shame, shame! Sin, sin…sin..."

And he half-stood to go. The pros, as compassionate as pretty, took pity on the precarious health of the brat and said softly and pretty sincerely, "You are too weak to move further, even five steps from here in this dark night. There is no hearth and home near where you can sojourn for the night. Please, put up here for the night and go tomorrow wherever you like! I do not have to stop you."

"What! Me staying further here in a whore's dwelling! Isn't it better death than this dishonour? You have spoiled my penance and persona by offering water. Now you volunteer to give me shelter! What nonsense! How do you dare to utter such rubbish, such sin?"

Pretty much politely but calmly, the prostitute said, "O learned brahmin youth! I have spoiled your caste, your culture. But there is a remedy for everything, even for this sin. That is this!" She brought out a bright yellow gold coin and put it before the hot-headed youth. The glittering coin seemed to wash the "sin" by the pros. He looked at the coin and mumbled, "Okay".

As the night advanced, the youth felt far hungrier. He thought of a plate of eatable then and there. But his *mithyachara* [hypocrisy] was the bar to bare his mind. The pros, on the other hand, was sure the fellow would have dinner at her place as much out of gut compulsion as out of greed for gold coin. Accordingly, she prepared ghee-soaked chapati and palatable curry. By 9 pm, the woman approached the youth and requested to sit for dinner. The youth roared with as much strength as he had and said, "Shall I have dinner here at a prostitute's place? What a sinful Satan are you going to make of me?"The prostitute was cool and said coolly, "O brahmin deity! Here are 2 gold mohurs for my sin. Pocket them and proceed inside for food!"

The boastful brahmin lad sat down for dinner and was about to eat when the pros whispered, "O young man! You are awfully weak to lift food to your mouth. Please sit comfortably! I shall feed you carefully and caressingly."

The youth once again cried about the sin: The sin of drinking water there, staying thereover for the night, agreeing to eat food from a lowly creature's hands and, finally, the sin of being requested by a prostitute to feed him with her hand. But the howling was hopelessly hollow. It was sound and fury, signifying nothing, an idiot's scowling. His hunger hamstrung him to say further "no" to the sumptuous dinner laid out with the hostess requesting to feed herself. The woman put 5 gold mohurs beside the braggart and fed him with her hand. Sex and hunger rules the world-they say. The dictate of the gut cannot be overridden by the guts of anyone, howsoever strong he/she may be in physique or personality.

Before asleep, the youth pondered- father's question is answered. The gold mohurs offered by the whore changed the whole spectacle. Hungry and hamstrung though I was, I would not have accepted water or chapati from the strumpet but for the glittering coins. My greed for gold dashed my guts, gutted my orthodoxy, to stand against the lady of the night. The whore is not so sinful as I am. She is a sex worker to satisfy others' sexual hunger and sensual pleasure. In turn, she earns money to maintain herself and offer charity to the needy and deserving. Gold, greed and sin; sin, greed and gold form a vicious circle that traps and torments us. Hypocrites that we are, we call the whore wholly unwholesome and me wholly sinless. Mithyachara! You stand unbeaten now and then and ubiquitous!

This obviously is the last verse of significance, ending the Krishna- Arjuna dialogue. This sloka suffices the whole of brahma vidya, the science of supreme spiritualism. Mahatma Gandhi says that in three places of the Gita there is clear command to surrender to the Lord totally, truthfully. Nobody misses or mistakes this; nobody can mistake or miss this unless he/she suffers from mental illness of the worst kind. How can Acharya Vinoba Bhave miss or not mind this pertinent point. He highlights this in section 108 of chapter 18 with the heading," Thou Alone…. Thou Alone". The Gita reader, the yogi, the bhakta should utter that single expression "Thou Alone...Thou Alone" umpteen times with heart and mind to realise and express "O Lord! I surrender to you; I submit to you; I take refuse in you." In the concluding words of Acharya Vinoba, "Now there is nothing but 'Thou Alone… Thou Alone'." He cites the curious case that a goat bleats mee mee mee… all through its life but when dead and silent, its bowels are used for strings of musical instrument. He quotes saint Dadu who says always utter "You alone, Alone"

How do we surrender to the Lord? What exactly is surrendering to the Almighty? It looks plain, simple, but is, in reality, extremely unachievable, undoable. People cite the case of Jajnyaseni's disrobing in the full view of all in the Kuru Sabha and the supply of thousands and thousands of sarees by Krishna to save Draupadi from denudement.

Draupadi's stripping is the most ignominious incident in the intensely enchanting epic Mahabharata. It is all the more ignominious because the disrobed Draupadi was subjected to such ignominy for no fault of hers. It is an abysmally abhorrent incident because the socio-moral stalwarts of the day like Bhishma, Drona and the monarch Dhritarashtra were insensitive witnesses of the show macabre. It is still more disdainful that gambling was so royal and so rampant in those days of apparently good socio-politico order, and, even Yudhishthira, the gem of a person and prince, was addicted to disdainful wager. The worst part of the disparaging episode was that a woman, the wife could be staked on wager.

Shakuni, the maternal uncle of Duryodhana, the crown prince of Hastina, was an exceptional expert in the game of dice. To deprive Yudhishthira of his kingdom, Indraprastha, Duryodhana prevailed upon his monarch father Dhritarastra and hosted the dice tournament between Duryodhana and Yudhisthira. Yudhisthira, a king of impeccable qualities, was ironically intoxicated to dice. He readily agreed to the dice duel. The game started. As conspired between the two, Shakuni played on behalf of Duryodhana with Yudhishthira's consent, of course. No doubt, Yudhishthira was a past master of the game but was unluckily unequal to Shakuni that day. The game commenced and Yudhishthira lost each cast, while Shakuni won each. As loser of each cast, Yudhistir cast off his wealth, jewellery, royal estates, mansions and manors and lo! his kingdom, in quick succession as a quirk of fate. That was not all. The match did not stop because the Pandava brothers never disagreed with or disobeyed the eldest of the Pandavas on the one hand and Bhishma, Drona etc were silenced by Duryodhana's intemperate, immodest and unbecoming outpouring on the other hand. The addicts, especially the loser, get madder with each stake lost and do not desist from further dice despite the diminishing luck. Yudhisthira was no exception. Karna and Dushasana instigated Duryodhana not to stop the game and Yudhisthira thought it cowardice and indignity to withdraw even from his losing game.

In next casts, Yudhishthira lost his four brothers one by one and, when there was nothing more for wager, he staked Draupadi, his wife and the Indraprastha empress, and lost. Then Duryodhana sent one of his bodyguards to get Draupadi out in the Kuru Sabha as she was lost to him as a maid. The guard failing, Dushasana was directed to get Draupadi down on the assembly hall.

Dushasana dragged Draupadi with her open locks in his fist when she resisted and refused to obey Duryodhana's dictate. The tormented, wailing Draupadi asked for justice to monarch Dhritarashtra, Bhishma, Drona and other counsellors. All of them articulated their acute helplessness.

Then down with despicable arrogance and insanity, Duryodhana asked Draupadi to come and sit on his robust and sexy thighs. What nonsense! Whatever wretched a woman may be, how can she sit on a man's thighs in the full view of full Kaurava imperial council! Draupadi failing and wailing, the devilish Duryodhana directed Dushasana to denude her. O my God! What a heinous crime on an innocent, noble and respectable woman! Dushasana did not delay or dither. His schadenfreude had a free play as were those of Shakuni, Karna and company.

Dushasana pulled away Draupadi's saree forcibly. He was sure, one pull and the saree peel off, and then Draupadi nude! But that did not happen. Draupadi clutched to her saree tightly with both hands and both legs. How strong is the frail, fair-sex woman called Draupadi to withstand

Dushasana's demonic pull? She stretched one leg on the impact of Dushasana's pulling impact. Then another leg, then one hand, then the other hand stretched out.... stretched feeble, faltering, failing. The stubborn pulling by Dushasana was weakening, devastating her body. Her legs and hands no more clutching her saree, Draupadi had the nightmare of being naked and nude in no time. Who can now come to her rescue? Who can protect her from pitiable indignity of nudity? Who? Who?

Hopeless and frightened, all the valiant Pandava husbands downing their heads in shame and shackle of the dice condition, Draupadi pondered that He alone can save. Then she prayed frantically but from the bottom of her heart, "Thou Alone...Thou Alone". Though Alone can save me, O Lord! Thou Alone can obviate my deplorable destitution. Her prayers were answered instantly and Lord Krishna in faraway Dvaraka rose to the occasion to supply unseen thousands and thousands of sarees cling to Draupadi's body. Her body could not be bare, try Dushasana as much, as forcefully, as frantically! Counsellors and elders, and the company of villains, the axis of Duryodhana, Karna and Shakuni, looked at the scene stupefied, stupidly; the first set with sense of hope and reassurance, the second set with shock and awe.

So long Draupadi believed in her strength, she could do nothing against the might of mighty Dushasana. As soon as she realised that the Almighty alone can crush the muscular and macabre might of Dushasana, she surrendered and uttered, "Thou Alone... Thou Alone"

Now it is time to chant with Acharya Vinoba Bhave, "Thou Alone...Thou Alone...Thou Alone...Thou Alone..."

TWENTY-TWO

**Man is mortal
Pundit's goat is not**

While speaking of surrender, of chanting "You Alone", the counsel of Mahatma Gandhi comes to mind. He said of Gita indicating absolute surrender to the Lord in three places. That sloka 66, chapter 18, is undoubtedly one and the ultimate one is indisputable. The other one could be seen in verse 62, Adhyaya 18,

*tam eva śharaṇaṁ gachchha sarva-bhāvena bhārata
tat-prasādāt parāṁ śhāntiṁ sthānaṁ prāpsyasi
śhāśhvatam [18.62]*

O Arjuna! seek refuse in Him by Whose grace you would get the ultimate and eternal place of peace.

The problem of peace and solution thereof is delineated in utterly simplified version; is stated in the most lucid language how to arrive at the unattainable objective of peace. Peace is plain and simple but is amply arduous to achieve, acquire, accomplish. In this verse Krishna asks Arjuna to surrender to the Lord by Whose mercy he could land in the paradise of peace. Only submission, surrender lands one in the realm of peace. Peace, everlasting and inerasable, can be reached by sheer submission to the Lord. So, surrender, sheer surrender, surrender sure and supreme, total and in toto, is the avenue to reach the venue of peace. As in 66/18, so here, forget everything and utter "Thou Alone". O scion of Bharata, the great, surrender to Him in all respect; in body, mind, heart and soul. Do not leave any stone unturned to surrender completely, comprehensively; not cosmetically or comically, not superficially or artificially nor ostentatiously or obliquely.

Verse 62/18 is the sequence of the preceding verse,

īśhvaraḥ sarva-bhūtānāṁ hṛid-deśhe 'rjuna tiṣhṭhati
bhrāmayan sarva-bhūtāni yantrārūḍhāni māyayā

[18.61]

O Arjuna! The Lord resides in everyone's heart but moves them in *Maya* as in a merry-go-round.

Only because beings are shrouded, clouded with Maya, they do not see, cannot see that their heart is the abode of God. Maya moves men and women constantly as a whirligig. So, we are unable to find or feel Ishvara in our hearts. If the carousel stops, then we can see and feel the ground beneath our feet. Otherwise, we feel flying fancifully in air, in the atmosphere. The Maya, the merry-go-round, the roundabout is His creation to entangle creatures with short-term, transitory, fictional, fanciful things in place of higher ideals, nobler notions, Truth. How to get rid of Maya? Is there a way out?

Yes, there is. There is the single way. There is only and one path. That path is paramount submission to Ishvara.

The Maya mischief and manipulation is immanent in men and women. Even an intellectual giant, bosom friend, faithful follower and astute assistant and aid of Krishna, Arjuna, succumbed to Maya in the nick of the moment. Not only did Arjuna fell, faltered and flabbergasted by Maya, he could not escape until he found refuse in the Lord.

If Arjuna could not sunder, snap the trap of ubiquitous Maya, how can we?

Maya is not mean or momentary. It is mighty and massive, all- inclusive and all enveloping, tolerable but unsurmountable. In a word, it is the hardest of the hard to hew or harm, to avoid or axe, to delude or denude, to conceive or deceive MAYA. It is not my word. I do not dare say this. This is said by Krishna to Arjuna, you know where. Yes, in the Kurukshetra battle field and here to us in verse 14, adhyaya 7,

daivī hyeṣhā guṇa-mayī mama māyā duratyayā
mām eva ye prapadyante māyām etām taranti te [7.14]

O Dhananjaya! The three-gunas-entwined Maya is unearthly, ethereal, extra natural, super natural, divine. It is very, very, very difficult to cross this ocean of Maya. None cannot swim across the Maya-ocean. [None? None?]. Only those who surrender to Me get across this Maya.

This verse has captivated Acharya Vinoba Bhave. Hence, he called his seventh chapter of the Gita as "Prapatti Or Surrender". To swim across the ocean of Maya, the only option available to all, to all of us, is to surrender to Ishvara, to take refuse in God.

Certainly, it is not easy to surrender, seek refuse in the Lord. It is extremely difficult and takes long, long time to render oneself eligible for surrender.

It is emphasised that only the wise who see the Lord in everybody, everything, reach Him after many lives.

*bahūnāṁ janmanām ante jñānavān māṁ prapadyate
vāsudevaḥ sarvam iti sa mahātmā su-durlabhaḥ [7.19]*

O Arjuna! I am available to the knowledgeable after many lives, who see Me in everything. While knowledgeable are few and far between, the seer of Vasudeva, the Lord, in all creation is rarest of the rare.

There is no doubt that the Lord is omnipresent. The scriptures and philosophies, the psalms and sermons, the epistles and epics harp on this persistently. The worldly-wise wise and otherwise wise people know from studies and sophistry that God exists everywhere, in everybody. Yet, in practice, they fail to feel the omnipresence of God, don't they? A story to the effect is worth retelling.

A poor farmworker named Madhava was assisted by his youthful son in earning extra income home and serving his parents in illness. The poor couple were a happy lot and dreaming of getting him married and bringing home a daughter-in-law who would help in kitchen and homemaking, and nurse them in disease and distress. But their dream was devastated when the son died suddenly of unknown disease. The mother of the boy under her veil and inside home wailed bitterly despite dutiful sympathetic consolation by the neighbourhood womenfolk. The poor farmhand Madhava failed miserably to console his wife and came out to the outer veranda of his modest home; and cried ceaselessly, cursed the death God, himself and his fate. The village folk gathered to condole the untimely death of the unassuming, well-behaving, robust youth. Nevertheless, there was no remission in the heart-broken, sky-rending wail of the poor couple.

The village priest, a brahmin of immense scholarship in scriptures and Samkhya, was out on the village road to the nearby river ghat for bathing, *tilatarpana* and due early morning worshipping of the Sun God and the riverside Lord Shiva. He was surprised at the early gathering of so many people in front of the lowly farmworker's nondescript house. The commotion close to the poor man's home was all the more intriguing to the pundit. The folk who thronged there were all reverence to the brahmin pundit to make way for him to head to the doorsteps of Madhava, where he sat crying and cursing. On seeing the pundit, the rustic farm-labourer Madhava stopped crying but sobbed still. On enquiry by the pundit, he replied with broken heart and in broken words and sentences that his only, youthful son died suddenly last night, shattering his sweet dreams and sweeter future.

The pundit dissimulated sheer sadness on hearing the sorrowful news. He said aha... oh... uh... as others usually say in such circumstances. But that was not enough nor new to assuage the grievously hurt feeling of the poor fellow. He as much as others hoped for some gainful, helpful words or acts of empathy from the pundit. The pundit was quick to gauge the gathering's mood of disapproval, if not disdain. Thus, he cleared his throat and said, "O fellow! The poor, illiterate fellow! I need must not talk to you people on such occasions as all of you, the poor, peasant villagers, are as far from religion and philosophy, Samkhya and Mimamsa, as the deer is from water or fish from forest. I open my mouth here because this uncouth, rustic, agricultural labour Madhava is simply unlike the whole lot of you. He is innocent, obedient and reverent. He is simple and humble. So, a hard-hearted pundit like me has a soft corner for him. His son was, as the puranas say, like father like son, even humbler and simpler than his father. Woe to the father that lost a son like him!"

Then, he paused for a minute or two and looked minutely at the innocent hearers who were happy to know that the great pundit was not so condescending as they usually thought of him to be.

Sensing the silence as the mood of agreement, he continued in direct address to the bereaved father Madhava, "O Madhava! You cannot undo what God has done; you cannot rewrite what fate has scripted for you. Have you not seen in the Mahabharata serial in which Lord Krishna had said umpteen times that He cannot override destiny of men and women? Yes, once He has earmarked our life circle, our fate triangle, he cannot erase that, can He? He has said so to Arjuna often in the holy Bhagavat Gita, hasn't He? All of you villagers are hopeless ignoramuses. You hardly read Bhagavat Gita, the most serene scripture of humankind. Alien to the Gita, how can you know A B C of Samkhya Yoga, the cream of the Gita."

He raised his voice and continued, "In the Samkhya Yoga, it is described vividly that the body is perishable, impermanent, now-here-now-not-here. All of us are mortal. We must die today or tomorrow, after a week or a year, or after some years. But death is must; death is our fate; death we cannot escape however strong or wise we may be. Our fathers and forefathers would have forborne death, had it been possible. Nor can our children however educated or intelligent would escape death, howsoever they progress in science or medicine."

"To an erring and wailing Arjuna, Krishna exhorted to battle, battling and belittling the former's doubts and dilemmas on killing *his svajana*", the pundit added, by quoting the eternal truths in the Samkhya yoga like,

dehino 'smin yathā dehe kaumāram yauvanam jarā
tathā dehāntara-prāptir dhīras tatra na muhyati [2.13]

jātasya hi dhruvo mrityur dhruvam janma mritasya cha
tasmād aparihārye 'rthe na tvam śhochitum arhasi [2.27]

To explain plainly, he went on, "As this body passes from childhood to youth and then to old age, so this body passes through death to bear another body. This progression of body by stages is inevitable, inescapable, unavoidable. Therefore, the wise do not mourn this stagewise progression of the perishable body. In sloka 27, Adhyaya 2, it is stressed that whoever is born must die and whoever dies dons another body. It is said that human body is a clothing article of the Self. As we throw away old apparel to dress in new, so does the Atman throws away this body and clothes itself in a new body. It is said in verse 22, chapter 2,

vāsānsi jīrṇāni yathā vihāya
navāni grihṇāti naro 'parāṇi
tathā sharīrāṇi vihāya jīrṇānya
nyāni sanyāti navāni dehī [2.22]

The hair-splitting haranguing by the pundit passed mostly over the hearers' heads. Slokas and Samkhya were not their daily bowel of cold rice. Of course, they understood the essence of the pundit's speech that we must die as we are born and poor Madhava's son was no exception to die last night. Madhava looking bogus and blockhead was better than others in grasping that his son's death was his inescapable, wretched fate.

Madhava stopped sobbing, was compelled to stop when the brahmin pundit patted him on the back and advised in soft, sympathetic tone, "Get up Madhava, get up! Go and take the corpse to the crematorium for the last rites of the departed soul."

Madhava rose and so did a dozen of neighbours to help him perform his son's last rites.

Time passed unstopped and uncareful of people's sorrows and satisfactions. Madhava resigned to his fate and reconciled to his fatal loss. The villagers forgot Madhava's woes of that day. One day Madhava was on his way to landlord's farm for the day's labour and wages. It was late in the morning. The brahmin hamlet is a bit away and isolated from the village. He heard the pundit-priest howling and cursing. He was astonished that a paragon of scriptures, the pundit was crying, that too as bitterly as he or other illiterate villagers did on their small or great losses. Madhava proceeded to brahmin hamlet to know what had happened. Reaching pundit's front-yard, he saw a dead goat at a distance and the pundit looking at the dead animal as often as he could, crying. Mustering enough courage, Madhava asked, "Pundit *mahapru*! What makes you cry so pathetically"

Pundit – "Can't you see block-head? The one-year-old goat raised with soft green grass, gravel and other edibles died suddenly. You fool cannot know the goat would weigh 8/10 kg meat that costs about ten thousand rupees. O Madhava! I tended the goat very much like my own child. What a great loss! Who can bear such huge loss? The loss as much of money as of a sweet, pet animal! Madhava, I am broken and gone!"

Madhava fumbled for words and kept quiet for quite some time. Then he consoled in his illiterate language but sincere feeling for some minutes. Thereafter to conclude, he was a bit quizzical, "Pundit *mahapru*! On my son's death, you very well said that whoever is born must die and it is not wise or useful to wail a death. You harped this so emphatically that I was perforce consoled, reconciled to my son's death. But you…."

The pundit stopped him from completing and howled, "Nonsense of the first order! What can you make of Samkhya Yoga or Bhagavat Gita? Since it was your son's death, your loss, I was vocal on the Bhagavat Gita. Today, it is my goat's death, my loss. How can I benefit from Gita lessons? How does the Gita apply to you and me equally? You are as much a man as me but isn't there no difference? Should the Shudra and Brahmin stand the same footing?" The Gita-ignorant, overall ignorant Madhava kept quiet. He could not quite comprehend what the scripture-competent pundit meant.

The illiterate Madhava was enlightened. He understood from the pundit's interpretation of Bhagavat Gita that the Gita is not to follow but is to create followers. What the preacher or pundit, teacher or rubble-rouser says does not follow. To them, the teaching, the lessons of Gita are hollow, hopeless, hyphen between learning and practicing.

Are these pundits or preachers *jnanavana* as said supra? Certainly not. And these people do never, can never surrender if they thunder the wonders of sloka 72/18 without blunder or flounder. But the *jnanavana* get the grace of God without harm or hinder. Who are they?

TWENTY-THREE

My witness?
Yes, Raghunath ji!
They are not far to seek. They are here and there, everywhere, though they have no inkling of their eligibility to surrender to the Lord. How can they think of their suitability to surrender to the Supreme, the Super Power? Where do they have the time or schooling? They are farmers and factory workers, rickshaw pullers and construction workers...Only because they have failed in formal schooling and learning; only because they endure fooling and conning by others without grudging and grumbling, they surrender to the Lord without knowing so.

A case in point. A poor peasant was indebted to the village usurer for certain some of money needed to defray some indispensable expenses. He paid off the debt on time with demanded interest. Illiterate and gullible that he was, he took the debtor's words that his debt was paid off and he was debt-free. But the shrewd usurer kept the loan instrument intact and, after a few months, asked the poor peasant to pay off the debt. Obviously, the debtor contested the claim. As is his wont, the usurer sought relief in the court of law. The case was heard. The judge asked the peasant debtor about who were present when he cleared the loan.

The debtor peasant repaid the loan with interest in front of the village Raghunath jew temple. Except for him and the naughty lender, no other villager was there then. The naïve debtor did not bother about availability of any witness. So, to the judge's question, he replied calmly that only three were there at the time of his debt repayment.

"Who are they?" the judge queried.

"The creditor, me and Raghunatha", the peasant replied.

As usual, the judge, without applying his mind and unmindful of absence of details of Raghunath, ordered the bench clerk to issue notice to Raghunatha to appear on the date fixed to render his testimony. Order carried, the court process server visited the village and enquired of Raghunatha's residence or whereabout. A noticeable number of villagers confirmed that nobody named Raghunatha resided in the village but the deity Raghunatha sits pretty on the cul-de-sac. The process server is nobody to judge the judge's order nor he bothered how Raghunatha, the village deity, would ever be a witness to mundane money matters. Of course, he thought that in this benighted rustic habitation, everything could be possible. So, he headed straight to the temple and handed a copy of the summons to the temple priest who gladly accepted the court order on behalf of Raghunatha.

He bothered a bit. For the first time in his servitor's career something of the sort had happened—Raghunatha had been summoned to the court. He never bothered about a number of miracles occurring at the behest of his Raghunatha. He knew of his power, charisma and compassion. He had seen people coming there with jewels, gifts, flowers, fruits, clothes, ornaments and whatnot. He had heard pilgrims and prostrators lying flat on the ground, praying and crying loudly to fulfil their desires, to relieve them of their distress. He had never seen court summons sent to Raghunatha.

OK. Let His will be done. On the appointed day, the priest dressed Raghunatha with the best of robes and adorned him with ample and sparkling ornaments.

While adorning his Lord, the priest mumbled and buzzed, "O Lord! You know it all. The poor fellow paid off the loan to the last pie. Yet, the bloody, blood-sucking usurer had drawn him to the dock. Do not be a lame duck in the witness box. You tell the truth to save the honest, humble peasant; you tell it all threadbare so that the greedy lender is bare of his falsehood and fake claims in the court."

The priest's prompting did it, didn't it? In the court on time appeared a pretty, positive, bluish figure with soft smile and unruffled candour. Straight in the box, He answered the judge's query quite clearly and convincingly that the loan was repaid and He was the sole witness. The judge did not doubt veracity of Raghunatha's testimony. Hence, he discharged the peasant of debt demand. Further, he sent the usurer to jail for false, fake, fabricated and fraudulent claims.

Raghunatha disappeared as soon as His testimony was over. The creditor was dragged by the police to the prison. Happy, the honest husbandry man was about to leave the court when he was beckoned to by the judge who asked, "Where did Raghunath go?"

"To his home. Why?"

"Who exactly is that Raghunatha?"

The rustic agriculturist pondered for a moment and

thought how come this judge, the dispenser of justice to all and sundry, does not know who Raghunatha is. O! he knows Raghunatha by Srirama, Satyasandha, Dasharathatanaya, Lokabhirama, Raghava, Ravanari...etc. Of course, how can he know Raghunatha Who stays with us, in our village and at the beck and call of our village priest? Nonetheless, the fellow has not read the Ramayana, has he? No Ramayana, No justice! Maybe he has read Bhagavat Gita.

"You didn't reply?" the judge asked.

"Yeh! He is that Raghunatha, son of Dasharatha, the emperor of Ayodhya, the crown of Raghu dynasty…"

"Ho! Do I enquire of you about Siyarama, Maryada Purushottama Rama? He is Raghupati Raghava Raja Rama, Patitapavana Sitarama… Who does not know of him? I ask who he is who gave testimony before me in your case a while ago? Who was that yellow-clothed, soft, subdued-smiling, regal fellow?"

"Oh! Ho! He is Raghunatha, our Raghunatha, our village Raghunatha, our priest's fancy, fond Raghunatha. He loves us; lives with us; says the truth and sides with the righteous, doesn't He? Didn't you see for yourself how he finished the usurer's falsity and fake demand?"

Disposing of the peasant, the judge sobbed inconsolably. He grieved that he saw the seesaw of Bhagavana Rama but could not see Srirama who stood before him for pretty long time, smiling and blessing.

The judge is enough qualified to surrender to the Lord. So is the debtor peasant and the professional priest. What about the pundit chiding Madhava? Would he ever be eligible to surrender or seek asylum? To be eligible, be gullible, not voluble!

TWENTY-FOUR

Mithyachara sa ucchyate....
You are not one certainly!

The pundit? The pundit?
"Mithyachara sa uchhyate."
Not only that pundit but plenty others who boast of being pundits are plainly fake, false, hypocritic.

karmendriyāṇi sanyamya ya āste manasā smaran
indriyārthān vimūḍhātmā mithyāchāraḥ sa uchyate [3.6]

O Arjuna! He who claims to have mastered the indriyas but acts according to the guidance of *his indriyas* harboured in his mind is a *mithyachari [hypocrite]*.
Gita tells who a hypocrite is. Hypocrites are not hard to find. But they could not be found right now in most cases. By the time, their hypocrisy is unearthed, the damage is done. Hypocrisy as *mithyachara* occurs in the Gita to describe the shrewd, the literate, the intellectual who make use of their bookish knowledge to fool simpletons like Madhava. But, as Madhava bared the pundit's hypocrisy sooner than later, so do others uncover the rank, risible, reproachable falsity, fakeness of other such pundits, professors, preachers and

propagandists. What Krishna advises is plain and simple. It is hard to harness, hammer or hew the *indriyas* which lead people astray. Until and unless you have controlled them, do not speak that you have subdued or supressed, subjugated or shackled your *indriyas*.

Without yoking indriyas, if you fake that you have fettered your indriyas, then you are a *mithyachari,* a hypocrite. If you say your hunger for mutton, biriyani or rasagollas is immense, insatiable, unbeatable, then you may be disliked or disdained for being a voracious eater, a gluttonous; but not be called a bluff, boastful, untruthful hypocrite. That state of being abnormally glutinous may be loathsome but is normal, natural for some people. On the contrary, if your weakness for sweets or chicken curry is huge but you desist from eating it in open for fear of others' criticism or dislike, you are a mithyachari, a hypocrite. You are more so, if you declare decisively that you do not eat chicken or eggs in the month of Karttika or Magha or Shravana, but eat it to your heart's content when you happen to be out of your neighbours', family's, friends' gaze. Some non-vegetarians refrain from eating fish, fowl and flesh in the pious month of Karttika but count the days when the month would end, when they would devour the 3 Fs stomach-full. Even some plan days and weeks before month end what they would buy from where in what quantity! *They are mithyacharis, hypocrites of the worst kind.*

What about the pundit who made light of Madhava's son's death but grieved unconsolably on his goat's death? They speak impressively on Gita, talk nonstop on Samkhya Yoga but hide their ulterior motives. They are double Dutch; they are gibberish and bank upon majority gullibility. They think they would go scot-free. No, they cannot escape the tentacles of their hypocrisy, their mithyachara. They cannot avail of French leave on dooms day, on the day of judgement.

Most of us, the literate, civilised lot are hyperbolic hypocrites, mithyacharis, are not we? Think of a courtroom in any Indian town or city where a witness is called to testify. In the witness box, he is asked to touch Gita and swear, "I swear in the name of God that the evidence I adduce in the court concerning the matter shall be truth, the whole truth, nothing but truth." And we all know well in how many cases the witnesses speak "the truth, the whole truth, nothing but truth."They swear by God and touch the Bhagavat Gita to tell the truth so that the judge would do justice to his job by delivering justice to the parties, to the litigants and to the general public for that matter. Since 7 out of each 10 witnesses adduce biased, false, untrue evidence, the judge is confused, fudged to find out the truth, deliver justice.

Gita is the book of faith, piety, truth. Gita is the book of honesty, not hypocrisy; Gita is the book of harmony, not hegemony; Gita is the book of honour and humility, not arrogance and snobbery. Gita is read, admired, adored from pretty primitive times by all-- from ascetics to agnostics, sceptics, monotheists, polytheists, atheists, anarchists; from pundits, preachers, professors, pujakas,to peasants, to pupils, preachers, traders, engineers, entrepreneurs, managers, motivators, orators, actors, movers & shakers, vacationers, vocationalists, vagabonds; from cult-worshipper to iconoclasts, from scientists to superstitious souls because Gita is all, has all equally, universally, unequivocally applicable to all conscientious creatures of all cultures, all climes, all conditions, all circumstances. Yet, swearing by

God above and with the Gita on hand to speak the truth, we tell lies, loathsome lies, lustful lies, damn lies, demonic lies, devilish lies...This is mighty, melancholic, morbid Mityachara, hypocrisy.

TWENTY-FIVE

What a shame to be a giver or doner!
If there is reference to hypocrisy, so is there allusion to theft. Who are the thieves?

iṣhṭān bhogān hi vo devā dāsyante yajña-bhāvitāḥ
tair dattān apradāyaibhyo yo bhuṅkte stena eva saḥ [3.12]

       O Partha! He who performs yajna to please deities and to get enough of goods, riches and pleasures is a Thief if he does not proffer much of the gift to the gods.
       It is a fantastic concept on charity, philanthropy. We get goods, good fortune by grace of gods. It is implied that the gods be given part of our fortune in shape of yajna, puja, and by extension in alms, charity and philanthropy. Most of us boast of our fortune, possessions, acquisitions and achievements. Though our treasures and accruals are results of our labour and exertion, due to our diligence and perseverance, there is also the unseen hand of God behind them and the invisible blessings and benevolence of the society at large. It is therefore imperative to part with our property and possessions to the gods and society as gratitude, isn't it?
       Bhagavat Gita, as we know well, is not orthodox or

iconoclast. It lauds rites and rituals like yajna. It is yajna that pleases the gods including the all-creating Prajapati. The gods in their turn pour rains to make the earth green and full of grains. It is a usual and useful give and take between humans and divines. He who breaks this give-take-give chain is a Thief, isn't he?

One may wonder about this proposition. One may dispute the proposition by saying that gods indeed take or want nothing. The gods [God] do not bother whether we make respectful offerings to the gods in gratitude or thanksgiving. This disputation, disrespectful to the orthodox, does not fall flat. Often and umpteen times, we have been said through Arjuna that God resides everywhere, in every being. Our respectful offerings to the gods shall be in form of assistance, alms, charity, gift and donation to the disadvantaged, to the suffering, to the needy, to the destitute, to the beggar, to seekers of help.

God dwells in everyone, in every creature, doesn't He? Not only does the Lord abide in all of us, we dwell well in the Lord. It is clear from

yo māṁ pashyati sarvatra sarvaṁ cha mayi pashyati
tasyāhaṁ na praṇashyāmi sa cha me na praṇashyati [6.30]

O Kounteya! He who sees Me everywhere and who sees all in Me, cannot lose sight of Me nor will I lose sight of him.

There is therefore no doubt that you have to give the best part of your wealth, health, strength in the service of others, to help others, to rescue others, to resurrect others. Mind it mindfully that what you are, what you have got and what you boast of is the gift, donation, charity, mercy of God. And when and what you give to the seeker, the sufferer, the needy, the deprived is spent honestly, honourably, nobly because it is given, offered to none else but God. Do not boast that you have given, you have done. You are simply the via media, the means of Lord's equitable distribution, delicate dispensation. The Lord overhead has bestowed upon you great opportunity and occasion to share yours with others.

In the illustrious Ishavasyopanishada, it is said,
Ishavasyamidam sarvam yatkinchityagatyam yagat
Ten tyaktena bhunjitha ma grudhah kasyaswitdhanam
[Mantra1, Isha Upanishad]

The humanity is addressed with this important mantra with the truth that all whatever moves in this moveable world is the abode of the Lord. You eat whatever is left by Him for you; do not steal, rob the property of other that is earned by the sweat of their brow.

The omnipresence, the all-existent aspect of God is manifest in this magnificent metaphor. He who owns a piece of property develops the sense of "my, mine" and tries to extend, expand his "my, mine". That is not enough, he intends and effects exclusion of others. God includes all, in exclusion to all others. Hence, you do not have to claim your property, your wealth as "yours", but as "God's". Whatever you earn, you own is not yours. All you can say is that you own, possess that "apparently", "superficially", "surreally", not really. And it is the "leftover" of the Lord. You enjoy a leftover; why do you boast of the crumb? You are at best a trustee, a caretaker. Nothing more, nothing better, maybe worse than that. To better your lot in respect of the property, the wealth, the riches, the estate, you seem or are said to own; say softly, soberly, humbly that you own, hold, take care the possession/acquisition/assets/properties on behalf of the Lord.

The legend of king Harishchandra of the famed Sun Dynasty to which Sriram belonged is enlightening.

Harishchandra was an illustrious ruler, always-win warrior, virtuous and learned. He was second to none as a magnificent, munificent monarch. But he stood out as a gifted giver. Whoever whenever approached him for riches, assistance, alms, gift and donation was given indiscriminately and illimitably. That was unique and incomparable, unsurpassable. That was not all. He was all cheer and humility when dispersing charity. And the wonder of wonders was that when he was gifting or assisting, helping or donating, he hung his head low as if he had committed a mistake or regretting a blunder!

Nobody, even none of his wise ministers, could make head or tail of this queer, quizzical gesture. None dared to ask the monarch of this odd, unexplainable behaviour. However, after some weeks or months asked the seniormost minister why the monarch hung the head low while giving out plentily, pleasantly, not reluctantly or meagrely.

The monarch smiled softly and asked soberly, "What kind of a minister you were for all these years? Didn't you see the embarrassment on my face caused by the grateful multitude?"

The minister fell flat. He was more puzzled by such question than before. He asked the monarch reverentially, "What embarrassment! The beneficiaries, the beggars, the bonus-getters, bonanza- receivers, the great-number of grateful souls who leap in joy, dance in boundless happiness cause embarrassment to the superior-most sovereign! Strange! Illogical regal reasoning, to say the least, to think like that!

Harishchandra smiled, "Cool down my honourable counsel! What do I give away? Foodstuff, coins, clothes, jewellery, land, facilities, amenities, luxuries, don't I?

"Yea my great lord!" nodded the minister.

Harishchandra added, "There lies the error; that exactly is the erroneous reasoning and belief of you my loyal royal courtiers and, the subjects in general and the beneficiaries in particular. Do I own a single silver coin or one head of bovine animal? Do I have a piece of ornament or an inch of land? All this I am the monarch of belongs to the Lord; all that I had given with my hands to the needy, suffering, deprived, disadvantaged over these years belonged to God. I am the custodian, trustee, caretaker of the vast estates, forests, quarries, cattle, horses, jewels, gems of that omnipresent, ombudsman, the Lord. Nevertheless, the pity is that the beneficiaries, the takers, the receivers construe all they get is "mine" and praise me profusely. Even you, the courtiers and councillors, generals and commanders, priests and professors, saints and strangers praise me in unison with the beneficiaries. Thus, each time I hand over something to a beggar or a seeker, I feel utterly ashamed! God owns, gives but I am overpraised for doing a humble act according to God's dictates! Each praise, each applaud on such gift, donation, assistance reminds me of my shame! So, to partially get rid of the undue appreciation and honour, I hang my head low!

Harishchandra was certainly aware of

dātavyam iti yad dānaṁ dīyate 'nupakāriṇe
deshe kāle cha pātre cha tad dānaṁ sāttvikaṁ smṛitam [17.20]

Here, Krishna advises Arjuna who a real, good, godly giver is. The first attribute of the giver is to believe, be convinced that "this gift", "this giving", "this assistance" is "my duty". This giving, this helping is my "duty". The second trait of gift is that the receiver did not give, help, assist me in the past or present. More important is that he would not give me, assist me, benefit me anyway in the foreseeable future. The gifts, presents we generally receive on the eve of Diwali, Christmas or on the New Year morn, or on a birthday etc are the worst kind of thing to talk about, boast of. The third characteristic of sattvic gift is that you consider the region, the time and the person who you are giving. Should you give money to a gambler, drunkard or womaniser? Should you assist an adversary of your country, club, society, region or family? And the person? Should he be amply able-bodied to work and earn his bread by the sweat of his brow but be begging? So, give; give to the needy; not to tom, dick and harry.

TWENTY-SIX

Father feasts on flesh of son
as he is Karna

When we have talked of *dana*, the tale of *danavira* Harishchandra, we may just casually think of two other danaviras who dominated the eras they lived and are deservingly remembered by posterity dutifully. They are *danavira* Karna and *mahadani* Vali.

Karna was begotten by unwed Kunti out of curiosity whether the rishi Durvasha's mantra of begetting a child at her own suit will would fructify. Ashamed and afraid of begetting a son before marriage, she put the newborn Karna in a casket and floated it on Yamuna. While bathing in Yamuna one early morning, Adhiratha, the Kaurava charioteer, found a newborn boy afloat. Childless since he was, he was overjoyed in spotting the abandoned baby and took him home. He brought up the child well who with the gene of his original father sun-god shone and showed promiscuous prowess in wrestling, boxing, duel, archery and mace wielding. The Pandava scions and sons of Dhritarastra taught martial arts and practices by indubitable Drona met for a friendly competition to showcase their superior martial skills. Of them, Bhima dominated mace fighting and Arjuna was incomparable in archery. That Arjuna is the best warrior of the then Bharata was announced by Drona and Bhishma. Karna who watched the Pandava, Kaurava princes' competition from a gallery corner could not digest the declaration. He came out to the royal stadium and asserted that he could compete with Arjuna and vanquish him. That he was charioteer Adinatha's son was the known secret. Hence, Arjuna with regal haughtiness dismissed the upcoming contender.

Karna was offended and was going back to visitor's gallery when Duryodhana came forward and declared that he is anointing Karna as the king of Anga kingdom. Prince Duryodhana was by birth king of Anga a feudatory kingdom of Hastina empire. He was jealous of the Pandavas from his childhood as the Pandavas excelled in learning, playing, fighting and in pleasing gurus, elders and the subjects of the empire in general. One day the 100 Kaurava scions were beaten badly by Bhima, Arjuna and the other trio. He wanted to beat the pandava princes at least in one martial event. He was glad that a lad was there to dare Arjuna. So, he anointed Karna king right there in the tournament stadium.

Bhishma, Drona and other elders who could sense of a senseless fight between Karna and Arjuna causing embarrassment and indecency declared the contest closed on the alibi of sunset. But Karna harboured a bitter grudge against Arjuna in particular and the Pandavas in general on the one hand and was emotionally, intensely grateful to Duryodhana in particular and his brothers in general on the other. Duryodhana exploited Karna's calibre to the extreme for this dana of a kingdom. Karna, an unwed mother's son by a heavenly hero sun-god, was obviously good and godly.

As king of Anga, Karna made a name as the invincible conqueror of kingdoms and castles. But his glory spread far and wide as a giver, donor of the first water so much so that he was called dani Karna or danavira Karna or Mahavira Karna.

He baths in the holy stream of Yamuna at sunrise, proffers holy river water to sun and the galaxy of other gods with pious prayers. Thereafter, he offers alms and assistance, gifts and presents in plentiful quantity and piteous sincerity. He would not say no to any beggar, any seeker, whatever the cost or consequences thereof might be. He did not depart from this noble nature at any cost.

The legend runs thus. The celestial beings were amazed at the stunning giving away attribute of Karna. Dharmaraja, the god of justice, once wanted to test Karna's unquenchable love for gifting and donating. So, he got down to the earth at an unearthly hour of the day when Karna and family and all others of his palace had had sumptuous lunch and were having midday siesta. The brahmin-turned Dharmaraja rang the palace bell. The estate sentry turning up, brahmin begged to meet the king Karna. Karna did not delay to meet the brahmin who were generally held in high esteem by his royal personage. On proper salutation, Karna asked what service he can render to the brahmin.

"I am hopelessly hungry for some days past; want a big plate of flesh and staples," the brahmin said.

"O so kind of you to have offered me this honourable opportunity to feed a hungry brahmin! Come in, sit down some minutes; I am getting your menu ready," replied Karna.

"Did you understand what I meant? I meant a plate of flesh," the brahmin added.

"Very much. Mutton, chicken, horse or elephant meat or doe or duck meat, whatever you hanker after would be supplied enough and spare," Karna confirmed.

"O poor fellow! It is human flesh. It is only human flesh that I relish. Can you arrange that quickly and adequately?" Karna was crest-fallen at the clear, cool but queer asking of the frail brahmin.

"I know you cannot, can you? And for your information, it is the meat of your young boy whose meat would be chopped, spiced, cooked and served by the queen-mother, none else."

Karna was about to fall fainting but for his physical, emotional and moral strength. In fact, the news, a bolt from the blue, was so hard, horrendous and harassing that Karna would have killed the seeker instantly, had he not been a reverend brahmin. Nonetheless, he sat the brahmin in the parlour and prevailed upon his lovely wife and only son's mother to act according to the brahmin's causeless, cruel desire to save his honour as the well-known giver.

The beautiful and dutiful wife-queen coalesced in being a draconian mother to the only son to uphold husband-king's unfailing giver honour. She was well aware of English poet Alexander Pope's lines,

Honour and shame from no condition rise
Act well your part; there all the honour lies

Karna's only son, Viswakeshana, a promising and promiscuous adolescent, was called home from play, was told the tale in detail. He was only too glad to lay his head for the feast of a brahmin-god and prevailed upon his mother to sharpen the knife, hone the cutleries, exhibit her culinary skill, cook and feed the hungry god without hesitation or hypocrisy.

The meat and meal were ready. Karna led the brahmin to the dining hall, sat him in the sprawling, sparkling dining table under glowing and glittering chandeliers. Brahmin looked at Karna and asked, "Only for me! Is it etiquette that the host does not give company to the guest? Please sit down or I go!"

"No, no, I sit to eat my son's meat, the wretched wart that I am on a father's face!" Karna sat down opposite the brahmin.

"O, yes! Where is your son? Must he not partake of the lavish, nutritious lunch," commented the brahmin.

Karna could not bear anymore and sobbed unbearably. His wife who had hardened her heart like a piece of stishovite or moissanite said soberly, "Brahmin- god! Our only son is roasted and spiced as your food. How can he partake of the party?"

"Are you teasing me queen? Who the hell can kill Karn's son for meat? Call him and lay a plate for him!"

Emotionally charged and grief-surcharged, the queen ran out to the front-yard and called out loud and long,

" Vi..swa..ke…sha…na….!"

"Why cry and impatient mom! Just a minute and I am there!"

The Karna couple cried unconsolably as Viswakeshana washed his hands, feet and face clean with clear water and sat down at the dining table in a chair between the brahmin and his father.

The brahmin rose up in his own form and frame to go and announced, "Karna! You are superb and spectacular as a giver. There was none or nor would be one to equal you in giving away in the manner and majesty as you can! To kill the only son for a brahmin's whim! Hail to you, victory to Karna! The great, glorious mahadani Karna!

The brahmin in disguise vanished as soon as possible appraising Karna's generous charity and praising him for his unequalled sacrifice and sagacity.

Karna is called the cruel, sadistic villain in the epic purana, the Mahabharata. But for him Duryodhana would not have dared the Pandavas to dice and Kurukshetra battle. Duryodhana was sure beyond a shred of doubt that where Karna is, there victory is. But more importantly, Karna is called the greatest giver, the tallest to gift, the noblest to sacrifice.

Karna's dana was diluted with egotism, divested of sattvic sagacity. He gifted generously, unbiasedly, indiscriminately because of the unsought, uncalled for, unexpected gift of a kingdom by Duryodhana. A valiant warrior, an undaunted kshatriya youth that Karna was, he was circumstantially indebted to Duryodhana. He repaid that debt to Duryodhana by kowtowing the latter through thick and thin and never differing with the latter whatever may be the price or public perception of him on the one hand and paying out profusely and promptly to the needy, seeking and distressed on the other hand to compensate that great, unsought gift by Duryodhana.

In such circumstance, Karna's giving could be rajasic dana as styled in,

yat tu pratyupakārārthaṁ phalam uddiśhya vā punaḥ
dīyate cha parikliṣhṭaṁ tad dānaṁ rājasaṁ smṛitam [17.21]

"O Arjuna! the gift made as gratitude or in expectation of future assets or assistance, with the motive of reaping earthly or ethereal pleasures like glory, good name, reputation or place in the paradise is rajasic dana. So is the donation made with physical pain and hardship to oneself or one's near and dear one's is rajasic dana."

If we analyse critically, Karna's being a great giver rested on his egoism, eccentricity and inferior complex. It is evident when he boasted,

Suta va sutaputra va jo ko va bhavamyaham

Daivayatam kule yanma madayatam cha pourusham[the Mahabharata]

A charioteer or son of a charioteer whoever I am, that I am due to my birth [as son of charioteer Adhiratha]. I cannot change my birth or parentage which is ordained by the gods but what I am as Karna now is my achievement, my doing.

TWENTY-SEVEN

Vali and Vaman
Dwarf and demon
What's our lesson?

Vali did not consider the "desha, kala, patra" [country or region, time and age of the donee] of the dwarf that stood before him. What kind of giver be called Vali?

adeśha-kāle yad dānam apātrebhyaśh cha dīyate
asat-kṛitam avajñātaṁ tat tāmasam udāhṛitam [17.22]

"O Dhananjaya! What is an example of tamasic dana? Without knowing anything about the seeker, his native place, the time of his seeking, his personality and his calling, if somebody grants great benefits to the seeker, then his gift is tamasic."

Then, what about Vali whose generosity crossed all parameters and all perimeters. His excesses in giving out indiscriminately earned him the disrepute in moral lessons,

Ati darpe hata lanka ati mane cha kourava
Ati dane valirvadha ati sarvatra gahirtram. [moral]

Ravana was too arrogant to ruin Lanka beyond recognition; the Kauravas were too conceited to get lost one and all; Vali died due to his excessive generosity. So, extreme is always indecently, inexcusably detrimental.

Arrogance, conceit are inexcusably bad traits of humans, demons and divines. They cause atrocious and arbitrary acts that cause suffering and losses, unhappiness and harassment to the masses. On the contrary, charity is virtue. Generosity is a genial quality of the ruler, the royal boss. Vali, a direct demon-descendant was undoubtedly divine in giving, granting, assisting, helping the poor, perturbed, helpless, hopeless, hapless. Notwithstanding that outstanding virtue, he suffered the same fate as arrogant Ravana or headstrong Duryodhana, didn't he? Why? Only because his charity did not stand the test of sloka 20, chapter 17 of the Bhagavat Gita. He gave out to one and all irrespective of the beggar's, the seeker's credentials. A giver should give free but not freely.

The Vali Vamana episode epitomises the best sort of gift by a giver to the seeker. For this exemplary charity, Vali became one of the seven immortals of earth, of humankind.

Ashwathama Valirvyaso hanumansha bibhishana
Krupah parashuramashcha saptaite chiramjeevinah .

Ashwathama, Vali, Vyasa, Hanuman, Bibhishana, Krupa and Parashurama are the seven who outlive deluge, dissolution. These seven immortals are unique and unequalled. In fact, they were not killed, could not be killed; they were out of the bounds of weapons or wizardry.

Among them, Vali alone was pressed purposefully down to the nether world by Vishnu in the Vamana incarnation. And that too for no fault of his. He was virtuous to a fault. Goodness, good qualities are per se not fault but are fault when exhibited or extended to a fault; riches breach the fault-line. Generosity, charity was hallmark, cream of his character. Regrettably, it was to a fault.

Vice is avoidable all through, in all measure, in all manner. The quantity, quality, instance, intensity, time, territory do not count in the consideration of vice, sin, impiety. Virtue, on the other hand, is significant and serene notwithstanding the case, custom, camaraderie, commotion or emotion. Virtue comprising charity needs no clarity that there should be no limit, no litmus test. But Vali's case was exception, example of "too much, too much of too much".

Vali was son of Vairochana, the diehard demon of distinguishable devilry though the latter was the son of Prahlada, the ardent Vishnu bhakta. Vali was partly Vairochana and partly Prahlada, the Prahlada part outweighing, overriding Vairochana part. So, succeeding Vairochana as the demon monarch, he went on military expeditions, winning and annexing territory after territory in the shortest of time. He won the war against devas and ravaged the paradise, subjected gods to ignoble snobbery and misery. Thereafter, he organised a great yajna to please the celestial forces and divine dimensions so that his subjugation of the three worlds would perpetuate without perturbance or trepidation by devas, humans or the nether or nocturnal destructive agents or anarchists.

Vali was like that. Valiant, vengeful and violent on the one hand and virtuous, philanthropic, kind, generous, genial, ritual and respectful on the other hand. Bountiful gift and donation to the beggars, the seekers, the sufferers, was accorded his number one priority. As a rule, he gifted goods, gold, cattle, castle, acreages to the needy, the disadvantaged, the depressed, the downtrodden, poets, pundits, professors, preachers, teachers, respectables and unearning socials. After the formidable, fashionable yajna was over, he was overjoyed to hand over whoever asked for whatever objects or ornaments, opportunity or amenity.

The gods tormented and subjugated abjectly by Vali prayed Vishnu to sort out the matter by one more sortie to the mundane world. Flattered and fondled by the divine friends, fans, followers, Vishnu considered doing away with Vali. But how? Vali was more divine in his royal, ritual, righteous obligations than the devas. His oppression, suppression, subjugation, domination was not condemnable as he made that up by good governance, do-gooder and glorious social, cultural, religious actions. All the same, Vishnu had to ditch Vali as a favour to the devas.

The yajna over, Vali would be indomitable, invincible. The amount of gifts, presents, giving away by him was simply superb and earned him unsurpassable, spectacular praise, blessing and good-wishes from beneficiaries and non-beneficiaries. Vishnu advented upon the earth in a queer dwarf avatar, embodiment. Vali was about to retire and rest when a 12- year-old dwarf with a large palm-leaf umbrella overhead, noticeable and nice tilak-paste spot over the forehead, a snow-white brahmin *upavita* across the left shoulder, approached in pretty little steps. His majesty Vali was bewitched by the beautiful boy's gait and gesture, was almost mesmerised when he looked up at the monarch and smiled softly, innocently [or intriguingly?].

Regaining his senses, he queried, "Where have you come from the godly brahmin lad? Seem worried and wanting, what would you have to be happy? Be free, frank and fearless to express your desire, your demand. Today is a special day after completion of the yajna and you're the special guest to be treated, feasted today and the rest of your life. Come on boy, come on!"

"Your generosity and charity is known across all worlds and is duly and deservingly declared so by beneficiaries and non-beneficiaries in equal measure, in equal number. So, I have come with a small request, will you oblige?" Vamana vented out slowly, sedately.

"Getting the heaven down on your little palms would be a little labour on my part. I can squeeze the quizzical universe in the cusp of your palm. 'Little or big' requests are requests for Vali who complies them completely, comprehensively. Come out!"

"I am afraid you might fail this time, this occasion. To assure me, you must swear by your gods that you will not swerve from your swearing, mustn't you?

"Why not? Astoundingly astonished and veritably vexed, Vali answered. "What kind of affidavit do you require, sweet little dove?"

"There is pure, pious Ganga water in this mine *kamandalu, [sacred bronze pitcher]. While I flow water therefrom, confirm aloud 'That I must give, I must give, I give must what the dwarf begs!'*"

Vali, disturbed to death but dissimulating bravado, swore aloud three times as Vamana poured water from his bronze pitcher,

"By my God I swear that I shall give, I shall give, I shall give what this dwarfish boy begs!"

"Wow, wow..." cried the spectators in unison, while Vamana smiled softly.

"Then" begged the Vamana, "give me three steps of land."

"Did you land in bedlam? O sweet boy! What is this that you are begging of mighty, majestic monarch Vali? You can ask for anything and everything from wealth to ornaments, from cattle to coins, from property to palace that can fling your poverty and wants to the furthest corner of the earth without impinging on my assets and authority, without creating any liability on me!"

"Yes, the mightiest of monarchs, the Kuber on earth! You have given enough over the period, yet have still enough to give. But I ask for nothing else than three steps of land measured by my tiny feet, will you impart or I shall depart sans grudge or grumble that you reneged on your avowed assurance?"

Vali fumbled for words by the humbling hint by the humble brahmin boy. He coaxed the dwarf, "Yea, measure this earth by your tiny foot to acquire the first step of land!"

Vamana stretched his right foot that covered the whole earth from the north pole to the south pole, from Chile's southernmost island to Siberia's northernmost tip. The people gathered by then numbering in several thousand saw to their amazement and amusement that a tiny foot of the dwarf covers the entire earth, as is if a vast scarf has fallen upon the earth. Vali was vexed whether it was real or nightmare that he saw with his own eyes in the presence of thousands of witnesses.

His bewilderment was bludgeoned when Vamana asked, "What about the second step of land?"

"O heaven! the whole heaven is very much mine, under my possession. There is none to dispute my suzerainty there. Take it!"

"Oh! Yes," said Vamana and extended his left foot

over heaven, the illimitable, infinite abode of the devas. Vali looked crushed, crestfallen that a tiny dwarf has roughed up his might, absolute authority over the three worlds in the winkling of an eye! What he is up to and what he has to do with this jugglery? What kind of deva or danava is this to dare me in my den, and as if for fun?"

He was interrupted when Vamana asked, "Where is the third step of land since heaven and earth is no longer in your title or possession?"

Vali was breaking; Vali was broken. He pondered for a moment and asked, "Where is your third foot? You dwarf have played enough mischief!"

"No mischief great Vali! See my third foot! I do have one, don't I?" And the third foot of the Vamana shot from his navel, a small navel, obviously a small navel of the small man. "Your land, Maharaj! Where is your land?

"It is here, it is here! Land your tiny step over there," Vali knelt down and hung his head low. Vamana put his navel-shot foot on Vali's large head that sank slowly beneath the earth.

Vali became great, eternal memory and immortal for his high, honourable gift of life. Nevertheless, this gift was faulty. Vali made the gift, not knowing who that queer creature was, wherefrom he arrived at the end of the yajna and after all gifts and donations were distributed...

In his immortal tale "How Much Land Does a Man Need", Count Lev Nikolayevich Tolstoy answered "Six Feet Land Is Enough." For a Christian's burial 6 feet land is adequate to contain the coffin of the person and the graveyard is crowded with coffins underground. For a Hindu dead, you need logs of wood, not land, that too 6 logs of wood. The Hindu ascending the pyre is fired, after which he is consigned to ashes, blown into the air, and forgotten, forgotten for good but for his good deeds done and good words said.

TWENTY-EIGHT

How much land does a man need?

Tolstoy asked the question in the tale and instilled the moral into our conscience, our conviction. It is worthwhile recalling the immortal moral tale of satisfaction and happiness in the beginning, marred by hunger for possession, more possession in the middle, and terrible tragic death in the end.

Two sisters in a Russian peasant family were married off to a town tradesman and a rural peasant respectively. After some years, they chatter on the pros and cons of town life vis-a-vis country life. Their sibling sweet-nothings ended as they went to sleep. But the Devil lurking behind and noting intently the town-denizen sister's snobbery, caught hold of younger sister's peasant husband, Pahom, who heard of their insufficiency in land and living. To the snubbish rubbish, he said to himself, "It is perfectly true. Busy as we are from childhood tilling mother earth, we peasants have no time to let any nonsense settle in our heads. Our only trouble is that we haven't land enough. If I had plenty of land, I shouldn't fear the Devil himself!"

The story develops with the Devil telling unheard, "I'll give you land enough; and by means of that land I will get you into my power."

Pahom, first of all, is troubled by the neighbouring estate steward who imposed fines for Pahom's cattle or horse trespassing into the estate. Then his hunger for land heightens when the estate is sold in fragments to the villagers. He desired to "buy twenty acres or so." "As life is becoming impossible," he conferred with his wife. But he did not have the wherewithal. To arrange money for the deal, he sold a colt, and half of his bees. Still wanting, he hired out a son as a labourer and got his wages in advance. Besides, he borrowed some money from his brother-in-law. The total was half of the value of the 20 acres land he purchased on down payment; the other half, as agreed to, was paid in future instalments.

Pahom was glad as his dream came true. He boasted of being owner of an estate comprising corn-land, forest, pasturage. But he was soon discontented by trespassing of cow, goats of the villagers and cutting of trees and shrubs by them, by neighbouring Simon in particular. He went to a court of law where he got no relief for want of concrete evidence. Enraged and indiscreet that he had become by now, he quarrelled with the judge and the village elders. This caused his indignity in the village Commune despite his owning land; in juxtaposition his respect before as a simple peasant was better and ample.

During those times, he came across hearsay that people were emigrating to new regions where land was plentiful and cheap but fertile, all the same. Initially, he dismissed the thought of his moving away. Instead, he thought of purchasing the migrants' land and expand his estate. Nevertheless, one evening, a stranger called at his residence, who spoke of cheap availability of abundant alluvial fertile land, vast pasturage. Pahom was motivated, moved. He thought to himself, "Why should I suffer in this narrow hole, if one can live so well elsewhere?"

In the coming summer, he started for the enviable location, first by steamer on Volga to Samara and then 480 kilometres on foot. Satisfied with what he saw, he came back, sold his land, cattle, household articles, homestead. On reaching the new place, he soon became Commune member. As Commune grant for his son and his, he owned 125 acres, apart from right to Communal pasture. It was 3 times his former land-hold, which made him immediately, immodestly happy. The huge pasture filled him with pride that he can tend as many heads of cattle as he may like.

But Pahom's discontent grew with quarrels with neighbours and constant concern for the rented corn-land far off. He pondered over his compact farm with homestead that would facilitate profitable and independent farming. He was planning purchasing a 1300 acres farm for 1500 rubbles when in a chance encounter with a far-off treader, he learnt that the latter bought 13000 acreages in a distant land with a paltry 1000 rubbles. Of course, the fortune would be his who courts the village chief's friendship with etiquette and gifts. The inhabitants were called Bashkirs who were as meek as sheep but land there was so vast that one cannot cover that if one walked nonstop for a full year.

Pahom was perturbed and pondered, "Why 1300 acres with my 1000 rubbles when I can get much more from the Bashkirs?" Ascertaining details of the region and the route chart, he set out with his man. In a town enroute, he stopped to buy presents for Bashkirs and their chief. On the 7th day and about 480 kms away, they saw the felt-covered Bashkirs tents on Steppes by a river. The treader did not tell a lie about the land or the people. They ate no bread to need tilling the land. Their cattle and horses grazed free in hordes over the vast Steppes. The colts were tethered to the tents, enforcing mares driven twice to milk. From mare milk, women made kumiss and cheese. The menfolk drank kumiss and tea, ate sheep mutton and played on their pipes playfully, peacefully. With an interpreter's instrumentality, the Bashkirs and Pahom exchanged their feelings and fraternity. To please the pleasant and positive hosts, Pahom gave them the gifts and tea. Then came the chief who was presented with the best dressing-gown and five pounds tea. Pahom prayed for land to the pleased Bashkirs and their chief to which the chief ruled that he could have as much land as he wished. For title deed thereof, it was customary that he would own as much land he could demarcate in a day.

Pahom could not believe his gatecrashing luck. Next morning, he started from a point on a hillock by putting his cap and money alongside the chief's fur-cap. As usual, he was to mark the perimeter at regular intervals with a turf-heap dug with his spade. The fully flat fertile land stretching out before his eyes were his were he to cover it before sunset! His gargantuan greed gyrated him to throw his legs fast and furiously, to digging earth to turf-heaping quickly one after one, and to cover all, the whole land before his eyes before sun setting! At the outset, he contemplated covering a formidable circle. Before long, he saw that he is fatigued and faltering and the sun declining over the western horizon. Instead of circular movement, he paced perpendicularly from that point. Tried as hard as he could, he could scarcely reach the hillock-foot whence he started by twilight. The

Bashkir chief and others were cheering him, caring for him, and encouraging him to reach the butt but he could not. Losing the coveted land that he never has had was not so important as the 1000 rubbles he staked. On his failure to circle the land before sunset, he would face double jeopardy.

He ran and ran and ran with his feeble feet to set foot on the butt anyhow anytime soon ere the sun sets! But his famished body and flustered mind did not give him company. He fell just near the butt, stretching his hand butt-ward. His servant helped him put his hand on his cap and money and the crowd cheered that he had done it!

But he was bitterly undone; he was dead and gone! The servant dug his grave with the six-feet-measuring land where Pahom fell dead to his greed, to his gerrymandering greed!

No one has ever asked the question: how much land can a man give? Nor has any one replied, has anyone? Of course, state governments have compelled portly landlords, zamindars to part with their vast estates and large acreages in compliance to laws like Estates Abolition Act, Land Reforms Act etc. That is not voluntary out of their volition. Voluntary land donations were made by kings of this country. But Acharya Vinoba Bhave, the saint, sadhak, satyagrahi and social reformer effected voluntary land gift by landlords, landowners in the Bhoodan Andolan initiated and immensely successful in in the 1950s.

Yet, Vamana asked Vali: how much land can you give?

Vali blasted: as much as you can seek. Vamana sought only three steps land and undone Vali was doomed to the nether land.

TWENTY-NINE

**All that glitters is not gold:
Gilded tombs do worms enfold**

Even an honest, honourable act of giving to the seeker could be faulted in the faultless Bhagavat Gita. Then what about other such activities like worship, tapa, yajna that we perform perforce? The 17th chapter of Bhagavat Gita is titled Shraddha Traya Vibhaga Yoga. Acharya Vinoba calls the chapter as the "Seeker's Programme". Since it is the last but one chapter, teachers and preachers, gurus and disciples feel bored and exhausted by the time they open this chapter. To Arjuna's query, Krishna replies that all people perform Worship, Yajna and Tapasya with fondness and fervour. How they discharge these jobs is important and that determines what grade of dana, worship, yajna, tapasya was done by the performer.

Of dana we have discussed supra [Sections TWENTY-SIX & TWENTY-SEVEN] and have concluded in accordance with Bhagavat Gita that dana is sattvic, rajasic or tamasic. Strange! Even in the noble virtue of gift and donation, there is classification. And the rajasic and tamasic dana suffers from noble mistake!

In case of worship, yajna and tapasya, the same

categorisation applies categorically. Mind it! The doers, the performers do not lack in or want in shraddha, due love or fervour for the dana, puja, yajna or tapasya. Yet, their dana, yajna, puja, tapasya is made or marred according to the paraphernalia and parameters. While the Sattvic earn kudos for yajna or puja, the Rajasic and Tamasic do not. We worship, we worship to whom/what? It is difficult to answer, isn't it? People speak of their or others' penance as easily as they speak of weather, sports, entertainment or election. Who exactly practice penance? Bhagavat Gita has long ago said about our puja in,

yajante sāttvikā devān yakṣha-rakṣhānsi rājasāḥ
pretān bhūta-gaṇānśh chānye yajante tāmasā janāḥ [17.4]

The Gita goes on to describe our penance, human penance in the next two slokas,

aśhāstra-vihitaṁ ghoraṁ tapyante ye tapo janāḥ
dambhāhankāra-sanyuktāḥ kāma-rāga-balānvitāḥ [17.5]

karṣhayantaḥ śharīra-sthaṁ bhūta-grāmam achetasaḥ
māṁ chaivāntaḥ śharīra-sthaṁ tān viddhy āsura-niśhchayān [17.6]

I am constrained by space to deal these in greater detail but do not refrain from hinting at these because these are mundane matters, earthly affairs, commoner's commodity. We worship day and night whenever we have time or need something or are in trouble, don't we? When we exert on difficult or long-term enterprise, our prayer is called penance, Tapasya.

The three verses above speak of classification of worship, of penance. The classification is quality-content, not quantity-rich.

Of puja, it is said,

The Sattvic worship gods; the Rajasic worship yaksha, rakshasa and the Tamasic worship spirits, evil spirits.

Gods mean literally, the gods and goddesses like Vishnu, Shiva, Brahma, Ganesh, Saraswati, Laxmi, Durga, Surya etc. But a Gita reader and practiser shall go beyond; should think beyond and worship their virtues, their attributes, there attainments. The gods and goddesses the sattvic worship are symbols and substance of superior sensibilities. Vishnu sleeps serene under a thousand-hooded snake in the seamless sea, indifferent to the possible trepidations by the snake and the sea. Shiv, on the other hand, meditates on the high Himalaya surrounded by thick sheets of snow, unmindful that snakes slither on his body smeared with cemetery ash while a bull is there at his beck and call. While he possesses an unusual third eye, the crescent moon crowns the top temple. The divine beings are not divine for being divine but are divine for their individual divine traits that are worthy of emulation, worship.

The rajasic run after money, gold, treasure trove. So, they worship gold and place goodness on gold. They think gold worship brings more gold and gold gets a seat among gods and goddesses. They forget or take the Shakespearean saying in the famous play, The Merchant of Venice, seriously,

"All that glitters is not gold-
Often have you heard that told:
Many a man his life hath sold:
Gilded tombs do worms enfold." [Scene VII, Act II]

Gold gets people mad to sell all, even one's life to acquire gold. Not gold but the desire to own gold is the cause of our insanity, insensitivity, irrationality. The attraction of gold is depicted therein in the inscription of the golden casket that prince of Morocco reads,

"Who chooseth me shall gain what many men desire."

It is our desire for the yellow metal, the queen metal, the malleable, majestic metal that morphs us, the crown of the Anthropocene, into arthropods, centipedes. It is hard and hard to be had by. Hard labour makes it had of to hoard. So, the mythological Midas prayed for the boon to turn whatever he touches to become burnishing gold, didn't he?

Midas was the Phrygian king of ancient Greece in the second millennia before Christ. Previously a peasant, king Midas chanced upon Silenus, the wise old teacher of Dionysus. Excessively inebriated, Silenus strayed into Phrygian peasants and was brought before the king. The king recognised him and treated him respectfully and lavishly. For ten days and ten nights, Midas entertained Silenus and his friends freely and fabulously. On the 11th day, he took back Silenus to Dionysus in Lydia. Dionysus was utmost delighted that his revered teacher had been hosted amply and aristocratically. Overpleased with Midas, Dionysus asked, "What do you desire, Midas! as return favour for taking so good care of my teacher? Whatever you ask for must be met with my miraculous power, don't dither!"

"If you are so pleased to favour me with your divine power, I humbly wish to be granted the boon that whatever I touch turns out to be bright shining gold! Only and pure gold, gold in the quantity no holds barred!"

"Yes, Midas! No holds barred whatever you touch is glittering gold!" Dionysus assured.

Back home on road, Midas was glad and giggled "Whatever I touch is gold; whatever Midas touches is turned to gold! Is it really so? Why not test and know!" He touched a dried oak twig and lo! it's very much, very real gold! Next, he touched a stone and that is gold! "Now it is proved that whatever I touch shall be intrinsic gold, instant gold! Dionysus cannot be false or fraud at any cost," thought Midas in joy.

Back home and overjoyed, he touched the roses in his favourite, fanciful garden. Dionysus would not prove wrong. All the fragrant red roses that Midas touched turned to lifeless, yellow flowers of gold sans scent and rosy beauty. He was sorry for the transformation of roses into gold. All the same, his pride knew no bounds on his rare feat of "golden touch". To celebrate the unique quality of his, he hosted a grand party for his palace people, counsellors and commanders. The servants laid out the lavish table. The assembled guests gossiped and giggled over the sumptuous dinner and the host's spectacular calibre. But the feast turned a nightmare when he touched the food-full plates of the guests out of courtesy or kindness.

The whole day, he could do nothing as whatever he touched was turned to tantalising gold. He could not eat or drink as the food he touched turned gold; the water or wine he wanted to drink was transformed to gold. The final blow came when his sweet little daughter turned to a golden doll; dull, lifeless like hell. The daughter came crying as the beautiful, 60-petals-each rose of his garden that grow naturally and transform the whole garden and surrounding with unrivalled beauty and fragrance were morphed to scentless, indecent flowers of gold. As soon as Midas held his daughter in his embrace to comfort with some effort, the girl was still, steely gold.

Now was the turn of Midas to cry and curse. Starvation and exhaustion, loss of several precious lives including his dearest daughter, and the irritating, immobile bright yellow colour of heaps of gold throughout thoroughly depressed and saddened him. Servants and employees ran away from him, dreadfully afraid of being transformed to inert, comatose, cold gold. Officers and counsellors who in the beginning thronged Midas and his palace shied away for fear of losing their lovely life to gaudy, goddam gold.

Gold kills the haves and have-nots, doesn't gold? Midas, the mighty and magnificent king, lost his all, inclusive of his dear daughter, and himself to the greed, hunger of gold. Knowing all that, we hanker after gold; we hunger for gold; we lose our honour and harmonious life at the altar of gold. We worship gods and goddesses to obtain gold, to obtain the 'golden touch'; to acquire 'Midas touch'. We forget that we lose the 'human touch' the moment we gain the 'Midas touch', the 'golden touch'. Yet, we run after Shakespearean gold casket inscription, "Who chooseth me shall gain what many men desire:" Men and women, rich and poor, learned and ignorant all over the world all the ages 'desire' gold, gold that they do not need for food, clothing, shelter or health. Gold is desired for luxury, luxurious living, not for cheerful, salubrious living. Gold is desired for ostentation, for arrogant, ostentatious living.

THIRTY

Nitai, who pulled up my ladder?

The Rajasic pray Yaksha and Rakshas. The Tamasic pray preta, bhoota. In this context the story of 'The Trust Property' by Viswakavi Rabindranath Thakur is pertinent.

Jagannath Kundu was so utterly miserly that he did not spend enough to feed, clothe his son, daughter-in-law, grandson or himself. He was so money-minded that he did not love his son or daughter-in-law as others in general in the village and elsewhere generally do. If he had any love for anybody, that was his 4-year-old grandson named Gokul Chandra. His son Brindavan did not see eye to eye with his close-fisted father and bickered bitterly occasionally when Jagannath denied him minimum expenses. Brindavan's wife was taken ill. The village Kaviraj suggested some common treatment [in Jagannath's computation, consideration] which was costly. As his wont, Jagannath dismissed spending money on purchase of drugs due to which the poor woman died prematurely, leaving bereaving Brindavan and her 4- year son at the mercy of the old haggard. Wife's death distressed Brindavan so much that he with Gokul deserted his miserly father.

While leaving home, he accused his father of being

the "murderer" of his wife. To which Jagannath retorted, "Nonsense! Don't people die even after swallowing all kinds of drugs? If costly medicines could save life, how is it that kings and emperors are not immortal? You don't expect your wife to die with more pomp and ceremony than did your mother and grandmother before her, do you?"

Brindavan was dismayed that his mother and grandmother died without treatment and medicines in a different era under different economic conditions. But the old haggard that his father was, was well off enough economically to spend a few rupees on his ailing wife. In a huff, he went out with the agile Gokul. But what will he do? His father's infamy was so well-known that the father-son duo would be disliked by their near and distant villagers for belonging to Jagannath Kundu. Hence, Brindavan put up the fake name of Damodar Pal and faked his son's name as Nitai Pal. Father and son stayed in some distance and Damodar made his both ends meet somehow. When he wanted to send Nitai to school, the latter took to the heels as far as Jagannath Kundu's village. There with the playing boys, he struck an agreeable chord, being extremely playful, prankster and lovely. He managed to put up with some playmate somehow or in a deserted, dilapidated structure or temple.

Jagannatha Kundu, on the other hand, grieved the departure of Gokula Chandra. Though, at times, he was utterly annoyed with the 4-year-olds' mischief and nuisance, he alone was an oasis in the dreary desert of Jagannatha's heart. Alone in the silent home, he recalled the many a mischief that the giggling Gokul made to make his home lively and lovely. In the absence of Brindavan and Gokula, Jagannatha grieved more and ate less; took less care of his body and bearing, clothing and shaving. With the passing of days, he became lean and thin and looked ghostlike with unkempt hair and unwashed dhoti, gamcha. He avoided the village folk and wandered lonely in the fields and groves bordering the village. One afternoon, he saw a stranger boy mingling and giggling freely and fearlessly with the village boys who follow him faithfully. Lovely and leaderlike, the stranger boy attracted Jagannatha's attention at once. While the village lads ran away in a hurry and with uproar "bhoota, bhoota", the new boy stood his ground.

Jagannatha was surprised at the courage and uncommon trait of the brat and gestured him to come toward him. The boy proceeded toward Jagannatha as much curiously as casually to strike a conversation with the strange ghostlike man. Jagannatha initiated the dialogue,

"What's your name, my boy?"

"Nitai Pal," the boy replied matter-of-factly.

"Where's your home?"

"Won't tell."

"What's your father's name?"

"Won't say."

"Why won't you say?"

"Because I have fled home?"

"Why fled home?"

"Father insisted I go to school."

Jagannatha smiled softly, delightfully. To him going to school is sheer waste of money and time. He was so much in love of the boy at the first sight that he wanted to keep the boy in home instead of sending to school by his father. He continued, "Then why not come with me and live happily without going to school and being seen by your father."

"OK!" said Nitai Pal playfully, pleasantly.

The errant stranger endeared Jagannatha with his actions, articulations, prankster and playful pleasant demeanour. No doubt, he demanded things of the close-fisted Jagannatha that the latter obliged unreluctantly to curry favour with the lovely brat who, hopefully, looked after and behaved like Gokula Chandra. Nitai was smart enough to take advantage of the old haggard's fondness for him and haggled hard and high for things he desired. The old man may part with his property but not with the lovely little brat that chatted day and night which was nightingale or lark's music to his ears.

Time passed happily for Jagannatha and Nitai despite the villagers' envy and anger toward both. Meantime, Jagannatha had declared to Nitai often in no uncertain terms that he would bequeath all his wealth consisting of silver coins and pitcher-full gold mohurs to him without any incumbrances except on the condition that he would ungrudgingly part with the same to Gokula Chandra Kundu, son of Brindavan and grandson of Jagannatha or the lineal progeny of Gokula Chandra, when they demand. Nitai understood but did not bother about the old man's sincerity or bequeathable bounty so long he lived, played and passed time happily with him.

One day a wayfarer told Jagannatha Kundu that one Damodar Pal was approaching the village in search of his missing son. Nitai who overheard their conversation was annoyed and was about to run away when Jagannatha assured him complete cover so that the neighbours nor the villagers would have any hint of Nitai's whereabout. Nitai by now trusted the old man fully and had no occasion to doubt his trustworthiness. The only point that stirred him was where he would be hidden that none could see him. As usual, his curiosity compelled him to query,

"Where would you hide me? Let me see where?"

The old man said calmly, "If we go there now, the villagers will see, won't they? Wait till night."

Nitai was delighted to hide from his father. He was excited that after his father's exit from the village, he would reappear from the hiding and play plentiful hide and seek with the village playmates. He imagined further how his father would search the whole village nook and corner but would fail to find a trace of Nitai, leading to excessive, rare fun.

From noon onwards, Jagannatha shut Nitai up inside his house and left for a while. Nitai impatiently waited for nightfall. As soon as the sun set, Nitai asked, "Grandfather! Shall we go now?"

Jagannatha said, "It's not yet night."

After a little while, Nitai repeated his request to move towards the hiding place. Jagannatha negatived Nitai, telling the villagers had not been to their beds. By rural bedtime, Nitai pleaded, "They are abed granddad! I am sure they had gone to bed. Let's now proceed."

Night had advanced. At least for Nitai, the night was deep and late by when he would have been in deep and undisturbed sleep any other day after a day's play and fun. Tonight, also he was almost sleepy despite his excitement and curiosity. At midnight when the village was asleep under cover of the dark night, Jagannatha led Nitai by holding his arm and walking through lanes and by-lanes to the barking of stray dogs and occasional twitting of nocturnal birds.

Nitai was afraid of the eerie silence and pitch darkness to fasten his arm around grandpa's hand. They walked on and on amidst farm fields converging on a village jungle. Inside the woods emerged a dilapidated temple before which the old man halted.

By then fully awakened, Nitai exclaimed, "What! Here!" he was honestly unsure that this kind of place was no place for hiding from the ransacking eyes of his father. He recalled that he haunted such places while on the run. Unmindful of what the brat was prattling, the old man moved out a slab from the middle of the temple floor beneath which a small room was lighted with a lamp. Wasting no time, Jagannatha descended underground by a ladder and Nitai followed suit with curiosity coupled with fear.

Nitai looked around to see brass pitchers on all sides. In the middle, an *asana* was spread in front whereof vermillion, sandal paste, flowers etc puja articles were arranged neatly. In a pitcher did Nitai see to his amazement coins and gold mohurs uncountable. Breaking Nitai's silence, Jagannatha said, "As I told you often earlier Nitai! I will hand over you all this wealth today."

"All! All of it!" Nitai danced with joy, "won't you take anything, not even a rupee?"

"If I take a single rupee" Jagannatha swore, "my hand will be struck with leprosy. But if Gokula Chandra or his son or grandson or any other legal progeny pass this way, you must have to pass these coins and gold mohurs to them." Nitai thought the old haggard had gone mad and said, "Yes, I must."

Then Jagannatha said, "Come and sit here on the asana."

"Why?" Nitai was inquisitive.

"Puja will be performed."

"Why puja?" the boy was upset.

"That is the law."

Even though not satisfied with the crypt reply, Nitai squatted on the asana, all the same, silently. Jagannatha smeared sandal paste on the boy's forehead and marked the middle of his eyebrows with vermillion spot. Nitai was wreathed with a flower garland and the old man recited mantras. Nitai was uneasy with the paraphernalia, particularly being treated like a god and whispered,

"Grandfather!".

Since the old man did not interrupt his recitation to hear him, the boy sat cool and Jagannatha hurried his incantations. Then, though with difficulty, he dragged each gold-laden pitcher before the boy and directed him to swear, "I do solemnly promise to hand over all this treasure to Gokula Chandra Kundu, son of Brindavan Kundu, grandson of Jagannatha Kundu or any other rightful heir in his progeny."

Nitai swore so ad verbatim after the old man. Since there were a number of pitchers and the old man repeated the ritual nonstop, Nitai was exhausted and almost stammered with his dry throat and desiccated tongue. The dingy den was asphyxiated with smoke of the burning wicks and exhaled carbon oxide of the two. The agile boy was enfeebled in the unenviable ambience. As the lamp was about to put out, Nitai heard the sound of the old man climbing out of the underground. He exclaimed,

"Grandpa! Where are you going?

"I am going now," uttered Jagannatha nonchalantly.

"No one can find you here. Remember the name Gokula Chandra, son of Brindavan, grandson of Jagannatha."Saying so, he pulled up the ladder out of the den.

"I want to be back with my father," cried the boy underground in a distressful tone and despondent agony."

Jagannatha covered the hole with the slab and put his ear unto the ground. He heard a faint and fatigued voice "Father". Then that was heard no more after sound of a heavy object falling with a thud.

Jagannatha placed his treasure with the yaksha and to ensure safety he placed broken bricks and loose mortar thereupon. Then he planted divots and weeds atop the covered slab. He did it repeatedly almost the entire night to make it foolproof. But whenever he put his ears upon the ground, he heard an agonised wailing of Nitai calling "Father…"

Jagannath left for his home through the fields and groves, hearing all the while the same heart-rending cry of the same boy. At home, he heard that only cry, only sound for days no end, that turned him half mad.

Then, one day after 4 years, Brindavan, his son met Jagannatha and enquired of Nitai, his son Gokula Chandra, Jagannatha's grandson, bearing the sham name of Nitai. Jagannatha was delirious. He dragged Brindavan to the temple to hear some sound from beneath the earth. When he said no, the delirious old was glad that his property was in the proper custody of Nitai in the dungeon to be returned to Gokula Chandra or his rightful heirs. Thereafter, the old man fell terribly sick and was bedridden since then.

In his dying delirium, he cried, "Nitai! Who pulled up my ladder?"

It is a queer case of rajasic and tamasic worship, isn't it? Never imitate Jagannatha Kundu, the wretched worshipper of gold! Never try to acquire the golden touch of Midas in lieu of your service, your goodness.

THIRTY-ONE

O, come stealing jackfruit!

Of worship, you have come across numerous instances that enrages and discourages you from worshipping divinities. They presume worshipping gods and worshipping gods with their [gods'] favourite objects, viz. flowers, is right, respectable duty which is richly remunerative. They not only allude to sloka 4/17 of Bhagavat Gita but also harp on,

patraṁ puṣhpaṁ phalaṁ toyaṁ yo me bhaktyā prayachchhati tadahaṁ bhaktyupahṛitam aśhnāmi prayatātmanaḥ[9.26]

O Arjuna! Those who offer Me leaves, flowers, fruits, water in devotion, I accept that fondly, fervently.

This is how Krishna tells Arjuna about the offering we make and how the Lord accepts that.

Leaves, flowers and water are generally and ubiquitously available aplenty. One does not have to labour hard or bother much to collect any number or amount of these objects to give and please the Lord. Country, indigenous and local fruits like citrus, banana, guava, custard apple, mango, jackfruit, coconut and what not are abundant in villages and backyards. These can be obtained for free if you are not able to pay for them for offering to God. And God savours these fruits to His heart's content, doesn't He?

Lord Jagannatha of Puri on the East Coast of Bay of Bengal is an incarnation of Vishnu. He is the Kaliyuga avatar of the Supreme, of God. He is directly descended from Krishna who was killed by the hunter's arrow hitting His toe thumb that looked soft and lively like a doe's ear. The hunter named Jara was aghast, seeing his sin of hunting out of ignorance a royal persona. To atone the offence and as directed by the hurt Krishna, Jara informed Pandavas of his infamy. The Pandavas sorrowed superlatively and burned the dead-body of Krishna, lying dead in a bushy sandy beach arrow-hunted by Jara by benign mistake. A bit at the navel remained unburnt behind the Pandavas' notice. That unburnt navel laden on a semi-burnt log floated for days from Dwarika coast to the coast of Puri. King Indradyumna of Malaba dreamt of this long voyage of the Lord and that He needed have the abode at Puri. Indradyumna acted upon the dreamy directive to reach Puri, locate the idol installed atop a hillock upstream Mahanadi near Kantilo. Therefrom, he kind of stole the idol and carted it to Puri to install the new 4-form image of the majestic god Jagannatha, viz; Jagannatha, Balabhadra, Subhadra and Sudarshana from out of the unburnt log. Jagannatha is called Vigrah Purushottam because He alone could be seen in Kaliyuga in an idol form [Vigrah] unlike preceding incarnates like Narasimha, Rama, Krishna. But his Leela is not unlike those of Krishna. In sheer mischief, He equals Krishna. The undermentioned incident would show the humanly naughtiness of Jagannatha.

Balarama Das, a 16th century Odia poet, saint, reformist was intense bhakta of Jagannatha. The eldest of the Pancha Sakha, he surpassed the contemporary, colleagues 4 in devotion and emotion to the Lord Jagannatha. He spent his days and nights in writing, penancing and reciting the glory and grandeur of Jagannatha. But he was steeped in abject poverty and did not get 2 square meals a day. For days, he starved if people stopped giving him alms, offerings or eatables by chance. How can he relish fruits or delicacies?

Jackfruit is a common favourite of Odias. All parts of the state are teemed with jackfruit trees, though people of Kandhamala, Rayagada, Koraput etc districts plant and harvest lion's share of this large, exterior-thorny, sweet fruit. In coastal Odisha, the taste and scent of ripe jackfruit in sultry summer makes cows and jackals crazy, what to speak of humans! Once this season, saint Balarama fervently desired a dish of ripe jackfruit. How can he get it? It was not his wont to beg or burglar. Somehow or other, the nice netizens of the town forgot to offer him a piece of the delicious fruit that season that far. For two or three days, he thought of the fruit fervently, frantically but slept hungry, wistfully. The dedicated devotee of Jagannatha that he was, how can he be deprived of so small a wish?

One night he is half asleep, while he heard a voice, "Bali! Won't we go for jackfruit thieving?

"Strange! Who is this fellow calling me at midnight to go on jackfruit stealing?"

But the smell of ripe jackfruit overpowered him to forget for the time being the moral dictum 'do not steal others' things.' Besides, it appeared to him that the voice was of none other than Jagannatha. And Lord Jagannatha is credited with and accustomed to such naughty and nefarious acts in company with and for His bhaktas.

"Why no or late," thought Balarama asleep and replied in dream, "Why not, my Lord! I am at your beck and call and ready to go, to go to hell; so good if it is to jackfruit grove!"

"Then just come on, we will be off to the Gajapati's grove in *Alasha* which bursts with sweet ripe jackfruits!"

Balarama somnambulated from the Lion's Gate of the Shreemandira where he lay asleep that night, following a yellow-robed, blackfaced brahmin fellow that came out of the temple in the dead of night and walked surreptitiously toward the Alasha grove of the Gajapati. Then they landed in the royal grove where the sentries were fast asleep, calmed by the soft, sea breeze that beat the summer heat and irritating humidity of Satyavadi area. Jagannatha said,

"Bali I cannot climb a tree, that too a huge jackfruit tree. You can climb the tree, can't you?"

Balarama replied, "Yes, my Lord!"

"Then you get up the tree, pluck a large ripe jackfruit and drop it down. I shall catch hold of it in my yellow *gamcha* to avoid it falling down on the ground and making sound," suggested Jagannatha.

Balarama climbed the tree quickly even in the pitch darkness and spotted faultlessly a large ripe jackfruit. He was about severing the fruit from the pedicel when the fruit fell to the ground due to its weight and ripeness. Since Balarama groped in the dark to trace the pedicel, the ripe fruit fell when he pulled away forcefully. The fruit fell to the ground with a thud. The sleeping sentries were awakened by the bang of the fruit hitting the ground. Jagannatha ran through bushes and shrubs of the grove and in the process had his costly yellow dhoti torn in places.

The sentries shouted "thief, thief, thief" uproariously and focussed their beacon among the branches to see Balarama. They shouted at and sounded to him to get down. When the frightened Balarama alighted the tree, he was beaten black and blue. Any other person would have fainted and bled white by the ruthless beating but Balarama bore it cooly muttering low and inaudible "Jagannatha, Jagannatha..."

The sentries collected the scattered pulp-coated jackfruit seeds, straightjacketed Balarama and led him to Gajapati's court. By then it was dawn and the temple opened to start the Mangala Alati. But servitors were started to see the costly ornate yellow dhoti that Jagannatha donned last night was torn and crimped at several places. Besides, the pratiharis guarding the temple reported to have heard the icon of the Lord was twisting and turning in inaudible agony as if someone was thrashing and beating the idol. Frightened and astonished, the servitors ran to the palace and reported about the surprising sound to the Gajapati. Gajapati, the greatest and most loyal bhakta of Lord Jagannatha, did not take a minute to comprehend the complexities of this Jagannatha Leela. He immediately freed Balarama and seated him in an aristocratic cushion. Being asked by the Gajapati, Balarama recounted the nocturnal errand of Lord Jagannatha and himself and the embarrassing incident.

To everybody's serendipity, while Jagannatha's staunch devotee Balarama bore no mark of injury or blood, Jagannatha twisted and turned in pain when Balarama was being beaten. Lord Jagannatha's dusty, shredded and crimped costly robes suggested beyond a speck of doubt that Jagannatha ran in the thorny, bushy, dusty jackfruit grove helter-skelter in the dark night. Jagannatha's bhakta Balarama was lauded for courting company of Jagannatha on a thieving errand. And Jagannatha set Himself a thief to help his bhakta eat jackfruit. And He ate that night and eats duly. What harm is there offering the jackfruit to your god, my god, our god, the universal, ubiquitous God? Certainly none.

THIRTY-TWO

O pundit! Why don't you give Me My coconut?

As He steals and eats jackfruit with the faithful Balarama Das, so He eats coconut from the downtrodden Dasia. Not only that, He asked the oblivious pilgrim brahmin why he was not handing Him over Dasia's coconut.

Dasia was born and lived in a wretched hut in Balisahi near Pipili, the place renowned worldwide for colourful and beautiful appliques from carry bag, umbrella, wallet, shamiana to decorative pieces, wall-hangings, toys. It is just 35 kilometres off Puri and villagers of Balisahi visited Puri on pious, festive occasions on foot, bullock carts. Nearby villagers and pilgrims from far off set off on the lifetime longing of Jagannatha Darshana on the dusty, muddy, paddy-field ridge-road of Balisahi. The village pilgrims talked frequently, even out of context, about Jagannatha, Shreemandira, Bada Danda, the numerous monasteries and charitable lodges and inns, numerous festivals of Lord Jagannatha, magnificent images of deities like Kashi Vishvanatha, Satyanarayana, Bata Ganesha, Mangala, Vimala, Kamala, Sakshi Gopinatha, Neela Madhava, Jameswara, Ishaneshvara, Kaka Bhushandi, Rohini Kunda, Laxmi Shrine, Vedi Hanuman, and sacred spots like the kitchen, Ananda Bazaar and Koili Vaikuntha in the sprawling precincts of Shreemandira. Dasia, the poorest of the poor, hardly made his both ends meet. How can he find time to go to Puri as the day he does not work in others farmland his family would go without food? Besides, he belonged to the lowly caste *Bauri* who were forbidden from entering Jagannatha temple.

All the same, Dasia was a bhakta par excellence. From what he heard from village pilgrims, he formed a vivid image of Jagannatha and His festivals. He was aware of the daily chores of lord Jagannatha and Balabhadra, Subhadra and Sudarshana. He could well imagine the offerings consisting of flowers, basil leaves, coconuts, banana, sweets etc handed to the head priest who made them over to the four-in-one image of Vishnu-Jagannatha. He was convinced Jagannatha does not discriminate on caste ground as his earliest and first priest and devotee was Vishvavasu, the *Shavara* chieftain of the mountains. Jagannatha was named Madhava closeted in the green mountain ranges on the right bank of Mahanadi. Madhava obliged his old priest Vishvavasu to come down to the riverside, then to Puri, at the behest of Indradyumna, the Malaba monarch.

So, Dasia decided to offer something to his Lord Jagannatha. What could he? He had a single coconut tree that bore fruits annually. He selected the best coconut of the lot for offering. Now how to transmit the fruit? A pious brahmin pundit of his village planned a pilgrimage to Puri shortly. On the morning the brahmin was to set out for Puri, he saw Dasia in front of his door. The brahmin queried,

"What is the matter, Das! Have you anything with me?"

"No, revered pundit! Nothing!"

"Don't fear! Tell what the matter is!"

Assured by the assuaging words of the respected pundit, Dasia ventured to say, "I want a small favour of you, wise pundit!"

"Yes, I shall oblige if possible. Let's see what's that."

"Will you kindly give this coconut to Lord Jagannatha when you're in the temple?"

Dasia brought out a coconut from the wrap of his greyish gamcha. The pundit was puzzled and pondered over the matter for some time and cleared his throat and said, "Dasia! You are a great devotee of Lord Jagannatha. A destitute beyond description, you have decided to offer a coconut to Lord Jagannatha through me because you can't go there yourself. Jagannatha is omniscient. He sees your devotion for, love of Him. I am glad to have the opportunity to do this for you."

Saying so, the pundit took the coconut and set for Puri after a while. By the late afternoon, he entered the shrine and completed his chores of visiting and bowing obsequiously to each idol, each image, buzzing slokas, mantras, hymns to them. All along he kept Dasia's coconut wrapped under his arm pit with a view to offering the same to Lord Jagannatha after his rounds and worships. He bowed before lord Jagannatha in the end of his errand as the customary go. Since it was getting late to go back, the pundit was in obvious hurry and turned his back to step out of the sanctum sanctorum.

Unfortunately, he was oblivious of Dasia's coconut in the temple-inside hurly-burly and out of haste to reach home early. He was just about to step out of the sanctum sanctorum when he heard a voice behind,

"O pundit! You are hurrying home, what about Dasia's coconut? Won't you give it to Me?"

Oblivious of Dasia's request and his coconut still under his armpit well wrapped, due to haste and forgetfulness, the pundit looked around to know who spoke to whom. He saw none and thought it was sheer delusion. He put his first foot forward when the same voice reminded,

"Pundit! Why don't you give My coconut sent by my dear Dasia of Balisahi?"

Pundit recalled Dasia's apologetic request and his fervent offering to Lord Jagannatha in the shape of a coconut from his tree. He looked back regretfully and witnessed the incredibly long hand of Jagannatha stretched toward him. Bowing down his head and pulling out the coconut from under his armpit, the brahmin showed the fruit. Lord Jagannatha snatched the same without a moment's late as eagerly as a baby snatches a chocolate.

"O my Lord!" the pundit cried and prostrated, "You certainly care for faithful like Dasia over the ages. For wretched and superficial like me, You will never care or shower your mercy or miracle. Yet, I am immensely happy that Dasia's coconut importuned me to witness your unimaginable grace for him, for mankind."

THIRTY-THREE

Why God after all asks of or accepts paltry or pitiable articles from us?

If God is so kind to steal jackfruit for His faithful, follower; if the Lord is so enthusiastic to snatch the coconut sent by His destitute devotee, why do you search for, steal flowers from the neighbour's plant or garden? Do you think stealing flowers is justified by verse 9/26 of the Gita? What does sloka 26, Adhyaya 9 say,

patraṁ puṣhpaṁ phalaṁ toyaṁ yo me bhaktyā prayachchhati tadahaṁ bhaktyupahṛitam aśhnāmi prayatātmanaḥ [9.26]

Whatever small, insignificant or free for all article you can lay your hands on is enough and important to offer to the Lord. The sloka does not list all such things of little or no value. The list is illustrative, not exhaustive. When you offer and offer with sincere devotion, not superficial, farcical show; God accepts that little-value, negligible object without objection. The Lord accepts, eats, enjoys the thing as it is given by a devotee with sincerity, from his/her heart.

You may ask: why after all God asks of or accepts paltry or pitiable articles from us? More so, when He has no need of these things or any other priceless, prized objects. Right! He needs nothing, needed nothing nor will ever need anything from anybody. He is fully full and fulfilled. His wants, if at all any, are met before the need, necessity begets. Then why this giving and grieving to giving things? Because it is his/her, your, mine, Tom,Dick and Harry's "giving", "offering", "gift" that He accepts, eats, enjoys since they are offered "in bhakti".

Flowers, no doubt, are His favourite if you say so. But that you will beg, borrow and burgle flowers to give to God is not your "*upahaara*" in the strict sense of the term. Worse is the case when you pluck flowers from the neighbour's flower plant behind his back, pluck flower and molest the stem or nip the bud. This kind of upahaara does not please God; for it is not upahaara at all. Of bhakti? How can you claim that you have given God such senselessly stolen flower in/with bhakti? This bhakti or this kind of bhakti does not do good to the giver, the bhakta nor the receiver, God, does it?

THIRTY-FOUR

Upahaara and shraddha

King Vishwambhara Birabara Mangaraja Mohapatra's precept and practice

Upahaara is a day-to-day word that people use indiscriminately. On social celebrations like marriage, birth, promotion in service cadre, purchase of property, upahaara is a must. Invitees, participants, guests grace the occasion with upahaara wrapped in coloured wrapper or put in attractive envelopes.

Upahaara is not a modern concept or practice. Unlike many of our habits, gracing a celebration with upahaara is entirely Indian and is as regal or aristocratic as common people's practice.

Kavichandra Dr Kalicharan Pattanaik is well known in Odisha and in some other parts of the country for his immense contribution to Odishi dance's recognition as a classical dance form of India. Besides, he was a poet, playwright, performing artiste of *paalaa, suanga, rasaleela,* Odishi, even *chou naacha* etc in youth. Later on, he wrote modern Odia plays on contemporary social topics as well as on popular mythological episodes. He directed and took part in the plays performed in theatres. He was talented but struggled a lot for the cultural and literary development of Odisha. His autobiography named "Kumbhara Chaka" meaning "The Potter's Wheel" is a masterpiece of the Odia autobiography genre. It portrays proficiently, profoundly but faithfully his strife and struggles, commitments and accomplishments in the cultural and dramatic domain of Odisha in very lucid yet standard Odia.

While recalling some incidents of his childhood, he describes a queer but provocative case of upahaara.

Badamba [Baramba] is a small ex-state sandwiched between primordial Mahanadi on the south and a long mountain range that is part of the Eastern Ghats on the north. The Badamba *gadajata*, as the ex-states are popularly called by the appellation "gadajata", was subservient to the Gajapati of Puri. It is believed that the Gajapati of Puri in the 14th century CE recruited robust wrestlers, archers for his military to safeguard Odisha from northern Islamic invaders. One Hattakeshwara Rout hailing from present day Singhbhum attracted the Gajapati's attention for his sturdy muscular manoeuvres and mentionable mental abilities. The Gajapati was so pleased that he settled Hattakeshwara in his kingdom with a grant of two villages. The two adjoining villages named Sankha and Mahuri on the Mahanadi riverbank were forcibly occupied by a *"Kandha"* chieftain. Hattakeshwara with his enormous prowess pushed the Kandha chieftain to the opposite bank of Mahanadi to the densely wooded jungles of present day Kandhamala. These two villages became one later on bearing the name Sankhameri that proudly stands on the majestic Mahanadi bank.

Hattakeshwara acquired the nearby villages to constitute a kingdom of his own under, of course, the suzerainty of the Puri Gajapati. Sankhameri situate on the open-banked riverbank was vulnerable to Kandha vicissitudes and unsuitable to house the kingdom's capital. Hence, Badamba, about 5 KMs north of Sankhameri, a tableland encircled by hillocks on all sides suited for the capital. In fact, most gadajata capitals stood on high ground surrounded by hills and mountainous ridges to defend the capital in general and the king and his family in particular from rebellious subjects or external invaders. Sankhameri had a hillock of its own on the river ridge with the temple of Swapneshwara [Shiva]. Badamba is a corruption of bada+amba, which is again corrupted from bruhat+ amba, meaning great+ mother. The "mother" alluded to here is "Bhattarika", the deity seated about 15 KMs upstream Sankhameri to the north-west corner of Badamba kingdom. The royal family is the chief devotee of the deity till today.

To the north-east corner of Badamba and atop a hill is the seat of the deity Mahakali which is a conjunction of two words, namely, maha+kali meaning great + kali. Both the goddesses stand for hugely fearful and ferocious power. And both seats are devotees' visit-must and tourists' paradise.

As customary, Hattakeshwara and his descendants excelling in martial abilities and military expeditions earned kudos from Gajapati and added appellations of Birabara [valorous], Mangaraja [rudder-veteran] and Mahapatra [great persona]. About half a millennia after the kingdom's founding, Vishwambhara Birabara Mangaraja Mahapatra reigned the kingdom. He was liberal and benevolent. He patronised establishment of a Middle English School in in

1933 in Badamba by Mohana Subudhi, native of Gopinathapur on Mahanadi bank 4 KMs downstream Sankhameri, and a rich trader who spent liberally on digging ponds for public use. King Vishwambhara set up a sun-dial in 1933 in his *darabara* premises that presently houses Badamba Tehsil office. Revenue collection-wise, Badamba was not wealthy since the kingdom comprised hills, hillocks, high grounds, rugged landscape substantially. But Vishwambhara was a benevolent ruler and spent the revenue judiciously. He was mostly austere, disciplinarian though compassionate. He was reputed for his bountiful gifts to the learned, brahmins and the poor.

Dr Kavichandra Kalicharan Pattanaik was approximately 10 years old when he acquired cordial access to the king's palace to hear gramophone-record-played music and witness festivals and folk performances in the palace with the king as the king was enchanted with the former's childlike mellifluous tone and recitation. That year the annual Ramlila was being organised. On the very first day, the king was about to retire in the afternoon after taking care of the ritual arrangements himself. Then a palace sentry ventured in and informed that a visitor was waiting for the king's call for quite some time. The king queried, "Who is he? What's his suit or grievance?

Sentry replied in usual manner, "Don't know lord! Looks very poor brahmin."

After a few minutes' pause, the king ordered, "Get him in!"

The sentry went out and reappeared soon escorting the waiting poor brahmin. As stated by the sentry, the brahmin was as poor as a rat. He pulled out a dirt-dense greyish, four-times folded gamcha from under his armpit, unfolded the gamcha wherefrom a large long yellow mango leaf appeared, put the same before the king, and uttered mantras and slokas in praise of and for divine blessings upon the king and his dynasty. Kalicharan and other boys laughed aside hilariously for some time but stopped laughing soon as they saw the king treated the brahmin respectfully and ritually.

This over, the king suggested to the brahmin, "Go, take your bath in this large pond, perform your evening rituals, stay in the common guest house and witness Ramlila performance here at night!"

The brahmin did not move. He seemed disappointed with this royal arrangement. The king could figure out the brahmin's predicament. So, he corrected himself, "O! you have not told your family of probable putting up in the Gada [castle, capital]. So, it would be inappropriate to stay overnight as palace guest. OK."

King called *Gantayata* Gati Mahapatra and ordered, "Gantayata! Give 50 Rupees and a handsome dish of Vishwambhara cake after evening *dhoopa* to this brahmin! His family would be awaiting him for what he will be taking from us. And take this mango leaf and place it on the parlour teapoy."

Astonished by the incident and to quell his boyish curiosity, Kalicharan asked politely, "*Chhamu! Why did he bring this ripe mango leaf and how did you praise profusely the paltry leaf?*"

King Vishwambhara Mangaraja clarified, "O son! it's unusual to come to king's palace emptyhanded. He is a poor brahmin. What could he get for a gift to the king? By chance, he saw this ripe mango leaf. Hence, he brought it as gift. The leaf is not common and is also beautiful. Of course, I paid him 50 Rupees not as the price of this leaf but as the value of his shraddha. Shraddha is priceless. This 50 Rupees is a token, nominal repayment of his shraddha. Shraddha is priceless and unrepayable. You can realise this when you grow up."

The incident as it occurred in the presence of the pre-adolescent Kavichandra Kalicharan Pattanaik concerning an unknown poor brahmin and the benevolent king Vishwambhara Birabara Mangaraja Mahapatra in Badamba in the early years of the 20th century is certainly an eye-opener to understand sloka 26 of 9th Adhyaya of Bhagavat Gita that God does not need anything from us but we can offer Him insignificant or useless things with deep devotion and sublime shraddha. Leaves, fruits, flowers those may be. Those valueless articles should signify the article of your faith. Leaves, flowers, fruits, water …are symbolic. Do not take them literally. If you cannot offer better, costlier articles, then you present the Lord with these cheap, commonplace things. If you offer things dearer, costlier to you, then it is better.

THIRTY-FIVE

Flowers are your daughters, aren't they?

Those who read sloka 26, Adhyaya 9 of Gita literally and indulge in pleasing God by offering flowers and flowers plucked from neighbour's, stranger's, friend's garden do no justice to Gita, do no service to God, do they? Even plucking a flower from your own garden to offer to the deity or God is no decent proposition. The garden may be yours; you may have watered the flower plants or flowerpots; you may have removed weeds obstructing or decapacitating the flower plant. Maybe the flower plant blossomed due to your sweat and sincerity. Yet, the flower is not yours. It belongs to all else, not you. That is the cardinal principle you should bear in mind when you mind planting a flower plant and seeing the plant in bloom.

What flowers are after all? Flowers are the eyes of nature. Plucking flowers blocks nature from seeing you, seeing your virtue, your value as a creature. Flowers blossom to beautify the world, to fill the earth with sweet, scintillating scent. You have read Gita and got its gist; then you must be aware of "Karmanyevadhikaraste****". You have a right to plant a flower plant but have no right to pluck the flower, have you? To pluck a flower is to pluck the eye of nature.

And when you pluck a flower, nature sheds a drop of tear like the Happy Prince's statue dropped a tear on the swallow in Oscar Wilde's immortal story "The Happy Prince".

Flowers are daughters of nature, daughters of society, daughters of humanity. And a flower is your own daughter. Your very own daughter. All the flowers you come across and all the flowers in full bloom are your daughter. And how precious is a daughter? How lovely is a daughter? You know it; know it more than I do. To pluck a blossomed flower is bad, sorrowful like the girl lost in the wild snow in William Wordsworth's poem "Lucy Gray". When Lucy Gray lost her path and was herself lost in the snowstorm,

"The wretched Parents all that night
Went shouting far and wide;
But there was neither sound or sight
To serve them for guide."

When you pluck a flower, you lose your sweet little girl and become wretchedlike Lucy Gray's parents, don't you? And to nip a flower in the bud is bad. To molest the stem or branch of the flower plant is worse, is worse than torturing a girl child, is worse than tormenting a daughter.

THIRTY-SIX

They[gods] show more care for us than we do for ourselves

In section 27 supra, we have cited sloka 5/17 and sloka 6/17 along with sloka 4/17, we may certainly shortly touch upon these two verses to see what Bhagavat Gita guidelines are on Tapasya.

Most people mostly speak of Tapasya to allude to deep concentration, singlemindedness. They are correct. But we should be wary of[not worried about] Tapasya per se. Tapasya, especially the spiritual, ascetic Tapasya [1] should not be in contravention of scriptures and specific texts,[2] should not be horribly and terribly practiced, [3] should not be smeared with desire, attachment, ego, physical strength, [4] the body, organs and limbs thereof should not be tormented, pained, punished during Tapasya,[5] so should extreme, severe pain to the body should be avoided because the body is the abode of the Lord and extremity and acuity of penance does not inflict pain on the human limbs alone but on God Who pervades and permeates the body wholly and wholesale.

Of penance with and within one's individual capacity, Lord Shiva advises penance-performant Parvati,

> Api kriyartham sulabham samitkrusham
> Jalaanyapi snanabidhikshamani te
> Api svashaktyaa tapasi pravartase
> Shariramadyam khalu dharmasadhanam
> [Sloka 33, Canto V, Kumaarasambhava by Kalidas]

Herein Shiva harps on the utility of human body, the perishable body of the individual. He dismisses the dictum "Shariram vaa patayet karyam vaa sadhayet". Between achievements- great, virtuous- achievements and the mortal, human body, the latter stands as number one; the former is number two or even lower in ranking. This is reiterated in Gita vide slokas 5/17 and 6/17.

Gita goes a step forward. It derides painstaking, painful penance on the reasoning that body is not ignoble, ignorable, negligible for the simple reason that Lord dwells the body. Painful, painstaking, punishing penance is menace to not only the individual but to God. The human body, the mortal body of men and women composed of the five eternal elements is construed as the consecrated temple of the Lord, isn't it? The Gita glorifies the body here so much so that those who undertake penance painstakingly, inflicting pain on their bodies, emaciating their bodies are asura, aren't they? They are asura who can threaten their bodies to premature, untimely end to extract a god/goddesses' blessing and bounty. Our puranas speak of asura Tapasya, Tapasya by asura enough and to spare.

We know for sure how hard Tapasya Ravana undertook to empower himself with indefatigable, invincible physical powers. Ravana became so powerful that he wrested the *puspaka vimana* from Kubera, his step brother and the god of gold and all material goods. He deployed the gods as his sweeper, scavenger, sentry, launderer, barber and so on. The gods/deities who unwaveringly believe in supreme, superior-most power of the puissant God, Vishnu, had to pray and beg Him to do away with Ravana. Vishnu descended to the earth in Rama avatar to slay the sinful demon, Ravana.

Like Ravana, Taraka underwent fierce, frightful penance to please Shiva. Shiva was pleased with Taraka for his fastidious, fast-un-to-death Tapasya, who immediately and most modestly but very shrewdly prayed for only one gift, the gift of being defeated or decimated by none else but Shiva's son. The erudite demon knew pretty well that by then Shive's wife Sati immolated Herself in the yajna-fire of Daksha, Her father, who, firstly, did not invite his son-in-law Shiva to the yajna and, secondly, reproached Her senselessly, shamelessly in the august celestial assembly of divines and rishis, for having visited the glorious yajna uninvited. Taraka supposed that Mahadeva would not remarry. Then how can He have a son? It is the mortal, material and moral law that begetting a son prerequires a wife, isn't it? But his whole hog went haywire. Maheswara married Parvati when the latter wholeheartedly and wholesomely contemplated to wed Shiva. And Kartikeya was born to defeat and do away with Taraka to save all in general and the devas in particular from Taraka's trepidations.

Tapasya of asuras and asura-like Tapasya are detestable and devoid. In present times, we come across cases when parents pressurise their wards to concentrate on their studies like undergoing Tapasya. The sweet and sensible days of the adolescent get lost in the quagmire of studies, studies not for knowledge or nobility but for being a doctor, engineer, technologist to earn a lot of money to own cars, bungalows, burgeoning bank balance. As a consequence, some youths commit suicide out of frustration by failing to cope with compeers who concentrate more and seem to be nearing the goal.

Those who argue for "shariram vaa patayet karyam vaa sadhayet" to achieve the goal against the contrary norm "shariramaadyam khalu dharmasadhanam" are mightily mistaken, aren't they? Who will you prefer to be- poor with good health or wealthy with diseased body? You are certainly not unaware of the classical Latin axiom, "mens sana in corpore sano", are you? But you perhaps did not know the complete sentence that reads, "Orandum es ut sit mens sana in corpore sano". What does this lustrous Latin sentence mean? It means- You should pray for a healthy mind in a healthy body. The writer of the immortal line was the Roman poet Decimus Junius Juveniles of the 1st-2nd century AD. The poet said so in the Satire X, The Vanity of Human Wishes, in lines 357 as in this translation,

> "Then you might pray for a
> sound mind in a healthy body."

It is interesting and equally enlightening that the poet does not advocate for prayer. Why? Is he an atheist or agnostic? No. He is more theistic and believer than you or I, isn't he? Yes, he is a believer of the best kind. We may quote him,

> "So is there nothing worth
> people praying for? If you'll take
> My advice, you'll allow the gods
> to determine what's right

For us, and what's likely to
benefit our situation; for
The gods grant us gifts that are
more fitting than nice."

As from these lines evident and, apparently according to the poet, "prayer" is worthless. If you do not "pray" you "allow gods" to "determine what is right for us". If gods are not distracted or disrupted on their chore, their routine, their daily do's, they will determine, decide what is "likely to benefit our situation". Undisturbed and unannoyed by our prayer, they will grant us "more fitting gifts", maybe not "nice" gifts. It is usual for gods to grant men and women appropriate gifts in consideration of "our situation". The god-granted gifts are befitting, may or may not be lucrative or interesting to the receiver or others around him/her.

He justifies his proposition by championing the creed that,

"They [gods] show more care for us
than we do for ourselves."

It is exceedingly true, isn't it? Isn't it said identically in Bhagavat Gita in sloka 22, Adhyaya IX?

"Ananyaaschintayo mam ye janaah paryupaasate
Teshaam nityaabhiyuktaanam yogakshemam vahaamyaham
[23/9]

O Arjuna! I take care of their daily needs and worldly uplift of them who always and without worldly thoughts contemplate and concentrate upon Me.

Decimus Junius juveniles in his Satire X composed about 120 AD echoes the same thing by saying that gods, our gods, take care of us without our knowing and praying.

The gods consider our predicaments carefully and grant gifts that suits the situation. The gift may not be pretty or pricy but certainly befitting, better.

He speaks of the futility or vanity of prayer. But does not outright reject one's interest in or intention of prayer per se. Aware of human nature, he says,

"Still, if you want a reason for
prayer, for offering...."

Know well that gods care more for us than we do care for us, that gods grant gifts to us in the nick of the time, befitting our case and condition and that gods endow us with appropriate gifts, maybe unattractive or unvaluable. Gods, our gods, God, serves us right at the right manner in the right measure. So, why pray gods, God, to redress our grievance, alleviate our suffering or things we wish to have?

Even then, Decimus Junius Juveniles concedes, if you like to go to the shrine to offer your prayer, offer gods' [or your] favourite food. Thereafter,

"Then you might pray for a
sound mind in a healthy body."

We can conclude that, if at all, whenever, we pray gods or God, we should pray for a healthy mind in a healthy body.

The English saying, "Health is wealth" reverberates in all languages of the world. In the Kalidas verse cited supra, the same norm, the same notion is reiterated. Shiva advises Parvati that it is OK you undergo hard penance to achieve the object of your desire. But acute, pernicious penance jeopardises the penance itself midway. Minimum good health is necessary to carry the penance forward. Good health is needed to take bath, to collect yajna-wood and flowers etc. The penance-performer should, first of all, realise that the body assumes first priority and dharma ranks below.

Those who dare to dispose of the body to achieve their goal, their mission, do no good, no justice to the goal or to themselves. "Shariram vaa patayet karyam vaa sadhayet" is idealistic, but no ideal worth the name; is emotional not rational; is theoretical, patriotic, zealotic, fanatic, frenetic; not practical, exemplar or worthy of imitation.

In short, such Tapasya is asuric, not celestial, divine, sattvic.

THIRTY-SEVEN

Live life king size

Tapasya is talk of the town nowadays as was in the hoary past. Tapasya was everybody's cup of tea in ancient Bharata. From brahmin to villain, from brahmachari to bourgeoise businessman, people resorted to Tapasya in the past. We know of many demons, asuras who assumed alarming power by dint of successful Tapasya. Brahma, Shiva etc were austere, fastidious. They spent their days and nights in yoga, with contemplation. But they showered lavish power to penance performants when pleased with flattering, hard penance. That was the motive, practice, especially by destructive demons.

Apart from asuras, others practised Tapasya. This Tapasya was generally desired and designed to get rid of earthly worries and anxieties initially and of repeated births and rebirths in the world in the long run. Even unblemished kings and mighty monarchs relinquished splendorous thrones to undergo penance. Kalidas in his immortal epic poem Raghuvamsa speaks of the kingly custom of the Raghu dynasty like this,

"Shaishaveabhyastavidyanaam
youvanevishayeshinaam

Vaardhakye munibruttinaam
yogenaantetanutyajyaam"
[Raghuvamsa, Canto, 1 Sloka 8]
It was the indispensable inclination of Raghu dynasty pedigree to learn shastras, warfare, administration, laws and morality in boyhood and adolescence; to marry and maintain household in youth; to practise ascetic, saintly life in old age, and to give up the ghost through yoga.

Obviously and incontrovertibly, this was the custom of royal dynasties of ancient Bharata. Kings and monarchs of repute and recognition spent the third stage of their lives in ascetic Tapasya.

Kharavela was a mighty and munificent monarch of present-day Odisha who annexed kingdoms in the north, south and east India. He was born into the Mahameghavahana dynasty in the year uncertain. His immediate predecessor and successor are also unknown. But he is well known and widely known for, as they say, "kirttiryasya sa jivati". Reigning in the 1st- 2nd century BC, well after Ashoka's invasion of Kaling in 262-1 BC, Kharavela carved a name for him in ancient Indian history for, among others, his Khandagiri and Udayagiri cave inscriptions in the nascent Prakrit. The twin hills encircled by dense green forests were worthy and admirable habitation for recluses, renouncers. And were nearby his capital Shishupala Gada, ruined remains of which could be seen not far off Bhubaneswar.

Of the two dozen of extant, responsibly restored though, caves, two named Ranigumpha and Hatigumpha i.e. the Queen's Cave and the Elephant Cave respectively in Udayagiri are the cynosure of tourists, archologists, historians, epigraphists, sculptors, engraving experts and

Jains. The other caves exhibit exquisite and elegant images of animals, deities, kings, soldiers, danseuses etc that glow in aesthetic, artistic exuberance. The rock inscriptions detail Kharavela's reign and stop with his renunciation. Historical details revealed from the inscriptions establish that he was declared heir apparent at the age of 16, was crowned when 24, and reigned for 13 years. Chronologically, the inscriptions describe the monarch's massive welfare projects as well as military expeditions.

Initiated to Jainism and in compliance to the codes and canons of the time, he spent time in these caves with spouse, and possibly with a couple of Jain saints and servants, engrossed in contemplation and Tapasya.

THIRTY-EIGHT

Buddham sharanam gachhami

Tapasya is not so much as traditionally understood or conventionally confined to. Tapasya, Gita elucidates, should be practiced in three planes, viz. physical, verbal and mental planes.

deva-dwija-guru-prājña- pūjanaṁ śhaucham ārjavam
brahmacharyam ahinsā cha śhārīraṁ tapa uchyate [17.14]

anudvega-karaṁ vākyaṁ satyaṁ priya-hitaṁ cha yat
svādhyāyābhyasanaṁ chaiva vāṅ-mayaṁ tapa uchyate
[17.15]

manaḥ-prasādaḥ saumyatvaṁ maunam ātma-vinigrahaḥ
bhāva-sanśhuddhir ity etat tapo mānasam uchyate [17.16]

The physical penance commences with worshipping deities, brahmins, gurus and the erudite. Cleanliness and humility as well as celibacy comprise physical penance or sharira [physical] Tapasya. At the physical plane, these characteristics or demeanour demonstrate Tapasya or penance. In the verbal plane of Tapasya come conversation or speech, language and words that is balanced, not biased; but truthful and delightful. Engaging in studies studiously comprise verbal penance [vangmay] Tapasya. In the mental, intellectual sphere, Tapasya refers to a cheerful [not fearful], tranquil, equipoised mind. [As far as possible] keeping mum and keeping off the worldly humdrum are elements of verbal penance. And so is distilling and discriminating thoughts and feelings.

Tapasya, the code and conundrum of yogis, yogic life, is a three-layered, three-faceted affair. It is easy and intelligible to the majority of laity and religious-minded. But most of them do not in spirit comprehend these traits and tenets. Most Sadhakas and Sannyasis overstate, exaggerate various virtues of Tapasya and brag of practicing penance for long periods. Their bravado is bafflingly bluff for the three-dimensional penance is very hard to attempt, advance and achieve success.

An instance of verbal Tapasya is germane.

Once Bhagawan Buddha, on abegging, stood silent on the front-door of an opulent householder. The latter came out a bit later and gorged out gargantuan expletives and abusive epithets on the Buddhist monk against Buddha and His bloody, bogus, blind followers. He was obviously unaware that the simple monk was the Buddha Himself. Exploding his expletives, the householder shouted,

"Are you dumb or deaf or both? After so much chiding and condemning, you keep silent as a statue. Can't you defend yourself or your damn Buddha or Buddhism with a word or two?"

Baffled by the tomblike silence of the shaven-headed, innocent monk in orange robe even after his intolerable, inhuman angry abuses, with curious and spurious sensibility, the householder implored, "For heaven's sake! Say something! How come you don't react to my disdainful, dehumanising verbiage?"

Smiling serenely as his wont, Buddha said "Should I say something, then listen to me! This begging bowl belongs to me, doesn't this? Suppose I give this to you and you flatly refuse to accept it, own it, then who is the owner thereof?"

"What rubbish! It was yours and now also it is yours. What the hell about it?" The householder hollered.

"Yea, that's so in case of your foulmouthed howling" said the monk softly, still smiling, and left the place peacefully for the next door.

The person felt uneasy at the easy reply of the easygoing monk. He was puzzled at the unpuzzled monk who just ignored his raucous reprimand without murmur as if nothing was being said or heard. He followed in the footsteps of the monk silently, stealthily. To his amazement, all his neighbours treated the begging monk respectfully, kindly and offered sweets, fruits, fine grains as soon as the monk appeared at their door. Finally, the monk disappeared into the congregation of orange-robed monks who, in a body and in unison saluted,

"Buddham sharanam gachhhami!"

The householder then housed no doubt that the mere monk whom he rebuked irrepressibly was none other than the Buddha, the great, glorious, godly Buddha who housed no animosity in his immensely calm and compassionate heart, hearty persona. No gainsaying, the man begged profuse apology for his irritating, indecent words and Buddha who had perfected vangmaya tapa embraced the offender and initiated him into Buddhism. In course of time, the man became a staunch follower of Buddha and preached Buddhism.

Buddha, here, no doubt, is a living illustration of verbal penance.

THIRTY-NINE

Speech is silvern, silence is golden
Apriyasya cha pathyasya vaktaa shrotaa cha durlabhah

Of all other things as enunciated in the Bhagavat Gita, "anudbegakaram vakyam satyam cha priyam hitam cha yat..[15/17] is extremely important for we common people. But vaangmaya tapa stated so simply, plainly, is scarcely pragmatic, practicable. How can one in the same breath speak true, likeable and useful? Truth is indelible, undeletable, undelusional, eternal, universal. You just can say what you have seen, heard, read or felt truthfully, without dilution or distortion. But that may not please many, may not be to the liking of many. And you do not know how useful what you say is to the hearer.

anudvega-karaṁ vākyaṁ satyaṁ priya-hitaṁ cha yat
svādhyāyābhyasanaṁ chaiva vāṅ-mayaṁ tapa uchyate
[17.15]

What may be sweet to the ears, may not be true or beneficial. In this context, what Maricha said to Ravana when the latter persuaded the former to help him kidnap Sita to avenge the disfigurement Suparnnakha wrought by Rama-Laxman duo is worth quoting,

> Sulabhah purushaa raajan satatam priyavaadinah
> Apriyasya cha pathyasya vaktaa shrotaa cha durlabhah
> [Ramayana, Book 3, Chapter 37, Sloka 2]

In Dandak forests, Rama, Laxman and Sita lived their pretty peaceful life in the ambience of unbroken greenery and enviable celestial scenery of nature. Ravana's sister Suparnnakha who, on her forest ambling, was infatuated by Rama's person coaxed Rama and then Laxman. Her cajoling failing to seduce either Rama or Laxman, she intended to kill Sita so that wifeless Rama would marry her. Enraged by her outrageous aspiration and subsequent attempt in this respect, Laxman severed the tip of her nose and helix of her ears. Bleeding and weeping, she approached her brother Khara, the demon king ruling the forest tracts. Khara sent Dhushan, Trishir and his 14000 strong demon soldiers in phases to perish at the hands of Rama. Finally, Khara fought with Rama to meet the same fate. This was reported to Ravana who wanted to avenge upon his sister's ignominy by kidnapping Sita to deprive Rama of his beautiful and virtuous wife. The might of Rama as evident from the crushing of Khara, Dhushan, Trishira and Khara's colossal demon army compelled Ravana to avoid direct fight. Instead, he planned to kidnap Sita in disguise and shrewdly.

So, he approached Maricha to morph as a golden doe, allure Sita whereby Rama, then Laxman would chase the unique, unprecedented golden doe. Thereafter emerging from hiding and faking himself as a sannyasi, Ravana would abduct Sita.

To justify his stance, Ravana spoke of Rama as

"Ashlilah karkasho murkho lubdho ajit indriyah
Tyakta dharmah tu adharma atma bhutanam ahite ratah"
[Ramayana, Book 3, Canto 36, Sloka 11]

In Ravana's words, Rama was vulgar, violent, ignoramus, greedy, debauch, apostate, impious and engrossed in the ill of all creatures. Maricha who had a narrow escape from the fierce arrows of Rama earlier was cocksure that another encounter with the mightily powerful Rama meant certain death. Besides, he was Ravana's well-wisher and did not wish Ravana's untimely end with the wishful thinking of kidnapping Sita.

So, he advised Ravan that people speaking untrue but pleasant to hear are aplenty but speaker and listener of unpleasant but true words are extremely rare.

This was reiterated by Vibhishana when Rama reached Lanka with a formidable army of monkeys and bears and was about to launch a massive assault on the demon kingdom. Other demon generals and commanders boastful of their brawny and brawly powers instigated Ravana to jump head on to war with Rama but Vibhishana was the lone dissenter. He cautioned against the demon generals' imprudence and impudence clothed in flattery and trumpery. So, he said,

"Sulabhah purushah rajan satat priyavadinah
Apriyasya cha pathyasya vakta shrota cha durlabhah
[Ramayana, Book 6, Canto 16, Sloka 21]

First Maricha and then Vibhishana proclaimed the eternal truths that there are numerous people to always utter utterly sweet words but bitter yet truthful words are rarely spoken or rarely heard.

Here in Gita, vangmaya tapa demands sweet but true and beneficial words. Unlike in Ramayana, in Gita we are advised to speak true, speak right or beneficial, speak nicely.

You need to strike a delicate balance between the apparently opposite principles of truth, palatability and utility. You have to choose if and when to utter the truth. You have to discern who must be told things in pleasant, sweet manner. How to convey what is right, useful despite being bitter, bad is the skill, the competence of the speaker. And you need to practice this solemnly, sincerely.

To start with this, you may have to keep in mind who you are talking to, why you are talking to, when you are talking to, how you are talking, and on what topic you are talking on/about.

"Speech is silvern, Silence is golden."

Was said by Thomas Carlyle, the 18th century English author in his novel "Sartor Resartus". He cited it from a Swiss inscription that reads "Speechen ist silbern, schweigen ist golden." It seems to have entered English language from Germanic which borrowed it from Spanish. The Spanish version was originated in medieval Arabic. It is believed that this truism originated in the east, essentially Bharata. The uncertain source of the saying shows that it was in vogue in the East, among the Jews, Arabians, from whence it moved to Spain, Germany and England almost in that order.

In both instances cited supra, Maricha and Vibhishana spoke out what was true, useful to Ravana, though not endearing to him.

FORTY

The food that is good is Ayuhsattvalarogyasukhapritivivardhanh

Adhyaya 17 of Bhagavat Gita deals in detail the three types of people we are; the three kinds of performance of the same activity by us. Sattva, rajas, tamas are the three attributes that divides us, that distinguishes us. As discussed supra in worship, tapa and gift, we people are not the same. So are we discriminated by our food. The sattvic do not eat the way the tamasic do nor do the rajasic eat the way sattvic do.

āyuḥ-sattva-balārogya-sukha-prīti-vivardhanāḥ
rasyāḥ snigdhāḥ sthirā hṛidyā āhārāḥ sāttvika-priyāḥ [17.8]

kaṭv-amla-lavaṇāty-uṣhṇa- tīkṣhṇa-rūkṣha-vidāhinaḥ
āhārā rājasasyeṣhṭā duḥkha-śhokāmaya-pradāḥ [17.9]

yāta-yāmaṁ gata-rasaṁ pūti paryuṣhitaṁ cha yat
uchchhiṣhṭam api chāmedhyaṁ bhojanaṁ tāmasa-priyam [17.10]

Our venerable Bhagavat Gita elucidates the kind of food humans eat and the classes they therefore belong to.

The eaters constitute three classes or we eaters are classified according to our food.

The first category people eat to acquire through/from/by food longevity, intelligence, strength, healthiness, satisfaction and savoury. The food is juicy, water-rich, soft, rich with food value and hearty. The sattvic eat with a view to attaining, sustaining and maintaining longevity, intelligence quotient, physical power, healthfulness, satisfaction of appetite and relish. Therefore, their food contains required amount of water; made soft with reasonable quantity of ghee, butter, cooking oil and fat; and suffused with protein, fibre, fruits, vitamins, minerals and calculated carbohydrates.

The rajasic eat strong, sour, salty, hot, hardened, spicy food that causes unease, illness and consequential pain and suffering.

The tamasic eat food prepared previous night, dry, stale and stinking, flesh and wine, and discarded leftovers and crumbs.

Food is the first and foremost requirement of humans and all other living beings. Raw and rudimentary food reigned supreme in the ancient times of our fore, fore, forefathers. They relished and cherished fruits and roots, seeds and flowers, corns and leaves. They also ate flesh, fowl, fish and eggs as and when they lay their hands on these edible articles. But things changed with cooking and invention of cooking appliances and culinary tricks. Condiments came to flavour foods. But further, regular and excessive conditioning of condiments and spicing spoiled the sport. Instead of enriching food value, they vilified food and the human systems that deal with food. Other living creatures, on the other hand, alien to cooking, devour and savour food as their ancestors did. They might starve, suffer or die for want of food but do not fall ill or suffer from the food they eat.

FORTY-ONE

He is the fire to consume your food

When we look at Gita prescription on food and classification of humans on what they eat and the way they eat, we are perforce drawn to

ahaṁ vaiśhvānaro bhūtvā prāṇināṁ deham āśhritaḥ
prāṇāpāna-samāyuktaḥ pachāmy annaṁ chatur-vidham
[15.14]

O Arjuna! I become the Fire and inhere in beings to digest the four kinds of food [eaten by mastication, swallowing, sucking and licking] by the conjunction of prana air and *apana* air.

Hunger, appetite reigns supreme in beings, in creatures. This is "fire". Only food quells this "fire" that is called *jathara agni*, brahma agni etc. Fire is one of the five elements that the universe is composed of. Fire is ferocious, furious, frightful, fastidious. It is fast and fabulous, indefinite, infinite and nebulous. It does not distinguish nor does discriminate. It is the same everywhere and from the time immemorial. It is friendly and fiendish. On the one hand it protects from quivering cold and deep darkness and it scorches, burns on the other. It ruins comprehensively, completely when it consumes. It is latent and potent. It is positive and destructive. The user has to decide how to employ fire. Employment of fire flowered human civilisation from the primitive barbaric state to the present polished state.

Without food life cannot subsist. But food, as it is, does not sustain beings. Food has to be suited to the need of the being by being burnt and assimilated into the system in toto. This complex process is performed by the Lord in the form of invisible, inherent hunger-fire of creatures. This all-consuming fire in aid with the air we breathe and that we fart out converts food to life-sustaining blood, bones, veins, vessels, cells etc. Food is primarily 4 kinds, viz. that we masticate, swallow, lick and suck. There cannot be any other. Food cannot be fruitful to the creatures until and unless burnt inside the intestines and other parts of the alimentary tract.

In this verse, it is evident that food is inevitable, indispensable. It is irresponsible to fie upon food or shun food. "To a hungry man food is God," goes the age old saying. We are all hungry all the time. Some could afford to satisfy hunger as soon as it is felt, some could not. The fewest who suffer from hunger far longer feel the presence of God in a morsel food and God's mercy when that morsel douses the "fire" in his body, being. The giver is certainly a form, an avatar of God to the hungry being. The food giver is not only satisfying a hungry creature but doing kind of Creator's job, isn't he? Anna dana is therefore the noblest gift, the noblest godly work.

As we must not abstain from food, as we must not refrain from eating, so should we not overeat or waste food.

We may feast and party to our heart's content but we must not waste a morsel, the tiniest amount of food in feasts, picnics or parties. Not for the hungry alone but for all of us food is God. Food availability, supply and abundant supply is the grace of God, the glory of God. We will be oblivious of God if we have no need of God. A good crop or rich harvest is attributed to the mercy of God. "annad bhavanti bhootani parjyanadannasambhavah*****" [14/3] is eloquent on food, life, rains, food production, yajna interrelation.

Food production is stressed stately by Jonathan Swift [1667-1745], Anglo-Irish satirist, author, essayist, political pamphleteer, poet, cleric, whose "Gulliver's Travels" has traversed time and space in popular appeal. In Gulliver's Travels, Chapter Seven, Voyage to Brobdingnag, he immortalises food production as the best vocation, noblest virtue in the statement, "Whoever could make two ears of corn, or two blades of grass, to grow upon a spot of ground where only one grew before, would deserve better of mankind, and do more essential service to his country, than the whole race of politicians put together." This may have been said to satirise the then British politicians- Whigs and Tories- quarrelling over the prevalent faminelike condition. All the same, the appreciation of food-growers, food producers is not exaggerated.

Food is God and sacred. Most people utter inaudibly "Vishnu" before gulping the first morsel. Even those who worship the dish with short worship, whisper "Vishnu" to initiate eating. It reminds us of the presence of Vishnu Vaishvanara inside.

The long and short of the 2 sections is that anna needs must cater to "ayuh sttvavalarogyasukhapritivivardhanah" considerations. Anna should be befitting, beneficial, incremental to our longevity, faculty, force, immunity, enjoyment and relish.

FORTY-TWO

Root bhook, Hit bhook, Mit bhook

Of the quality and quantity of food we need to take, there is an interesting and enlightening story. And the story appertains to Charaka and his foremost disciple Vana Bhatta's dialogue on food.

Charaka, the charismatic, talismanic physician of ancient India died. One day his spirit became curious about what happened to the precious principles of health, hygiene, medicine, dieting and treating he so strenuously learnt, practised and imparted to his pupils.

"Are they being followed, practiced and handed down to posterity or distorted, diluted and debased?" he pondered.

To clear his doubt, he planned to go around Bharata and spot the worthy disciples wedded to his teachings and procedures. In the camouflage of a crow, he flew all over Bharata, especially the assemblies of pundits, residence of quacks and institutions of apothecaries. And, like a common crow, he cawed continuously wherever he flew over. From pundits to common folks, none took note of the solitary crow or it's a bit different caw...caw....

The crow-Charaka was cawing differently though indistinctly. Heard with caution and erudition, the caw was "*ko aruk*", that meant who is disease-deficit, disease-devoid?

Most hearers thought that it was usual crow cawing meaning nothing to men and women; some others could decode the "caw" as "ko aruk" but could not make head or tail of it. Still others who could decisively decipher the poser could not find out the proper answer. They wondered, "Who could be without ailment or illness? Men and women could ill afford not to be ill and disease-devoid as they are destined to be diseased as they are destined to die. The human physique, they critiqued, is a mine of ailment, a fountain of diseases, a storehouse of corporeal uneasiness. Everybody, everybody owns a body that is prone to disease, vagaries of illness. Who could be free from disease?"

They did not agree on some plausible answers. But they did not disagree that the unusual crow with the intricate question was a god in disguise to test the health and hygiene taste of humans.

Vana Bhatta, an eminent poet and physician, was offering water-oblation to Sun about 9 AM in the morning in a Banaras ghat. He was astonished at the crow querying an intricate health issue. He guessed that the crow was not a common or commonplace crow. The "ko aruk" means who devoid of disease is. The answer, thought Vana Bhatta, is "root bhook, hit bhook, mit bhook." And he said so aloud, looking upward at the crow.

The crow descended on the bank and morphed into the mortal frame of Charaka. Vana came up the bank and prostrated before the veteran physician, while Charaka held and hugged Vana in deep embrace. Charaka expressed joie de vivre that Vana answered his query accurately and that his lessons and health and healing conclusions were not lost in desert sands of ignorance and perversion of health and healing practitioners.

Food makes us healthy and immune to diseases. But quality and quantity of food we take determines our disease-free body, healthy life. First criterion is root bhook. The food we eat must be earned by the sweat of our own brow. We must labour to fill our *"udara"*. We must not be parasites on someone's income, labour. We must not beg, borrow or burgle our food, must we? Prestige lies in earning your own bread. For bread and butter, we have to work more, haven't we?

The second criterion is that the food that suits your body, your taste, your temperament is the only food you should take. An Indian must not be tempted to take American, European, Japanese, Chinese, Korean or Manchurian dish or delicacy. Your constitution, climate, country conditions compel you to be accustomed to the eatables you eat. Of course, "While in Rome, do as the Romans do." When in Rome, Berlin, Sydney or Seol, you may relish local dishes and delicacies for facility, for the fun of it, for some time.

The third criterion is the amount of food we eat should be moderate. It should not be excessive or grossly insufficient. The stomach should not be full, overstocked. The food we eat must be moderate, not the most. Our forefathers spoke of and practiced that 1/2 of the stomach be filled with food, while ¼ should be full with water and the remainder ¼ shall be vacant for air. That exactly is what Vana Bhatta spoke as "mita bhook". An old saying goes, "Stop eating while you are still hungry." It is apt and appropriate today, always, isn't it?

FORTY-THREE

Yuktahariviharasya yuktachestaya karmasu
the golden mean

The Charaka Vana Bhatta story echoes from the venerable Bhagavat Gita in chapter 6 slokas 16 and 17.

nātyaśhnatastu yogo 'sti na chaikāntam anaśhnataḥ
na chāti-svapna-śhīlasya jāgrato naiva chārjuna [6.16]

yuktāhāra-vihārasya yukta-cheṣhṭasya karmasu
yukta-svapnāvabodhasya yogo bhavati duḥkha-hā [6.17]

Of yogi's food, rest, waking, working and, even dreaming, Krishna counsels Arjuna with comforting course of action, practice, sadhana.

O Arjuna! A yogi should not abstain from food nor should eat excessively; nor should he sleep soundly to snore and dream nor keep awake without a wink of sleep. Extremities in eating, sleeping, performing and practicing brings about suffering and stymying.

In other words, the yogi should eat and sleep moderately, modestly. While he should eat, drink, sleep and awake in right, required measure, he should also act and attempt moderately. Excesses in these physical activities and attempts thwarts yoga, causes pain and suffering to the yogi.

We are not alien to overeating and oversleeping. It is said that Romans in their heyday of glory and aggrandizement were gourmet giants. Romans in general and senators, tribunes, magistrates, nobles and generals in particular ate sumptuously for 4 days a week so much and so rich food that they fasted for the next 3 days. Overeating, exuberant and indigestible eating, in other words, crapulence, is extremely indecent. Even, the plebeians had their day and did the nobles' way on days of festivity and days of plenty. Elsewhere it was almost the same tendency to eat unrestricted if the food is fascinating and friendly to the taste buds while supply seemingly seamless.

Our mythological personae Bhima and Kumbhakarna are cases in point. Bhima, a paragon of virtues and dearest to Pandavas, was a voracious eater. He could eat and eat and eat…He ate most of the food served by mother Kunti to her 5 sons. She was partial to Bhima in serving far more than his $1/5^{th}$ share. In spite of that, Bhima also took away forcibly from Nakul and Sahadev's share and plates. Yudhisthira and Arjuna offered a handsome handful from their share to satisfy staggering appetite of their voracious but lovely brother. Notwithstanding the lion's share, Bhima remained hungry most of the time. Bhima's unsatiable appetite for food manifested when the boyish Bhima ate a lot of poisoned Ladoo offered by Duryodhana, that too behind the back of his brothers, a thing he scarcely did before.

The other story concerning his voracity shows how he volunteered to take cartloads of sweety and tasty foods to the cave-dwelling, maneater, Vakasura, near Ekachakra Nagar. When their host wailed to send their only son to the maneater monster with the cartload of food, Kunti concurred in Bhima's willingness to go the giant because of her infallible belief that Bhima would crush the demon to death on the one hand and that he would in a long time have a feast of sufficient and salivating food.

Kumbhakarna surpassed Bhima in eating. While Bhima restrained from eating even when hungry due to his sense of shame and other considerations like insufficiency of eatables for others, especially his brothers; Kumbhakarna did not. The all-eating, nonstop eater demon that he was, he would eat and eat and eat till he fell asleep out of the weight of the food he gulped. Then he slept and slept until he was hungry again or was forced awake. Once awake, he ate and ate and ate till he was approached for a favour or he was served with an order of Ravana to go on an errand.

Men and women are no meaner eaters. There are people who eat to their heart's content and more when delicacies and dishes are not in short supply. In parties and picnics, they eat a lot, overeat no doubt. These frenzied eaters are called Kumbhakarna jokingly. Their case is comprehensible. Free foods are ungrudgingly available and the usually-home-unavailable delicacies are available in good quantity. Men and women have the universal and uniform weakness for good food and goodness leads to excess. Of course, in partying and picnic, overeating not bad or belittling.

FORTY-FOUR

The more He eats, the hungrier He becomes!

Bhima is godly, a godly soul by all accounts. Do gods eat or overeat? Why not? If gods behave humanly, why cannot they eat or overeat like men and women? A legend in this context is worth quoting.

Lord Jagannatha of Puri is popularly, endearingly called *"badakhia thakura"* in Odia, which means the *fabulous- eater deity.* His daily consumption consisting of 56 staple foods like rice, dal, curry, curd etc coupled with special delicacies on festivities weigh 60 *pautis*. A pauti is the measurement unit of grains like rice, paddy, of pulses like black gram, green gram, brown gram et al. A pauti can conveniently be converted to a quintal in metric measurement system. Lord Jagannatha is credited with eating 60 pauti food a day. In other words, the total foodstuff consumed by the badakhia thakura is 60 quintals a day. The *Prasad* offered to Lord Jagannatha comprises quantity of oblation dedicated by the Gajapati, the monarch of Utkala[ancient Odisha], the monasteries in service of the Lord and the temple servitors engaged in the deity's distinct, unique kitchen.

Some of the monasteries wedded to Jagannatha's

festivities and rituals enjoy huge landed property granted by the Gajapati. In lieu of the service rendered, the abbots were lords of the Lord's grant lands. They took care of these landholdings through leases and sharecropping pattern cultivation and collected the grain produced. That was utilised by the mahant to offer daily *bhoga* to Jagannatha, Balabhadra, Subhadra and Sudarshana idols installed in the monastery; to feed his monastic establishment comprising some regular and other irregular mendicants, needy pilgrims to the town, destitute and the like.

One such mahant had a large chunk of land in Khandapara, an ex-princely state now in Nayagarh district, famous for the birthplace of astrologer and astronomer of international repute, Mahamahopadhyaya Chandrasekhara Singh Samanta; and the seat of Nila Madhava, the predecessor deity of Jagannatha, at Kantilo. The mahant, on a grain-gathering errand, visited a village near Khandapara where the villagers congregated to chitchat with the mahant. By the by, they informed him of a poor but do-gooder teen in want of employment. The mahant was in for one to serve him as personal attendant, bodyguard, errand boy rolled into one. The villagers were glad to suggest the adolescent's candidature with, of course, a rider that the adolescent, a big eater, would settle for no less than *paancha paa* rice daily. Paancha means 5 and paa means $1/4^{th}$ of a seer, totalling 1.7 kilogram. It was a big amount of rice per capita even for rural adults of that time. Since the mahant was master of a large kitchen cooking, say, half a quintal rice daily, he did not disagree.

The juvenile was taken to Puri and accommodated in the sprawling math. He ate rice cooked of 1.7 Kilogram raw rice and was happy. He was strong and stout and his physical strength was spectacular. The mahant was very fond of him very soon due to his obedience, loyalty and efficient service. Soon came Ekadashi, the 11th day of the fortnight when the math kitchen had the customary shutdown for the day and night. Worried over the matter, the mahant called for *paanchapaa* [that was his nickname by now given due to the amount of rice he ate] and spoke about the problem. The mahant then suggested that he should go outside to the far-off backyard of the math, with the required ration and utensils, cook himself for himself, eat, wash plates and utensils, and come back. Paanchapaa readily agreed to the kindly proposal. The mahant advised that after cooking, he should first offer food to Jagannatha and then eat. Paanchapaa went to the backyard, quickly collected dry twigs, tree branches, fronds, dead leaves for fuelwood and ignited his hearth. Well and on time, rice, dal and curry were cooked and ready to eat. He was reminded of mahant's caution of offering cooked food first to Jagannatha. But he had not an iota of idea about what or who Jagannatha was. All the same, in compliance to mahant's instruction, he called out,

"O Jagannatha! Please come, food is ready and I am very hungry by now!"

He guessed that Jagannatha was a man like him or you or me whom the mahant offered food before taking his meal.

After a few minutes, a dark-skinned, big dark-eyed but decent person appeared and sat near paanchapaa. The latter laid two banana leaves and served eatables on both plates. Both ate happily. The dark-faced person left hurriedly after eating. Paanchapaa cared the least about his coming, eating, vanishing.

Back in the math, mahant curiously queried how Paanchapaa's outdoor feast was. He narrated his first-time culinary experience in detail but concluded casually he could not eat satisfactorily owing to insufficiency of food.

"Why? You had paanchapaa rice as usual, hadn't you?" the mahant asked.

"Yea, I had. It would have been adequate for me but for Jagannatha."

"Jagannatha! Which Jagannatha?" mahant was askance.

"You forget so soon, don't you? You cautioned me to invite Jagannatha to partake of my meal. As I invited him, he arrived; sat down, ate and went his way. What is great or baffling about it?" Paanchapaa poured his heart out without pause or punctuation.

The quick-witted mahant nodded in agreement. "You can take more rice next Ekadashi," he comforted the stupid Paanchapaa. On next fortnight Ekadashi, Paanchapaa proceeded to the math backyard with his ration including more rice, dal and vegetables, culinary articles and equipment. He completed cooking and called out,

"Jagannatha! Meal is ready. Come early!"

No sooner did he utter his coarse-voiced but cordial invite than Jagannatha accompanied with his companion, a well-built, whitish-white- complexioned person, appeared and sat down to eat. Unhappy a bit yet ungrudgingly, Paanchapaa laid out three banana leaves and distributed the delicacies among the three. The threesome had had hearty meals. By the time Paanchapaa was preparing his journey back, the twosome gave a silent slip.

"Today's ration was adequate for you and your friend, wasn't that?" asked the mahant.

"How? Had not Jagannatha had his friend with him, we would have enough," quipped the simpleton.

"Friend!" mahant wondered.

"Yea, friend or brother whatever you may say. But the new- comer was all white and handsome in contrast to Jagannatha's all black. Otherwise, both looked like the same mother's son. Next Ekadashi, you give me supplies sufficient for three, won't you?"

"Yea, yea", the mahant said nervously. He was sure the innocent chap was not playing prank with him nor was sharing his food with some friend he has made meantime. Paanchapaa was not prone to suspicion on the one hand and his description of Jagannatha, Balabhadra was not spin-doctored on the other. The third Ekadashi, he took ration enough for three.

Back in math, mahant questioned sweetly,

"Today you three had enough and to spare, hadn't you?"

"No, *Mahapru!*" said Paanchapaa rather pensively, and added, "your Jagannatha is naughty and playing mischief with me. Today he was accompanied with a golden-yellow-faced, extremely beautiful virgin apart from his white-skinned male friend. And all three ate to their heart's content and kept to their heels."

The mahant was stunned. He looked at the youth with emotions rising and ebbing in his heart. The Jagannatha Leela and lore are well known and empirical to numerous bhaktas. He was amazed at and all praise for the untutored, rural youth whose simplicity is simply superb. The mahant yearned to witness the earthly play of Jagannatha in close vicinity.

Next Ekadashi, he gave bountiful supplies for 4 people and followed Paanchapaa stealthily. Paanchapaa cooked under a jackfruit tree, while the mahant holed him up in nearby bushes and shrubs. Cooking over, he called out loud and clear. Jagannatha, Balabhadra, Subhadra advented from nowhere, sat down, had lunch, and melted in thin air as the mahant headed noiselessly and stealthily to the picnic spot. From some distance and due to obstructions in between, the mahant saw the threesome silhouetted on the semiwild and smoke-screened landscape. All the same, he was sure Jagannatha, Balabhadra, Subhadra partook of Paanchapaa's picnic cordially and commoner-like. Needless to say, the overwhelmed mahant embraced the simpleton in admiration and adoration. He taught him alphabets and arithmetic, initiated him Pachanga and religious paraphernalia. As the successor in waiting, Paanchapaa remained there. After demise of the mahant, he was anointed as mahant. Later on, the legend spread among Jagannatha devotees who named the math "Paanchapaa Math." On widening of the Jagannatha temple outer perimeter, the math, like dozen others, was demolished to untraceable dust, burying with it a beautiful legend of Jagannatha glory.

FORTY-FIVE

Trividham narakyasyedam dwaram nashanamatmanah

While we have discussed on 3 types of worship, gift, eating etc, we may look at 3 in another context in another verse that speaks of hell. Hell is hailed in holler, hate. "Go to hell!" is the common refrain by friends and foes in joke, jealousy. Hell is as much part of our scriptures and puranas as of epics and folktales. You can do without heaven but not without hell. When you are hellbent upon curing and purifying, you head for heaven. What about hell in Gita then? Gita speaks of the 3 gates of hell.

tri-vidham narakasyedam dvāram nāśhanam ātmanaḥ
kāmaḥ krodhas tathā lobhas tasmād etat trayam tyajet
[16.21]

Krishna apprises Arjuna of the 3 gates to hell and they are desire, anger and greed. Since entry in hell definitely destroys one, one needs must abjure these 3.

There is no gainsaying that these 3 ungainly traits in humans mars their lovely march to heaven, to paradise, to the palace of peace and bliss in afterlife. In fact, these 3, separately and collectively, destroy one in this life, in this worldly life. If at all, you still course through the rough and tumble of this life with these Satan on your side, as your guide, you would be dragged down, drawn down to hell. These 3, severally and synchronously, are the one-way way to hell.

Desire, anger and greed are your creed as men and women. You can't, you must not abjure these 3 since they are your flesh and blood. They appear in you some months after you appear in the world and they mount the pyre with you, not a day before. The only caution is required of you is leashing them, keeping them under wraps so that they do not wreck and ruin you.

FORTY-SIX

Sadbhavapratipannanam vanchane kim vidgadhatam?

In the preceding section, we browsed upon the gates to hell, the 3 no-return, one-way gates of hell. Desire, anger and greed; unleashed and uncontrolled, un-reigned and un-reined desire, anger and greed are inevitable and veritable entrances to hell. It will not be out of context to quest who the hell go to hell?

Kalidas, the crown of poets of Bharata composed a verse to tell who go to hell. And they are,

Mitradrohi krutaghnasch je sch vishwasaghatakah
Trayaste narakam yanti yavatabhutasamplavam
[verse attributed to Kalidas]

Those who harm or handicap friends, the ungrateful and the betrayers, traitors are the ones who go to hell till the world is inhabited by creatures of all kinds. The story behind the moral verse is interesting.

Once a prince with a pack of pals and hordes of servants went on hunting. As they entered un-surveyed dense forests, they were disarrayed to lose paths and one another. Somehow or other the prince's companions made their way out of the deep woods. But the prince was alone and trapped in the wild wilderness when sunset thickened the darkness.

Hopeless of moving out of the forest, the prince climbed a tree to shelter himself at night from nocturnal beasts of prey. Alas! when he was on the tree, he saw a bear hunkered there. The prince realised that he was unequal to the terrible wild flesh-eater in darkness due to his exhaustion in daylong scrambling and futile labour in finding friends and path out of woods. But the bear, much against his violent nature, spoke coolly,

"O man! Do not be afraid of me; I will not harm you because I am not harm's way from the ferocious tiger lying in wait beneath to kill me anytime should he get the slightest chance. He will no doubt kill and eat you if you disembark the tree anytime now. He is awfully hungry and will feast upon either of us, maybe both and maybe before dawn."

"Since we face the common enemy," the bear went on, "we should be friends for the night to fight our fright. At dawn when the tiger is gone, we will be on our own separate ways."

The prince nodded in agreement. He thought of being between Scylla and Charybdis- prey to the bear on the tree and feast of the tiger under the tree. Since "A known devil is better than an unknown one," the prince settled for being with the bear come what may. After some time, the bear began,

"O prince! After the daylong trial and tribulations to find your way out, you would be awfully tired and would need some sleep. So do I need. But both of us cannot take a nap at the same time as the tiger is likely to attack us when asleep. Since sleep we must, we must do that alternately. I do not mind if you sleep first by putting your head on my lap. After you wake up, I shall sleep in your lap."

The prince had no other alternative to agreeing to the seemingly sensible proposal of the bear. It was a catch-22 predicament. Hoping for the best, the prince reclined in the bear's lap. No sooner had he closed his lids than he fell fast asleep. The tiger emerged from the bushes and said,

"O foolish bear! How do you dare save and shelter a human from me? Don't you know that the humans are our enemy number 1 and killer eternal? They kill us for their fun, sport and bravado for no fault of ours, don't they? They deprive us of our food, habitat and happiness by constant encroachments to the vast, virgin woods and wastelands, greenery and grasslands to deplete our food, fodder and fairyland, don't they? Yet, you bloody fool let a foolish prince sleep and snore on your lap lest he should be preyed upon by a waiting tiger."

"O nonsense, foolish beast!" the tiger scolded, "I was hopelessly hungry and chased you to slaughter and satisfy my hunger. Now that you climbed the tree and that a better prey obtained, isn't it your duty to push the prince down for my feast on the one hand and save your skin on the other? You bogus beast! Instead of saving your paternal life by sacrificing our common foe, you opt for the double jeopardy of my anger now and betrayal by the prince when he comes down at dawn. Don't you know that the prince at daybreak will break your bones with his physical prowess and mental superiority since you are a beast of prey? Pray push him down so that I eat his lungs and limbs and go!"

The bear was unmoved by the tiger's instigations and motivations, and replied that he had befriended the prince and had struck a deal with him to save each other. Come what may, he would not betray the human friend to danger and likely death. The tiger kept mum. He awaited the prince's turn. As mutually agreed, about midnight the bear awakened the prince to let himself take rest. While the bear slept and snored on the prince's lap, the tiger reappeared to say,

"Hi prince! How do you do? You are prince of a state and I am prince of the forest. Thus, we are similarly placed, aren't we? As of royal lineage, our credo is 'Might is right' and we abide by that right, don't we? This bear that has befriended you this night out of my fright is a base, bedevilling beast. At daybreak, he breaks the dissimulated friendship to breakfast on you. For the sake of you, I have spared him so far. No more. You push him down and I do the rest! Then you rest on the tree free of fear of me or the bear and find your way to the kingdom at daybreak to break free of the frightening forest. Though you are a wise prince, you have committed this unroyal, silly error of trusting a cursing beast of prey that does not look straight, act straight but clutches and claws his prey straight in the face to peel off the prey's eyes, ears, nose, nostrils and what not. They say and rightly so that a human can escape a tiger's assault but not a bear's blitzkrieg. Why late, act fast lest the bear should wake up to play spoil sport to the plot!"

The prince pleaded pusillanimously not to throw the bear down. "You are as much vulgar as violent," said the prince to the tiger, "how and why shall I betray the bear who has saved and sheltered me in this deep, dreadful jungle? It is inhuman and unbecoming of royalty."

But the tiger persevered and persisted with sweet flattery and sweetened treachery to which the prince succumbed reluctantly. As the prince was offloading the bear of his lap and just when the bear was to fall, he woke up, clung to the tree-trunk with his sharp and strong claws. The tiger beneath left the spot as he realised that all his endeavours ended in smoke.

The bear chided the prince for his beastly betrayal and unbecoming behaviour. He scolded the prince, wondering while a beast of prey, a wild bear, kept his promise to save a human despite tempting persuasion by the tiger; the human, ironically, fell a prey to the tiger's poisonous persuasions. Since day was breaking on the distant horizon and human noise was being heard nearby, the bear told the prince to go his way. Before clawing his descent, the bear pulled out the prince's tongue to write with the former's fingernails,

> Sadbhavapratipannanam vanchane ka vidagdhata
> Ankamaruhyasuptanam hantum kim nam paurusham.
> Setum gatwa samudrasya gangasagarasangam
> Brahmahapi pramucchyate mitradrohi na muchyate.
> Mitradrohikrutaghnascha yaschavishaswasaghatakah
> Trayaste narakam yanti yavadabhutasamplavam.
> Rajendra nijaputrasy yadi kalyanamichhashi
> Dehidanamdwijatibhyah devataradhana kuru.
> [verses attributed to Kalidas]

On daybreak, the prince alighted from the tree and, luckily, soon found his lost itinerary. But to everyone's wonder and worry, the prince uttered only one word, that too incoherently, "*sasemira*". The prince chanted that very same unintelligible word "sasemira" all along, without stop, comma or colon.In the capital and palace, he continued the same bogus blabbering, unmindful of eating, drinking, playing, sleeping. The king was annoyed with the vexatious verbiage of the prince and sent for quacks and pundits to treat the prince but to no avail.

Finally came poet Kalidas in a guise. He guessed the nocturnal hazard to the scion, pulled his tongue out, and uttered the first verse supra. Then the scion uttered "*semira semira*...", dropping the first letter from sasemira. Kalidas went on like 3 times more by composing the 3 slokas one after another. The prince stopped blabbering sasemira further and regained consciousness.

The first sloka means it is not prudent to cheat someone who had reposed trust in you. To kill someone asleep on your lap is not a manifestation of manhood.

The 2nd verse says a brahmin-assassin may be absolved of his gruesome killing by pilgrimaging to Rameshwaram where a bridge was built by Rama on the sea or the holy Gangasagara confluence where Ganga falls into the sea, but a friend's betrayer would not wash out his sins after pilgrimaging to these sacred sites.

The 3rd sloka says the 3 who go to hell. They are – *mitradrohi, krutaghna* and *vishwasaghataka* i.e. who harms a friend, the ungrateful and the trust breacher.

The 4th sloka advised the king to worship deities, give presents to brahmins in furtherance of welfare of the scion.

FORTY-SEVEN

Who else is there like me?

We talked of the 3 gates to the hell and, incidentally, quoted Kalidas to ascertain who go to hell. Bhagavat Gita does not ignore reference to hell and it is there in,

āḍhyo 'bhijanavān asmi ko 'nyo 'sti sadṛiśho mayā
yakṣhye dāsyāmi modiṣhya ity ajñāna-vimohitāḥ [16.15]

aneka-citta-vibhrāntā moha-jāla-samāvṛtāḥ
prasaktāḥ kāma-bhogeṣu patanti narake 'śucau [16.16]

O Arjuna! Those who boast of their wealth, of their clan; those who brag, 'Who else there is like me'; those who boast, 'OK, I shall worship such and such deities'; those who say proudly, 'I shall give and gift, shall enjoy myself massively' are utterly ignorant creatures to utter so and are trapped. Those fellows are unmindful that they are full mental fools and have been snared in the knotty net of Moha. These Moha-maddened madcaps womanise and waste life and fortunes wantonly. As a result, they go to the ugly, unclean, sorrowful HELL.

Kalidas had listed the persons who fall to the fell,

foul Hell. They are the betrayers, the amicicides and the ungrateful. The friendly malefactors cannot absolve their ghastly sins even after long and arduous tirtha tours. Hence, they would go to Hell. The list is illustrative, not exhaustive. The Gita list of Hell-goers, Hell bound humans, is given above. Those who boast of their property and pelf, their wealth and weight in gold, go to Hell. So do they who assert that there is none like him/her. Those who speak of worship lightly, egotistically go to Hell. So do they who speak of gifts and donations in unhumble, highhanded tone and temper. And wanton, wasteful enjoyment including addiction to drinks, drugs, prostitution leads to HELL.

This may look improper. Why not speak, speak highly of one's property or pedigree? What harm is there to say 'I am going to temple or I worship Shiva or Siddhi Vinayaka?' How could it be bad or beastly to say, 'Let me give alms to this beggar or a blanket to that cold-cursed destitute?'

Apparently not. Between the lines remains the crux. You must speak of, speak well of your forefathers, your wealth and estate. But your language, your manner, the context and the necessity is the thing. You may say, not show; you may speak high of but with humility and contextual propriety. But why speak of your pedigree or property at all. What did Karna say of clan or lineage?

Daivayatakulejanma madayatam cha pourusham

It is divine play to be born to certain parents or pedigree but manhood is the manifestation of the quality and accomplishments of the man/woman.

It is indisputable that destiny determines people's parents, family but the person concerned determines, designs his/her fate, fortune, fame.

Wealth is a weighty responsibility, socio-cultural obligation. Wealth diminishes, evaporates as swiftly, as steadily as it accrues, accumulates. Wealth does not last long. Our scriptures and morals therefore thrust upon useful utilisation of riches and resources. Our good old saying says,

"Dhanani jivitani cha pararthe prajna utsrujet
Sannimitte varam tyago vinashe niyata sati"

Life and riches are destined to decay, destruction. The wise take the cue to utilise these for good cause, noble cause, memorable mission.

It is further said,

"Vidya vivadaya dhanam maday
Shakti presham parapidanayam
Khalasya sadhunam viparitametat
Jnanay danaya cha rakshanaya"

The evil-minded use their knowledge only to disagree and debate, their wealth on addiction to narcotics, psychotropic substances, liquor and womanization, and their power to torment others. The good people, on the contrary, use knowledge to enhance enlightenment, wealth to give to the needy, and power to protect people from cruelty and against injustice.

Hence, in the best case, our wealth is a trust property. You are the present keeper, caretaker. Maybe a bad caretaker like Jagannatha Kundu in Rabindra Nath Tagore's telltale story "The Trust Property" or a good caretaker like the great king Harishchandra. So, where is the occasion to brag of your wealth?

FORTY-EIGHT

If there is no God, who created the world?

Hell is home to devils listed above. Do you think the Hell is so thinly populated? No, not at all. Hell is the natural habitat of a lot more inhabitants. For instance,

> pravṛittiṁ cha nivṛittiṁ cha janā na vidur āsurāḥ
> na śhauchaṁ nāpi chāchāro na satyaṁ teṣhu vidyate [16.7]

> asatyam apratiṣhṭhaṁ te jagad āhur anīśhvaram
> aparaspara-sambhūtaṁ kim anyat kāma-haitukam [16.8]

    These Hell-habitant devils do not know what profession, vocation, activity should be pursued and what not. They are not clean nor do they follow good habits. To cap it all, they are alien to speaking the truth.

    They hold that all the good, ideal truths, traditions, systems, customs, cultures are untrue and unfounded. There is nothing like the universe nor there is any God. The creatures are created out of sexual intercourse between opposite sexes.

    The devils, the demons, the demonic humans do not know what is right and what is wrong. They possess unclean body and impure mind. How then can they be clean in spirit? How can they be pious and religious? This degraded, degenerate state of theirs is due to their disbelief in truth, their disinclination for truth. So, the devastating demonic vices breed in humans' qualities to denounce and disparage truth. Truly speaking, adherence to truth, abiding by truth, makes all the difference. While you may be a devil, your neighbour is not; while you maybe demonic, your friend may be divine.

The devil, the demonic, deny the existence of the universe and of God. Things written or talked about the universe and about God are untrue and unestablished for them. The age-old principles and practices, the universal beliefs and books, are absolutely bogus—they pronounce and preach. If there is no God, who created the world? Simple, they say, the opposite sexes cohabit, consummate and intercourse out of sexual urge to create creatures.

FORTY-NINE

Who is God?

The list does not end with the aforesaid devils. Rather it starts with as them as hereunder. You say devil, the devil is here.

idam adya mayā labdham imaṁ prāpsye manoratham
idam astīdam api me bhaviṣhyati punar dhanam [16.13]

asau mayā hataḥ śhatrur haniṣhye chāparān api
īśhvaro 'ham ahaṁ bhogī siddho 'haṁ balavān sukhī [16.14]

Krishna speaks to Arjuna what the devils do and how they speak about what they have done, are doing and will do next, in future.

'I have got this much, this amount of money, pleasure, ease and success. But this is not enough. I want more, furthermore, still more. I want riches and treasure troves, jewelleries and estates, palatial buildings and sprawling estates, luxury vehicles, ranches, yachts, choppers, chauffeurs, chuffers, serves, servants. Since I want, I must have it,' says the devil, even though you did not ask anything on it. Even though you have nothing to do with the devil's what-he-has or what-he-hasn't, he goes on speaking, goes on speaking like, 'I rode a bicycle, but in a year, I owned a motor bike, didn't I? But a motor bike was not suitable for my long ride. So, I purchased a Maruti van. Just after a year, I was fed up with that small car and I bought Hyundai City. Yet, I am not satisfied, I shall purchase an Audi or Ferrari, won't I?' He cares least that you had nothing to do with his bicycle nor would you have anything to do with his Mercedes Benzo. So nonstop he talks on his bank balance, bungalow, plots of homestead, agricultural acreages, farm houses, jewellery etc that you simply want to escape from the conversation, even the encounter.

Of physical prowess, he speaks and speaks more dangerously like, 'I killed tom, dick and harry...the bloody fools do not know who I am. They defied and disobeyed me or competed and contested with me. Do you think they will go unpunished? And you know, for trifling of an offence, I do inflict the severest punishment, don't I? And why other smoother punishment for my foes? I just push them away from my path for good. I do not kill my enemy; I nip the bud, don't I?'

The devil goes on boasting, 'Govind's farmhouse adjoins mine. I have persuaded him to part with that for any amount of consideration that pleases him. The foolish fellow refuses flatly to sell his farmhouse to me. Shall I spare him? I shall murder him and merge his estate with mine. Who is there to hinder me? Am I afraid of police, courts or caustic backbiting by neighbours and locals? Who cares for social criticism or cordial censure? If you care for courtesy or criticism, can you advance in life? Can you accumulate, property, power and prestige? 2 or 3 others are bitterly opposed to my business. Their hostility is often covert but clearly manifest in their motives and manners, actions and attitude. I must murder them. It would be too late for them to realise how dangerous it is to act against my interest, my ambitions, my designs and devices.'

The devil brags, 'I am God. I am Lord of all I survey. If there is God, it is me, me alone. None else but me is God, is the Lord. I have enjoyed enough myself and will still enjoy myself all that remains and for all time to come. I am siddha. I am siddha purusha. I am the strongest, stoutest, sturdiest. And I am the happiest, am not I?'

So, what is the devil not? He is getting things and would get what he has not. Not will get, but get he must! He has wiped out enemies and will eliminate the remaining ones. He is not the murderer but God. He is mightier than the mightiest and a sage, seer or the most accomplished person. His enjoyments are boundless and limitless and timeless. Last but not least, he is the happiest, the gladdest.

The devil's version is he is all. He has all. He has achieved all. He will be what he is not. He will do what he has not done as yet. He will have the remainder of his want.

You will be vexed at the devil's blowing hot and cold at the same time. In verse 8, chapter 16, he says there is no God. In verse 14, chapter 16, he avers he is God. Is the devil contradictory in regard to God? No, he is not. The devil does not contradict himself with regard to God. In sloka 8/16, he denies God. He is atheist. He is anarchist, nihilist. In sloka 14/16, he speaks of your God, my God, others' God. He is in no need of God but needs must fulfil our God requirement. He can do without God but we cannot. So, he volunteers to fill the vacancy of our God. Of course, he is a goddam fool who fails to understand that there can be no vacancy of God and that the God we adore has not asked us to recognise Him as such.

More importantly, when the devil declares that he is God, he thinks God is the powerhouse, storehouse of all pleasures, riches, powers, popularity, dignity, authority et all. God is undoubtedly all that but is incomprehensibly, incredibly, unimaginably, indescribably full of other virtues and vibes. The devil vilifies God by boasting of being God and that exactly is the devil's demeanour.

FIFTY

Hell is empty and all the devils are here

You may assume that the list of devils or the vices of devils have been exhaustive by now. No, how can that be so soon?

In "The Tempest", the last play of eminent Elizabethan playwright and poet, William Shakespeare, appears the famous saying that English-knowing people from all parts of the world quote quietly, "***was the first man that leap'd; cried, 'hell is empty, And all the devils are here'." In Act I, Scene 2 of the play, Ariel, the loyal spirit enslaved to Prospero, the banished Milan duke dwelling in an almost deserted, desolate island, reports what he did to the king of Naples and his itinerary that were sailing on sea nearby. Ariel raised a violent tempest that tossed and turned the ship frequently and frighteningly. The voyagers were bedevilled by waves, strong currents, tall waves and menacing marine creatures. Finally, the ship sank and the cruisers and crew of the ship were drowned. Ferdinand, the Napolitan prince, was the first person to leap out of the sinking ship. On trying his luck against the ferocious surf, surge and sea, Ferdinand cried, "Hell is empty, And all the devils are here."

Ferdinand and his co-voyagers' tempest- struck,

precarious condition as reported by Ariel to Prospero is described thus,

> "Prospero- hast thou, spirit,
> Perform'd to point the tempest I bade thee?
> Ariel- To every article.
> I boarded the king's ship; now on the beak,
> Now in the waste, the deck, in every cabin,
> I flamm'd amazement: sometime I'd divide,
> And burn in many places, on the topmast,
> The yards, the bowsprit, would I flame distinctly,
> Then meet, and join. Jove's lightnings, the precursors
> O' the dreadful thunder-claps, more momentary
> And sight-turning were not: the fire, and cracks
> Of sulphurous roaring, the most mighty Neptune
> Seem'd to besiege, and make his bold waves tremble,
> Yea, his dead trident shake.
> Prospero – my brave spirit!
> Who was so firm, constant, that this coil
> Would not infect his reason?
> Ariel- not a soul
> But felt a fever of the mad, and played
> Some tricks of desperation. All but mariners
> Plung'd in the foaming brine, and quit the vessel,
> Then all a-fire with me: the king's son, Ferdinand,
> With hair up-staring, -then like reeds, not hair, --
> Was the first man that leap'd; cried, 'Hell is empty,
> And all the devils are here'."

FIFTY-ONE

Born you be must innumerable times

Of the unseen, unheard, un-mitigating, agitating turbulent sea, storm, Ferdinand spoke of devils, devils emptying the Hell.

Here, Hell is not yet empty nor all devils have been out as yet.

ahankāraṁ balaṁ darpaṁ kāmaṁ krodhaṁ cha sanśhritāḥ
mām ātma-para-deheṣhu pradviṣhanto 'bhyasūyakāḥ [16.18]

tān ahaṁ dviṣhataḥ krūrān sansāreṣhu narādhamān
kṣhipāmy ajasram aśhubhān āsurīṣhv eva yoniṣhu [16.19]

Krishna tells Arjuna that the devils adopt, avouch, adhere to egotism, physical prowess, pride, ambition and anger. By that, they become inimical to themselves, others, and even God.

What happens then, thereafter? They had their day, as they say; have achieved what they wished by means fair and foul [frankly speaking, only foul]. Will they go scot-free or on French leave? It sounds unfair the devils' wheel-dealing, the wheedling devils ditch the doomsday. Then?

Krishna tells Arjuna what He does about the devils. These worst, cruel humankind-malefactors and fallen humans, who decry, desecrate Me and are anathematic to Me and the animal kingdom, other humans and other creatures are duly dealt with by being made to be born umpteen times in lowly, devilish wombs.

In the end the chickens have come home to roost. The devil is made to rollercoaster in demonic and degraded embryos unendingly. He cannot find salvation from the sadistic, insatiable, insane hunger and desire for more and more and more ephemeral, evaporating pleasures and pelf, pride and aggrandizement.

Your mother knows the labour pain, the pain of miscarriage, the pathos of pregnancy termination, abortion. You do not know the cold, dark chamber of mother's uterus where you struggle to come out, to see daylight, to find freedom and fresh air. You liken the uterus stay with hell, don't you? Yes, it is hell, hell full of raw, rotten flesh, blood, putrid, stale slabbering mucus and membrane. The pathos of the pathos is that your bones and veins, your skin, skeleton and skull, your blood, bosom and brain become reality in this hell. Of course, you are fortunate to have a human birth, become a human baby. Once out of mother's uterus, you are showered with love, nourishment, enjoyment, education. If you so like, you can attain enlightenment because you are born intelligent and conscious to cognitive, conscious parents, society and world. What would happen if you descend to a dog, donkey, insect, worm womb? What would happen if you intrude a woman's womb in an isolated island or deserted Tundra village where you would be perennially deprived of food, clothes, safe shelter, education, healthcare and healing words of human fraternity? That is why, God's severest punishment lies in you lying in mother's embryo innumerable times.

Is it a cock and bull story? No. Let us cite a tale.

Dhruva, in the high heaven, was once, unfortunately, had a flash of pride to feel that he could see God when only 5 years old and ascended heaven through a single life's actions and accomplishments, while sages and seers seek God's grace and heaven but fail frequently. Dhruva, certainly serene and sheltered-in-God, forgot as soon as it flashed across his vision's horizon. He went around his daily chores and rested for the night. Next morning when awakened, he was astonished to see a lean and thin ascetic-like figure not afar. Dhruva proceeded toward that fellow who stood tomblike where he was. Dhruva, saluting him solemnly, asked,

"Mahatma! you won't mind if I put you a question, will you?"

"No," was the prompt, nonchalant reply.

"Who are you and what do you do here?" Dhruva queried, in a puzzle-plastered face.

"I am the sexton, the cemetery- sentry," pat came the reply.

"Cemeterial caretaker, burial boss here in heaven! Made me laugh Mahatma! You certainly did not mean that, did you?" Dhruva added.

"Come on to comprehend what I mean!" the mystique with a silhouetted physique nearly commanded and ambled toward the hazy horizon.

Dhruva followed suit kind of compulsively, wondering about the almost apparition. They reached a well-upkept burial ground or cemetery and standing afar, looked at heaps of bones, bone-dry and decently desiccated.

Dhruva was crestfallen at the fantastic, kind of funny sight in paradise. Stunned by the spectacle and pointing to a tall bone-heap, Dhruva queried,

"Mahatma! Will you not oblige me by divulging whose bone-hill that is?

"Yours, whose else? The mystique smiled meaningfully.

"Do you think you landed here by virtue of your virtues of this life? No, no, not at all," he emphasized, "you have been born and reborn innumerable times in different yonis[uteruses] and have, no doubt, improved upon your actions and attitudes so much so that in this life you were granted God's grace to ascend heaven as a rarefied feat."

Dhruva was thunder-struck and swiftly recollected the cold, colossal pride that overcast him for a fraction of a moment. He prostrated flat at the feet of the faint physique. When he opened his eyes, Dhruva saw the phantom disappearing away to dissolve in the distant horizon.

FIFTY-TWO

Lead kindly light amid the encircling gloom

Rebirth is not exclusive to Hinduism. Other religions believe in and behave according to rebirth. Nearer home, Jainism and Buddhism which dismiss polytheism, caste-classification, supremacy of Veds, paraphernalia of worship etc, the core creeds of Hinduism, are at one with Hinduism in regard to rebirth. Buddhism prides in its jataka stories that parades a thousand previous lives of the Buddha. Buddha like Dhruva underwent innumerable lives, numerous uterine imprisonments, uncountable embryonic sufferings, to attain enlightenment. He was born into fish, fowl, flesh-eater, deer, donkey, monkey, moneylender, vendor, cloth-launderer, barber, beggar, farmer, teacher, priest, preacher, merchant, mendicant and whatnot.

What was the Buddha's enlightenment? The light that lighted his darkened, buried past. On the banks of river Niranjana in moonlit Vaisakha Poornima, struggling, penance-punished Gautam sat cross-legged under the murmuring leaves of a huge Pipal tree to seek the supreme truth, the reasons and objects of life. He recounted the penance and painstaking search for knowledge for the last 12 years and the futility thereof. Scriptures and teachers, pundits and professors professed the theoretical and theological, speculative and hypothetical, philosophical and theosophical lessons of life. Interesting and enlightening though they were, they did not supply the cue to attain truth. The practical was lacking; the how-to-do demonstration was wanting; the do-it-yourself guidance was unavailable. So, Gautam sat determined to do it of himself, by himself and, obviously, for himself. And he did it himself when he saw in his mind's eye his recent past, distant past, the past of his predecessors, the past of his state, society and the whole world. He saw for himself the birth after birth he had been subjected to and susceptible to in the future. He was at the end of the tunnel; he was in the realm of light; he was the Buddha.

This life, this earthly life, this earthy life of ours is darkened, blurred, bewitching. Our ancient mantra says, "tamaso mam jyotirgamaya!"; O God! Lead me from darkness to light! We grope in the dark, in the darkness of ignorance of Truth, the only truth, the ultimate, immanent truth. The English poet, saint, John Henry Newman, recovering from a severe fatal fever, wrote in 1833 the hymnal lyric, "Lead kindly light...," on boat from the Italian city Palermo to French city Marseilles on way home to England. The poet saint echoes our mantra when he sings,

"lead kindly light, amid the encircling gloom
Lead though me on
The night is dark, and I am far from home
Lead though me on
*******"

Home here is not home in the popular sense of the term but our home proper, humankind's home proper; the home where we are bred, fed, clothed, sheltered and shielded. It is that home where we met Dhruva. This home may not even be high heaven. It is God's shelter, sanctuary from assault from all quarters. Nonetheless, as Newman so all men and women are far, far away from this home. When they say 'Home sweet home', they mean as much this home as the earthly home, family home we are born into. There is no sweeter home than this home, is there?

FIFTY-THREE

Flight of the Light

Our scriptures and stories, epics and epistles underlie rebirth. Science speaks of indestructibility of matter, energy. How can Atma, Self, the Spirit in us be destructible? It is more than matter and energy, and something still more. Constraint of space confines us to a skimpy discussion. In Bhagavat Gita, there is a pretty metaphor on rebirth.

śharīraṁ yad avāpnoti yach chāpy utkrāmatīśhvaraḥ
gṛihītvaitāni sanyāti vāyur gandhān ivāśhayāt [15.8]

śhrotraṁ chakṣhuḥ sparśhanaṁ cha rasanaṁ ghrāṇam eva
cha adhiṣhṭhāya manaśh chāyaṁ viṣhayān upasevate [15.9]

O Arjuna! As air travels with the scent of flower, so do Ishvara leaves one mortal frame to another with the mental faculties and five sensory organs' attributes to function with in the host body.

It is to note that air travels with the scent of the flower, not the concrete flower alive or withered. Similarly, Ishvara travels from one body to another with the mental faculties along with visual, auditory, olfactory, gustatory and tactile characteristics of the former frame. Like scent of flower, the scent or abstract attributes of the previous body are carried on along by Ishvara to install them there for the host body's enjoyment.

In sloka 14/15, God, Ishvara speaks of chopping, chewing, sucking and licking, digesting food, in short, in the form of fire. Here, Ishvara harps on the intricate aspect of transmigration of Jivatma, Self, from body to body with the sensory properties of the former frame. Herein lies the crux of acts and attitudes of Jiva in this life, in this earthly life. The good you do promote you in your next body, next life; the bad you do demote you in the next life. It is not a short or simple process. The evolution of species, according to Charles Darwin, takes years and years. It is slow and steady and wins the race of evolution, promotion. Not all species pass the evolution, promotion test. Some, no, many fail, fail pathetically, and face extinction. Hence, the famous Darwinian adage, "Survival of the fittest." The fittest survive and the unfit bury themselves in oblivion, in past, in fossils.

Unlike Darwinian evolution, Gita evolution and demotion, degradation go hand in hand. As the species struggle and fight for their existence, improvement, so the Jiva struggle and exert themselves to improve, develop their existential status. You inherit your past properties incognito. You start with them to live, lead your present life. Nevertheless, you have scope and capabilities enough to improve upon, move higher in the hierarchy of existence, consciousness. From a crow or cow to more sentient creature, you could be as the Buddha jataka stories demonstrate.

FIFTY-FOUR

Where do you go when you go? Flower falls off: scent travels

Reference to rebirth is made again in Gita in,

yam yam vāpi smaran bhāvam tyajatyante kalevaram
tam tam evaiti kaunteya sadā tad-bhāva-bhāvitaḥ [8.6]

ā-brahma-bhuvanāl lokāḥ punar āvartino 'rjuna
mām upetya tu kaunteya punar janma na vidyate [8.16]

na tvevāham jātu nāsam na tvam neme janādhipāḥ
na chaiva na bhavishyāmaḥ sarve vayamataḥ param [2.12]

jātasya hi dhruvo mṛityur dhruvam janma mṛitasya cha
tasmād aparihārye 'rthe na tvam śhochitum arhasi [2.27]

In the first sloka herein [6/8] Arjuna is enlightened with the truth that when a Jiva, the individual Self leaves, it leaves for the host of which he thought at the time of departure, death. Like the flower's scent, his last thought, feeling, infatuation flies to and enforces entry into the host of his feeling, fancy, infatuation. And the last thought, fancy, infatuation does not flash like a lightning. It is there with us from early life most of the time. It is the idee fix, the dominant thought. It is the persistent, persevering pursuit. That is why people in the know of this truth chant "Rama, Rama, Krushna, Krushna, Radhe, Radhe" etc. They know as we all know pretty well that death arrives without notice, intimation, information and on any logic or uniform policy. Death is confirmed but does conform to no rule, pattern, parameter, procedure, practice or paraphernalia. They chant the names of their holy gods for quite some time past to ensure that the name of Rama, Krushna, Shiva, Vishnu, Durga, Radha might be on their lips by the time of death.

In the second verse herein [16/8], rebirth is emphasized. It is stated that all creatures of earth have to die and be reborn. Those pious persons who have been elevated to Deva Loka, Shiva Loka or Brahma Loka are not exempt from rebirth. Their rebirth may take a recession but rebirth must they experience, be subjected to. Exemption is available to only those who secure a place in, take refuse in God, the Lord. Only those who shelter in, plunge in, merge with God, are entitled to immunity. Notwithstanding the all-inclusive, universal, uniform canon of rebirth, there is only exception, only one exception, and that is immediate emigration to/in God. Subject to only this rider, all are subject to rebirth.

In the 3rd sloka quoted from 2nd Adhyaya, Krishna chides Arjuna for the latter's insensible sentimentality, cheap sentimentality to suppose as if none of the kings nor them were ever there in the past nor would there ever be in future. Krishna implied that all the kings, commanders, warriors, generals arrayed against Arjuna were there for ages, for eons and would invariably be there for innumerable years ahead.

In verse 27/2 cited supra, Krishna counsels his comrade in arm, Arjuna, that that is born must die and that that dies must be reborn.

Rebirth, the most critical quiz of scriptures and epics, folk lore and faery tales from Egyptian, Graco-Roman to Indian civilisations, finds its preeminent position in Gita. The crux of the matter is that rebirth is a must and is in a link in an unbroken chain. The essence of the present life springs from the past and would manifest in the next life. The third thing about rebirth is that you can act upon, improve upon the essence of life to make your future existence better, prettier.

FIFTY-FIVE

Let us, then, be up and doing,
With a heart for any fate;

We have to, we need to improve upon our essence to enhance our existential prospects, needn't we? Gita has, in its pragmatic wisdom, exhorted to embark upon the path of progress, improvement in,

uddhared ātmanātmānaṁ nātmānam avasādayet
ātmaiva hyātmano bandhur ātmaiva ripur ātmanaḥ [6.5]

bandhur ātmātmanas tasya yenātmaivātmanā jitaḥ
anātmanas tu śhatrutve vartetātmaiva śhatru-vat [6.6]

Most modern Gita readers, metropolitans place top position to sloka 5/6 as their favourite, as the most important verse of Bhagavat Gita. Others in general accord most significant verse tag to this verse after verse No 66/18.

In the simplest, literal meaning of these two verses, Krishna addresses Arjuna to say,

O Arjuna! You alone have to rescue your Atma, Self from the worldly bondage, birth-suffering-death cyclic snare. It is your lookout not to demote, debase your Atma, individual Spirit to lowlier, baser life, the vicious cycle of rebirth. You alone are your friend if you have controlled, mastered your *indriya*s. If you fail to discipline your *indriya*s, rein in your *indriya*s, reign upon your indriyas, you become your enemy, don't you?

It seems "you" have been given a free hand to deal with your acts, your life, your future, your fate, haven't you? Apparently, you should care for none as nobody is your friend or foe. You suffer or prosper due to your meritorious deeds or fail or lag behind due to your mediocratic methods or modus operandi. Your virtues or vices dictate your ascension or descension. More importantly, you alone are responsible to rescue or redeem your Atma from the painful, pathetic life on earth and rebirth. The onus lies on you to rise and fall, to pass and fail.

This is echoed in others' sayings and sermons. In the well-read poem "Invictus" by William Ernest Henley [1849-1903], the oft-quoted concluding lines assert,

"I am the master of my fate,

I am the captain of my soul."

Similarly, sings the famous 19th century American poet, Henry Wadsworth Longfellow [1807-1882] in "A Psalm of Life",

"In the world's broad field of battle,

In the bivouac of Life,

Be not like dumb, driven cattle!

Be a hero in the strife!"

Most people most often say that life is analogous to a battle. So does the popular poet H W Longfellow in his inimitable way. What he says more is that you be a hero, not

a hero-worshipper; you lead, not be led like dumb bovine herd driven by a whip or whistle. He advises,
"Let us, then, be up and doing,
With a heart for any fate; ***"
Neither Henly nor Henry deny God or His hand. But they exhort people to proceed positively on this worldly path of life.

FIFTY-SIX

From death row to kingship- possible?

The position, predicament of humans in saving them, redeeming them could be illustrated from a simple story.

Long, long ago, there was a king who had plentiful of everything mortals hanker for except for one, a son. His wishes and worships to be blessed with a son were all in vain. Finally, a crafty or knowledgeable fakir suggested to the king that the latter's queen would be begetting a boy, should the king offer the blood and bones of a young boy in the altar of Kali couched in a corner of the dense forest of his kingdom. He hopefully hinted about the long, windy, narrow path in the impregnable jungle to the seat of goddess Kali. The king was usually kindly to his subjects and was humane. He did not force parents to part with their son to sacrifice before the forest goddess in order to beget a son. He therefore declared that handsome compensation be paid to parents who volunteered to sacrificing their young son.

A poor person with a couple of children including 4/5 sons conspired with his wife to sacrifice their youngest 10-year-old son in lieu of the huge cash compensation. They heard people whispering that the benevolent and compassionate king would give them more in donations and gifts to ingratiate for the unprecedented voluntary sacrifice. The poor couple had 11/12 mouths to feed and their daily food need could hardly be met with all their assets and exertions. The compensation amount would be a dream come true for the poor family to eat, clothe happily for a couple months, even years. The poor young boy was made over to the king's courtiers and constables.

The boy was kept in safe confinement in the palace guest house till the next propitious Tuesday when he would be worshipped and sacrificed on the Devi's altar. The boy lived life king size, forgetting that in the recent past he did not have two square meals a day for many days and a hearty treat was never his luck back home all his life. Though he was well aware that his days were numbered, he did not grudge, grumble or groan for the inevitable, imminent end. On the contrary, he enjoyed his life with the newfound store of luxuries, believing, probably in the Longfellowian sermon, "***Let the dead Past bury its dead!

Act, - act in the living Present! ***"

The opportune moment of the appointed day arrived. The king in the company of a handful confidantes and escorts reached the goddesses' seat. Puja was performed by the priest with profound sincerity and serenity. The mantras chanted echoed the pristine forest corners. The boy dressed in new clothes, garlanded with fresh, scented flowers and vermillion mark in a string of sandal paste dots on the forehead, was sitting still except for murmuring a word or two here and there to the direction and dictation of the purohit. The butcher was a little away with a sharp, shinning sword that can sever the boy's supple neck by a single stroke.

Everything was right and ready. The purohit gestured to the butcher to raise the sword and severe the boy's head, when, suddenly but surprisingly, the king commanded,

"Purohit! Stop a while. Let us ask him of his last wish as is the ancient custom of this kingdom!"

To the statue like boy, he said softly and reassuringly,

"Beta! Tell freely and frankly what your last wish is. I must fulfil that desire of yours come what may."

The boy looked up unemotionally yet a bit happily and replied,

"What can I do with what you grant my most majestic monarch since in seconds hence I won't be there in this world? Yet to honour your honour's pleasure and piety, I ask that I may be provided with 4 small wooden toy houses right now."

Everyone was aghast and vexed. The king was moved by mountains of mercy at the thought that a lovely, young soul would be felled prematurely and preposterously to see his heir apparent arrive at the behest of goddess Kali. His sense of shame and sin sunk him in juxtaposition of his selfish, senseless desire. He decided that he would spare the boy should he so wish. But the boy is up to none of these. He ordered those 4 wooden toy houses be brought immediately. The boy was dismounted from the alter to a nearby enclosure to sit and do what he pleased to do with the quadruple wooden toy houses. Others inclusive of the king were anxious and expectant, while the boy sat non-plussed. Some moments marched on the highway of Time.

Toy houses brought, the boy picked up one, tossed it up 3 or 4 times fondly but flippantly. Then he smashed the toy to shreds.

Next, he lifted another, did likewise and broke it into pieces. Onlookers there looked at the spectacle without interfering in the frivolous deeds or unspoken words due definitely to the august presence of the king who maintained an austere silence.

The boy picked up the 3rd toy house, tossed it up and down 2 or 3 times as before. Then he looked at it a bit indignantly, yet smiled soberly, and smashed the toy.

Lastly, he lifted the last toy house, held it up in the cusp of his left palm, looked at it intently, smiled a bit gravely, maybe sanguinely, and then kept it aside carefully.

"My most merciful monarch! It is all over. I have nothing more to say or do or wish. Now it is as you wish!"

None, not excepting the king, made head or tale of the tale. Some thought it was simply a childish or even childlike ploy to buy some time. Some others fumbled about the mystery or myth lurking behind the scene. Still others imagined that the boy was an angel in disguise and his sacrificial death would bode disaster for the kingdom and the king. The purohit was readying to restart the paraphernalia from the interregnum. The boy awaited what the king would do or say. Breaking the stifling silence and stupendous stupefaction, the king queried calmly of the lad,

"O son! What was it all about? You could have wished anything and everything for your parents, siblings, yourself. You did nothing of the sort. Instead, and awkwardly, you asked for 4 wooden toy houses, tossed 3 of those up and about, then shattered those to shreds in sheer snobbery. In case of the $4^{th,}$ you seemed to be different, discriminating and discerning. I am afraid all of us adults who witnessed this your play played fools not to grasp a grain of the substance or significance of this. Will you please enlighten us?"

"No, my great king! There is nothing great or glossy about it. I was apprised of my imminent end when I was handed over to you. On the Devi's altar, I was composed and awaiting severance of my tender head anytime. In the nick of time, you interceded to grant me my last wish. What could I have wished for and why? Instead, it struck me how unprotected I had been when I could have been protected by all means."

"The 1st house stood for myself," the boy continued, "and I was entirely undone to save myself from premature death. So, I broke the 1st toy house as unworthy, useless."

"The 2nd stood for my parents who begotten me, brought up with difficulties and distress. But they surrendered me to death for some coins and comforts for them and their other children. Parents traditionally stake their lives to protect their son. In my case, you know what they did. Orphans and urchins have relatives and friends, neighbours and near and dear ones to protect them. I have some of them, so many of them in my vicinity, in my village, in this vast kingdom. But nobody volunteered to plead for me, protect me from the king's butcher.Nobody, nobody, made even a feeble attempt, a fanciful attempt to protect me from the king's claws, save me from death's jaws. Hence, I demolished the 2nd house with disgust."

The 3rd wooden toy house stood for the king, the sovereign of all his subjects, the saver, the rescuer of all subjects irrespective of their nativity, caste, creed, colour, calling. Here the king was the slayer of a simple, stupid, child subject to fulfil his dream, his goal of securing a son successor to his throne. Where does, therefore, the question of his saving a guiltless subject arise? I had to break the 3rd house which was as bad as, or even worse than, the other two."

The boy paused but to douse the emotion- charged, expectant hearers' excitement added,

"The 4th house signifies God. I wondered what God had in store for me. He is famed to have fended for all defenceless, destitute, distressed in their time of need and in the face of acute adversity. It looked everything was over for me. Even then, I could not dare to break the 4th wooden toy house that represents God since His ways are incomprehensible, inscrutable to humans and no one knows when and how He employs His means and manoeuvres to miracle escapes and exits from adversity, troubles, trepidations, death."

All the king's men [there obviously were not a single woman, not even the queen] were taken aback at the plain philosophical explanation of an apparently childish act or play. The king and his itinerary were delighted with the light that the boy threw upon them by breaking the lightly crafted wooden houses except one. The king was dismayed at his great guilt in planning to behead a young son's head for no fault of his and for petty gains of a son of his own. He repented and rebuked himself silently for having been morbidly selfish of the worst sort. He set the boy at large forthwith and, overtly overjoyed, held him in deep, passionate embrace. Needless to say, the boy was adopted by appropriate royal decree and declared publicly heir apparent to the marvel and mirth of the kingdom's subjects.

You can draw your conclusion on who saved the boy.

FIFTY-SEVEN

Everyone is conduit

Most readers and scholars of Bhagavat Gita may argue that the boy saved himself by his ingenuity and intelligence. Some others not unjustifiably credit the king with saving the boy from certain death, arguing inter alia, that his initial action in dragging the boy to the sacrificial altar was an excusable regal error. Others, not still others but most others including the two sets of readers and scholars referred to herein, will aver vehemently that God saved the boy. The boy, the king and others of his itinerary, were mere means, means to the end of God. None else can take any credit for their conduct, for everyone is a conduit.

FIFTY-EIGHT

He is Kaala- how cruel?

Are all of us conduits, more precisely, a conduit, nothing more? Don't we have anything of our own? We just carry, convey, conduct His will willingly or willy-nilly?

śhrī-bhagavān uvācha
kālo 'smi loka-kṣhaya-kṛit pravṛiddho
lokān samāhartum iha pravṛittaḥ
ṛite 'pi tvāṁ na bhaviṣhyanti sarve
ye 'vasthitāḥ pratyanīkeṣhu yodhāḥ [11.32]

tasmāt tvam uttiṣhṭha yaśho labhasva
jitvā śhatrūn bhuṅkṣhva rājyaṁ samṛiddham
mayaivaite nihatāḥ pūrvam eva
nimitta-mātraṁ bhava savya-sāchin [11.33]

Krishna says,

O Arjuna! I am Kaala, the terrible, tremendous, destructive Time. I am here to collect living beings by Death. If you desert the Pandava army, then even none in the opposite army would go back home alive, live in the future. Therefore, you rise, earn fame, enjoy the vast empire. These warriors in the opposite camp arrayed against you have all been Killed by Me beforehand. You just become a Means, Medium to that end, Savyasachi!

God, the Lord, is the cause of Death. Here we come across a very negative, usually unheard-of aspect of God, the Lord, that He is here to collect, herd the living beings through Death. In our scriptures and epics, puranas and postulates, Death is described as the act or attribute of Shiva, Mahadeva, Maheshwar. Of the topmost 3 gods, of the triumvirate- Brahma, Vishnu, Maheshwar- Maheshwar is the cause of dissolution. Maheshwar is the cause of wholesale, universal, inevitable dissolution, deluge as Brahma is the cause of Creation and Vishnu the cause of Sustenance. But here Krishna- Vishnu, God, the Lord- appropriates the cause, the case of Death to Himself. Of course, the triumvirate is in essence One and the One manifests in three forms or functions- is the belief, is the explanation by the sadhakas and seers, pundits and philosophers.

FIFTY-NINE

Yasoda, Akura, Arjuna- how do they compare?

There are arguments for the existence of God. Some impressive and speculative points are made by the erudite and theologians to prove their case. Perhaps none harp on the point -since there is Death, so there is God. God is, of course, death to the destructive demons, to the destabilising, devilish humans, inhuman dictators. It is well known or axiomatically believed. God is devoid of Death and Birth but He takes birth to save saintly souls from oppression and suffocating subjugation by the evil elements, doesn't He?

yadā yadā hi dharmasya glānir bhavati bhārata
abhyutthānam adharmasya tadātmānaṁ sṛijāmyaham [4.7]

paritrāṇāya sādhūnāṁ vināśhāya cha duṣhkṛitām
dharma-sansthāpanārthāya sambhavāmi yuge yuge [4.8]

O Bharata! When dharma wanes, slips, crashes and adharma ascends, rises, surges, then I create Myself to protect and rescue the good, the virtuous, the just, the righteous, the pious on the one hand and to crush, flush, fluster, flunk, flummox and finish the evil, uncivil, the devil, the vicious, tyrannous, unjust, unrighteous on the other. From time to time, I shall recreate Me to establish dharma.

Hence, as discussed in section 59, not Arjuna but He would kill the Kauravas and their cohorts and companions. Arjuna is His weapon, His pawn, His means, His medium, His conduit. He would kill the unjust, unrighteous, adharmic Kauravas and their kith and kin through/by/with Arjuna. Should Arjuna flee, not fight, no problem; they would be destroyed anyway on the very Kurukshetra battle field. Apparently, Arjuna would do to death the dozens and dozens of valiant warriors like Bhishma, Drona, Karna, Duryodhana, Dushasana et all; while, actually all of them would be vanquished and pulverised to dust by Him. No doubt, the mass and massive destruction of enemies of the Pandavas would be attributed to, actuated by Arjuna; but the Kaala, the Killer cosmos lurks behind every destruction, every death. What we do or is done to us is the reenactment of the Kaala, Kaala's cosmic play.

It is interesting that Arjuna sees the war and its outcome long before it happened. Arjuna saw, Arjuna saw, not the trailer but the premier show of the Mahabharata War, the Kurukshetra Battle. Arjuna saw, Arjuna saw Arjuna killing Bhishma in collusion with Sikhandi; Arjuna saw Arjuna raining inexhaustible arrows on exhausted, without-weapon and woefully-weeping Drona being hacked by Dhristadyumna; and Arjuna witnessed Arjuna reluctantly but vengefully lashing innumerable arrows on invincible Karna whose chariot was mired in a bloody muddy swamp and whose charioteer stood beside giggling instead of lending a helping hand.

Where did Arjuna see these scenes? Inside the

unfathomable depth of Krishna's mouth cavity, where else? No, it was not inside Krishna's wide-open mouth, belly or abdomen. It was the skyscape of Kala, Mahakala, Time. Of course, Krishna is the creator, cause, custodian, caretaker of Kaala, Mahakala, Time.

This Kaala kaleidoscope was shown 3 times to worthy 3 in Krishna avatar. Yashoda was the first to witness the cosmic, Kaala kaleidoscope inside infant Krishna's mouth cavity to find out whether the latter tasted and swallowed clay particles or pieces. She saw, she swooned, and she soon forgot what she had seen as if she saw nothing.

The second was Akura who saw the Kaala, cosmic kaleidoscope underwater while bathing in Yamuna river enroute Mathura. He saw and smiled; laughed at his foolishness of thinking that Krishna, Balarama gave him a slip from the chariot in fear of the ferocious Kamsa. But he kept the secret close to his chest to the best possible extent for the rest of his life.

Arjuna was the 3rd witness to the gargantuan, gory aspect of the Kaala kaleidoscope that was utterly unlike the ones seen by Yashoda and Akura. Arjuna was intimidated and frightened by the fierce, ferocious, fearful sights and scenes. Yashoda and Akura were witness to subtle, sweet aspects of the Krishna Cosmic spectrum and were shut from the scenery and stage-show before they could respond or react. In fact, they had nothing to react or respond. Arjuna, on the other hand, shivered and shuddered at the unheard, unseen, unread Cosmic Dimensions and Depths of his dearest friend, philosopher and guide, Keshava staring, scarring, sparring at him in the most unkindly and unlikely manner and manoeuvre.

SIXTY

Who is pious, who is *paapi*?

While dealing with "uddharedatmanam****[5/6]", we were drawn to "kaaloasmi lokakshayakrutpravruddho****[32/11]" to ascertain who rescued the boy in the story from Death.
That Krishna, the Cosmic Spirit, the Supreme Spirit, is Kaala, Death is alluded to in,

mṛityuḥ sarva-haraśh chāham udbhavaśh cha bhaviṣhyatām kīrtiḥ śhrīr vāk cha nārīṇāṁ smṛitir medhā dhṛitiḥ kṣhamā
[10.34]

O Arjuna! I am the all-remover, all-eliminator, all-destroyer, all-leveller- DEATH. I am what all will rise, arise, erupt and exist in future. I am the 7 lovely traits, characteristics, attributes-beauty, sweet voice, memory, intelligence, fortitude and forgiveness- of women.

So, God, the Lord, is Death; death the leveller, the equaliser, the remover of pain and pleasure, inequality and injustice, prejudice and perversion. Death is must to the powerful and the pusillanimous equally well and in equal measure. You cannot beat death; you cannot ditch death; you cannot dodge death; you cannot avoid death; you cannot evade death; you cannot defy death; you cannot falsify death because death is "sarvaharah". Mrutyu will take all, break all. In the verse cited from chapter 10, Krishna tells Arjuna that He is Death. In the next chapter Arjuna sees for himself the frightening, ferocious Death in Vishnu. Arjuna sees the all-remover, all-inclusive Death, the Death that draws all and the Death to which all join in the rat race, the mad race.

yathā nadīnāṁ bahavo 'mbu-vegāḥ
samudram evābhimukhā dravanti
tathā tavāmī nara-loka-vīrā
viśhanti vaktrāṇy abhivijvalanti [11.28]

yathā pradīptaṁ jvalanaṁ pataṅgā
viśhanti nāśhāya samṛiddha-vegāḥ
tathaiva nāśhāya viśhanti lokās
tavāpi vaktrāṇi samṛiddha-vegāḥ [11.29]

lelihyase grasamānaḥ samantā
l lokān samagrān vadanair jvaladbhiḥ
tejobhir āpūrya jagat samagraṁ
bhāsas tavogrāḥ pratapanti viṣhṇo[11.30]

O Krishna! I see creatures hurrying here and there for some time to meet, to mingle in You as streams and rivers run to meet the sea. As insects fly fast to blazing flames to burn themselves to Death, so do the valiant warriors are hurrying and entering Your burning mouths. O Vishnu! The terrible fire of your mouth spreads in all directions and burns, wipes the whole world.

Death is death-certain but certainly uncertain- in its coming, in its knocking, its breaking in, its barging in. That uncertainty about Death's certainty is the quiz and curio down the ages. To Yaksha's query what the most astonishing thing in this world is, the wisecrack Yudhishthira responded,
"Ahanyabhootani gacchantiha yamalayam
Sheshah sthavarmicchanti kimascharyamatah param"
[Mahabharata, Vana Parva, 313/116]

Yudhisthira implied that so many surprising events and actions take place daily. People often tend to be bizarre, bogus, abnormal, awesome and, thus, surprising, stunning. But the most wonderful thing about not only humans but all creatures, living beings is that irrespective of their respective knowledge that *they must die, they behave, act, as if they would not die.*

On death, let us waste a little of our breath. In the past when generally people were mostly poor but righteous and pious to the core, a group of labourers headed for a river-embankment earthwork a few kilometres off their village. They dug earth the whole day with a little lunchbreak and returned home in the evening. Since it was hot May, an unexpected thunderstorm accompanied by a heavy shower hindered their journey home. For fear of being drenched and catching cold, they took temporary shelter in a thatched house, school building at the end of the nearby village. They thought of resuming journey after rain and thunder ceased. But the rains lashed hard and heavy and, thunder and lightning roared and danced around the school campus incessantly. Cessation of rain and lightning was not in sight. On the contrary, fury of the shower and thunder intensified as night and darkness advanced. It seemed lightning would strike and engulf the thatched roof anytime, charring the 30 plus hapless inmates to ashes. They were accustomed to unseasonal, untimely thundershower and lightning in the hot summer days once a while in intervals. But those outpours arrived abruptly and stopped as quickly. This evening, they presumed, Indra, the god of rain and thunder, was bent upon punishing them.

They wondered who among them the culprit was that Indra willed to punish. Poor and innocent as they were, all of them were subject to the same kind of vices and wrongdoings like stealing green-leaves or a bunch of pumpkin flowers or half a dozen ladies-fingers out of curiosity, not animosity; out of attraction, not of greed. They criticised and backbit neighbours at times as a usual pastoral pastime or regular rural recreation, not out of envy or fault-finding, never with mens rea. So, who was the black sheep that thunder-god wish to punish?

Pondering the matter pensively for pretty long time they decided that one by one should go out to the open in the rain and stand for minutes. If lightning strikes him dead, it is well and good. He would die due to his sin and others be spared of Indra's anger to go home as the rain stops forthwith. The idea struck root as unequivocal, unanimous decision and one by one went out to face rain and lightning in the open in front of the wretched thatched school building. Each one was initially afraid of being lightning-struck for his small mischief or minimal misdeed. After standing for a few seconds when one was unscathed by lightning and thunder, he hurried to the safety of the thatched roof and was reassured that he was guiltless, no wonder. One by one went out and came back unhurt and unharmed. The remainder 4 or 5 wondered and looked at each other as to who of them the vicious sinner was.

By and by, all the labourer inmates except one drenched in the rain and came back unscathed. The thunder and rain were still raging intimidatingly, more intensely than initially. It was certain for the last one to think that he was the most vicious, worst sinner of the lot who now must face the music of the lightning god's wrath. That wretched rat was definitely better than the lot in being right, just and pious despite his abject poverty. Yet, who knows the ways of the gods? They punish for petty crimes and small mischiefs while closing eyes to hefty and heinous crimes, don't they?

The last man convinced of certain death punishment for his known or unknown crime or sin went out to the open. While others stood nearer the school building and for as short a period as possible, this fellow went away further from the thatched roof and stood longer awaiting nonchalantly lightning strike. And after some time, in the midst of deafening thunder and thrashing rains struck a terrible lightning! A terrible, blinding lightning with smashing rains and exploding thunder struck the thatched school building! Lo and behold! To the utter amazement and wonder, the school thatched roof was aflame and all his poor brother labourers were consumed clean by the enraged inferno.

SIXTY-ONE

Kaala- the killer of creatures

Death defies all calculations, all logic, all permutations and combinations, doesn't Death?

An umpteen-times told and retold puranic story is still more interesting, intriguing. Garud, the mount of Vishnu, as his wont, sat in front the sprawling palace of Vishnu in Vaikuntha. Yama arrived. To Garud's salutation, Yama responded courteously and proceeded towards the door. Just before entering, he saw something and smiled quizzically. Garud was annoyed and anxious. Yama's laugh was no good omen for living things. He wondered about what mortal stuff was thereabout. Finding none, he ran swiftly, detained Yama respectfully and enquired the cause of his laugh. Without hitch or half-truth, Yama indicated to a minuscule, tiny birdlike creature clutching to a corner of the door.

"What is a big deal about it, lord Yama? Once Vishnu graces, elephants to amoeba can find a place in Vaikuntha and enjoy the illimitable bliss and peace prevalent here."

"No, Garud! That is not the case. None, not even me can displace or demolish a creature here in Vaikuntha. In the eerie and awkward instant case here, this birdie is destined to die in minutes hence far, far away. I wonder how that could happen. But it must happen. It is not protected or promoted by Vishnu and its Kaala is complete to compel it die in just minutes from now. OK, I am late for Darshana and let me go."

Garud was taken aback. Such a tiny creature cannot escape death, the curse and course of Kaala even in the cocoon of Vaikuntha! Wasting no time, he rose swiftly and caught hold of the birdling carefully and flew. Garud flew innumerable kilometres before he embarked upon the summit of a sky-scrapping mountain, searched for and soon secured a small, hard rock cave, housed the birdie there and flew back. By the time Yama was out of Vishnu's chamber, Garud was there where he previously was. Yama looked at the spot the birdie perched and smiled again.

"You smiled again, my lord Yama?"

"Yes, Garud! I smiled because you put all your might to play in lifting the birdling from here, ensconcing safely it in the high Himalayan cave, assuming it would definitely be inaccessible to my couriers and carriers to reach there and kill the creature. You scarcely knew that that very spot was verily earmarked as its death spot by Kaala. A snake in hiding in that cave killed the birdling soon after you left. You cannot undo the prescription and providence by Kaala, Garud, can you? You cannot nor anyone else in your place. Not even me for that matter is any better in this matter. Can I do anything about it?" Not at all.

SIXTY-TWO

Do you act or made to act?

If, even the mightiest of the mighty, valiant warrior Arjuna is a mere means, a hapless pawn in the hands of, in the design of predetermined destiny, providence, fate, how can we "uddharadetmnanatmanam na atmanamavasadayet***?" [5/6]. How can we rescue our Atma, our Jivatma, our individual Spirit by ourselves, not degrade, devalue? It is breathing hot and cold in the same breath, isn't it? The erudite may reconcile the contradictory stands with irrefutable metaphysical reasoning, but what about the ignoramus whose cup of coffee is not speculative pedantry? To him it is easy and easily assimilable that he is a mere, nominal, nameless pawn in the grand design of things manufactured, monitored and mastered by God or by Kaala. He can therefore have no business in interfering with the scheme of things. He will not find fault in his wrongdoing nor appraise his so-called praiseworthy deed or decency. He will leave things to God. His motto will be,

"Tvaya Hrushikesha hrudisthiten yatha niyuktoasmi tatha karomi".

It is reverberating in 61/18, isn't it?

The wise do not act or advise unwise when they say

the onus lies on you to protect and promote your Individual Self, Spirit, the Jivatma by yourself. The Gita enjoins this upon you. Krishna calls upon Arjuna to act, work, perform his job not perfunctorily but consciously,

> sarva-karmāṇy api sadā kurvā ?mad-vyapāśhrayaḥ
> mat-prasādād avāpnoti śhāśhvataṁ padam avyayam[18.56]

> chetasā sarva-karmāṇi mayi sannyasya mat-paraḥ
> buddhi-yogam upāśhritya mach-chittaḥ satataṁ bhava [18.57]

O Arjuna! He who does all his duties always by taking refuge in Me, he shall be blessed by Me and shall get the ever-blissful place. You dedicate your duties to Me, submit yourself to Me, and act applying your mind, conscience with intellect in yoga.

It will therefore appear that there is no carte blanche to act according to your will, whim, fancy and caprice. You should remember that you are pawn, a piece in the grand design of things, in the inscrutable scheme of things. At the same time, you cannot escape your responsibility in the omission and commission of what you do; you cannot wash your hands clean of the faults and fallacies, your infirmities, your ignominies; because you are sentient; you are conscious; you are cognitive. Unlike other creatures, you are endowed with mind, mental faculty of judging right and wrong, just and unjust, piety and impiety.

Hence, in 5/6, the ball is in your court. You can play fair or foul. Naturally, you play free, frank, fair and fearless, when you submit to norms of the game, rules of the game. In most cases in that case, you win and lift the trophy, don't you? Though in the beginning, middle or end, you never cared or bothered about the trophy. You lift the winners' cup, because you have dedicated your play, your prowess, your proficiency, your skill and expertise to God.

Those who criticise the concept of *nishkama karma* [duty without minding outcome] as negative, pessimistic, unrealistic, fictional or imaginary are absolutely erroneous. They forget that Gita enjoins strenuous efforts. Gita exhorts to play and win. As here in 5/6, you play and possess the prize. You alone, none else, will secure the trophy for you.

And the game is not short or single; it is long and a series. False, faulty, foul play may win you a small, single, cheap trophy. On the other hand, fair, friendly, festive play with full confidence in yourself and total dedication to the Lord wins you trophies and prizes positively, as many as you can count.

SIXTY-THREE

Do sattvic win trophies?

When we speak so much about game, play, you may wonder what exactly we are heading for. You may wonder whether we have wandered into the blundering world of sports from the spiritual world of discourse on Bhagavat Gita. No, we have not blundered nor have wrongfully wandered in to the sports ground. We have stood our ground, the Gita ground, the spiritualism high-ground, haven't we?

We have, no doubt, talked of play and winning. We have talked of excellence in games and of unwavering adherence to the rule of the game, haven't we? We have spoken of winning the game and winning the trophy, haven't we?

When playing, one is aware of the prize, the trophy at stake. The more valuable, the more prestigious, the more praiseworthy the trophy at stake is, the more is the competition, the stiffer is the contest, the bitterer is the fight. And obviously, happier is the winner; richer becomes the winner; more popular becomes the winner; more dignified becomes the winner; more respectable, more powerful, more influencer becomes the winner. On the other hand, winner of a village level, local, school or college level tournament does not count much. Most people do not care for the winner or the loser there. The winner is forgotten as early as the loser. The trophy or cup gathers dust due to neglect and carelessness of the winner, what to speak of others. So, knowledge about the prize is paramount about the trophy. The more people know of a prestigious game or competition, the more are the participants, contestants, competitors. When more knowledgeable participants join the race, the brighter becomes the trophy. Imagine of an Olympic Games in Mars or Moon, do we care about those? Since we are ignorant of those Olympics, we care least for those, even though those Olympics might be mightily popular; more attractive, more cutthroat competitive than ours. It is the knowledge of Olympics that adds charm, chrome and fame to the games, their participants, their prizes, isn't it?

karmaṇaḥ sukṛitasyāhuḥ sāttvikaṁ nirmalaṁ phalam
rajasas tu phalaṁ duḥkham ajñānaṁ tamasaḥ phalam[14.16]

sattvāt sañjāyate jñānaṁ rajaso lobha eva cha
pramāda-mohau tamaso bhavato 'jñānam eva cha[14.17]

ūrdhvaṁ gachchhanti sattva-sthā madhye tiṣhṭhanti rājasāḥ
jaghanya-guṇa-vṛitti-sthā adho gachchhanti tāmasāḥ [14.18]

O Arjuna! The sattvic's actions are virtuous, truthful and honest. Hence, they reap pure, positive and praiseworthy results. The rajasic's activities end in failure, suffering and pain, whereas the tamasic kind of people land in ignorance due to their efforts, their acts. Whenever the sattvic work, they inter alia acquire knowledge. Whatever the sattvic do is enlightening, brightening. Whatever the rajasic do enhances their longing, greed, lust. What the tamasic do leads to delusion, attachment and ignorance. As such, due to their jobs and jest, the sattvic go up, while the rajasic hang midair. The tamasic, on account of their heinous and hateful vocation and vices, go down.

"Going up" is spoken of modestly for going up to heaven, paradise or the palace and parlour of Parameswara. "Going down" is the mild, kindly language for going to hell, for being deprived of human gene and genre for lives after lives, for eons and eons with intimate and intense pain, suffering and affliction of the acute, cruellest sort. The rajasic hang midair. They cannot go up nor fall down. Their struggles and strife, their trials and tribulations, their efforts and exertions continue unabated and unstopped but they do not succeed achieving what they will. Since they are active and positive, they do not fall. But their case, their predicament is pitiable, precarious. Their rise and fall hangs overhead like the sword of Damocles. They are hunted by the fear to fall anytime, all the time. At the same time, they are not hopeless, hapless. They cannot choose to fall nor are they forced to fall. They may fall, fall deep down to the hell. Nonetheless, they might improvise upon their curse and condition to rise up, up to the paradise.

SIXTY-FOUR

Uneasy lies the head that wears a crown

In the preceding section, we have compared rajasic's predicament to sword of Damocles. It will be worth our while to recount the high moral story to appreciate rajasic's agony well.

In ancient Greece, reigned Dionysius I. Damocles was a courtier excelling in exaggeration, flattery. He used to praise Dionysus I with flattery of the first order. The theme of his refrain was, "O monarch! Your majesty is really fortunate as a great person of power and authority that is greater than all his peers and competitors. And his highness was encircled by opulence, magnificence, munificence and popularity." The wise king did not take the overpraising kindly. He wanted to teach Damocles a lesson. So, he suggested that Damocles occupy his seat and him Damocles'. The latter was only too happy to role in the luxury and authority he was infatuated with so long.

Damocles sat in the ornate royal throne with embroidered rug laid out in front and on sides. Flowers and perfumes permeated the air and sweetened the atmosphere. Smart and swift-to-act attendants were there to carry out orders. But Dionysus ensured that a sharp sword hanged overhead. The pity was that the sword hung with a strand of a horsetail hair. It was likely to fall and pierce Damocles' head in the middle anytime with slightest touch, pressure, force or wind-movement. Damocles sat, sat for some time, with his attention constantly veering on the sword overhead. He could not sit comfortably or coolly, what to speak of enjoying the enormous power at his disposal. Each second, he imagined the sword falling straight on his head, piercing his skull and killing him instantly. Pitiably, he prayed the king to set him free from the peril.

The legend explains well the troubles and trepidations associated with power. Dionysus is stated to be very powerful as well as full of enemies. He could hardly enjoy the power, pelf, luxuries and facilities at his command as he was in constant fear of being deposed by his enemies who were many. We who struggle hard to own and enjoy need not forget that adversity, death hangs overhead like sword of Damocles. Never follow in the footsteps of Damocles to envy others' property, power, position.

This is equally well explained in Act III, Scene I of Shakespearean play, King Henry IV Part II, where the king himself says,

> "How many thousands of my poorest subjects
> Are at this hour asleep! - O sleep, O gentle sleep,
> Nature's soft nurse, how have I frighted thee,
> That thou no more wilt my eyelids down
> And sleep my senses in forgetfulness?
> Why rather, sleep, liest thou in smoky cribs?
> Upon uneasy pallets stretching thee,
> And husht with buzzing night-flies to thy slumber,
> Than in the perfumed chambers of the great,

Under the canopies of costly state,
And lull'd with sound of sweetest melody?
O thou dull god, why liest thou with the vile
In loathsome beds, and leavest the kingly couch
A watch-house or a common 'larum-bell?
Wilt thou upon the high and giddy mast
Seal up the ship-boy's eyes, and rock his brains
In cradle of the rude imperious surge,
And in the visitations of the winds,
Who take the ruffian billows by the top,
Curling their monstrous heads, and hanging them
With deafening clamour in the slippery shrouds,
That, with the hurly, death itself awakes? -
Canst thou, O partial sleep, give thy repose
To the wet sea-boy in an hour so rude;
And in the calmest and most stillest night
With all appliances and means to boot,
Deny it to a king? Then happy low, lie down!
Uneasy lies the head that wears a crown."

In this moving soliloquy, King Henry IV, old and ailing is awake late into night owing to rebellion in the kingdom and an irresponsible vagabond-like prince. Sleep is called 'nature's soft nurse' and is described to opt for the poor's filthy bed than kingly couch. While the 'low' lie happily, a king is deprived of, denied the privilege, the opportunity to sleep happily. The sea-boy could sleep, could be forced to sleep even for an hour in a turbulent sea voyage, risking death, whereas as a king like him could not have a wink of sleep even though his bed and bedroom are beautifully and bewitchingly furnished to induce instant and deep sleep. As Damocles felt constant and threatening fear under the sword, so a person wearing a crown, the king, the monarch is tormented restless and irate to sleep peacefully.

The Gita readers could decode from the above that the sattvic could sleep peacefully, happily, whereas the rajasic could not as they are disturbed and intimidated like king Henry IV or Damocles. Ensure sound, peaceful sleep and worship sleep 'the gentle sleep' and 'nature's soft nurse'. It is more useful and advisable to parents who deprive their young children 'gentle sleep', 'nature's soft nurse' in the abhorrent alibi of keeping them awake long hours to read and read...

SIXTY-FIVE

Even in sports, you have sattvic, rajasic and tamasic?

What we spoke of sports and play kind of playfully and sportively applies well, holds good to all other arenas and realms, worlds and spheres from agriculture to fishery, from sericulture to forestry, from entrepreneurship to entertainment industry, from scientific research to active politics, from spiritual discourse to space technology, from aeronautics to occultists. Fair play, holding hard and fast to rules of the game is the crux of the matter, is the mantra of success.

If the means is pure, unalloyed, right and pious, the end must be pure, lighting and delightful. If you set foot on the right path, you must reach your right destination. If you pursue the right, reasonable and intelligible course, you shall arrive at the aspirational venue. There is no shortcut to your goal, your destination. That should always be borne in mind.

The just and right- the sattvic- run their race and win the competition. The egoistic, crafty, cunning-the rajasic- run the race and lose. The sattvic participate in the event as a duty, as worthy contestant, aware of the aftermath of the competition. Since they give out their best in the best possible manner, they are expected to secure the best possible slot, the best possible position. The rajasic, on the other hand, jump on the bandwagon to win the race, to win the shield. They consider the cup important, not the game, the contestants. They disregard and envy others' skill, acumen and expertise unlike the sattvic who consider and care for the game; respect, not rue, the opponents. The rajasic seek the cup anyhow, by hook or crook, by means fair and foul. As a result, they scarcely succeed in securing the first position, the top position. If anyhow, through manipulation and machination, through manoeuvre and masquerading, they win; the win loses its sinews and shine soon. It is short-lived and not satisfying. It increases the craze for more prizes. It inflates the ego and infuriates future losses. It causes self-aggrandizement and illusion of being the "best", when, in reality, it is not the case.

The tamasic- the lazy, laggard, lousy- are averse, alien, unwilling to the game, its rules, its glory. And competition and winning. They lack in knowledge, zeal and skill. They do not bother about the race or the result; its rewards and reputation. They do not bother about other players or participants. Made to sprint or play, they sigh and while away!

SIXTY-SIX

Good and bad: He is all

We have arrived here from 5/6, uddharedatmanitmana****

If we extend this discussion a little further and in respect of games and sports, we will find the way to win and win in total righteous and just manner. What is that or how is that? By practice and perseverance. By adopting and adhering to the "Slow and steady wins the race" maxim. *Abhyasa, abhyasa is the crux of the matter. If we do not have adequate calibre for, commendable concentration on the discipline of the game or sport, what happens? We lack in consistency*; we suffer from sustained consistency. Our performance per force becomes as often failure as fluke or flash. To improvise consistency, to ensure concentration, and to sustain both; we should persevere and persist on abhyasa, practice, shouldn't we? Abhyasa improvises and empowers.

abhyāsa-yoga-yuktena chetasā nānya-gāminā
paramaṁ puruṣhaṁ divyaṁ yāti pārthānuchintayan [8.8]

O Partha! Through constant and contemplative practice coupled with single-minded devotion and without diversion and digression, one achieves the highest degree and kind of success, the divine attainments and Me, provided one keeps Me in mind all along, all through.

In the preceding verse, it is clearer,

tasmāt sarveṣhu kāleṣhu mām anusmara yudhya cha
mayyarpita-mano-buddhir mām evaiṣhyasyasanśhayam
[8.7]

[Therefore,] O Partha! At all times, always fight out, fight on bearing Me in mind. Those who fix their mind and intellect on Me must be as good as Me, must reach Me; there is no doubt about it.

Reaching the peak in the realm of your activity and attention is not unworthy but praiseworthy. To stand on the summit of your calling or curiosity is laudable, loveable. *The best begets best* in the best possible manner among the best number of humans. *Best is the manifestation of God*, of the Lord. The best, the excellent, represent, symbolise, signify God. Arjuna is told so in,

bījaṁ māṁ sarva-bhūtānāṁ viddhi pārtha sanātanam
buddhir buddhimatām asmi tejas tejasvinām aham [7.10]

balaṁ balavatāṁ chāhaṁ kāma-rāga-vivarjitam
dharmāviruddho bhūteṣhu kāmo 'smi bharatarṣhabha [7.11]

O Partha! I am the eternal seed of all creatures, all beings. I am the intelligence of the intellectuals and I am lustre of the lustrous. I am power of the powerful. I am the desireless, anger-less of the pious, *while I am the desire in the impious*.

That God is the guiding force of, that God guides, goads, and that God is the friend, philosopher and guide of the best, the excellent, the extraordinary, the most successful, is evident in,

dyūtaṁ chhalayatām asmi tejas tejasvinām aham
jayo 'smi vyavasāyo 'smi sattvaṁ sattvavatām aham [10.36]

Krishna tells Arjuna that in notorious and nefarious deals, He stands for dice. He is the strength and brilliance of the most brilliant and buoyant. He is victory of all fights and contests; He is the most illustrious and exemplary businessperson. He is truth of the truthful.

Good or bad- in all efforts, industry, exercises and enterprises- **God's grace and glamour glitters and is ingrained**. Business, industry, trade and commerce are human activity, God's activity. To excel and outrun others in industry, commerce, trade does not spring from, is not resultant of one or a group's hard work and honesty. **There is God's hand.** In fact, *that excellence, that illustrious eminence, is God Himself.* He who casts dice and wins invariably, outsmarting opponents miraculously is no less symbolic of God. It, of course, does not imply through any stretch of imagination that you should fall for power and pelf through unfair, false, fraudulent, foul methods, means or modus operandi.

The quickly, unfairly earned riches and resources wane and wither as quickly as gained. No pains, no gains- is axiomatic in trade, commerce and business. You explore new avenues, expand and extend your existing enterprises and investments and earn your profit, your wealth. *Do not extract from and exploit others.*

Krishna is victory. He is winning. When you are His show piece, you need have to, you should have to win. *Failure and frustration are not your fate.* The sattvic has to win and win. The rajasic wins less and fail more. The tamasic sigh and self-blame in frustration.

SIXTY-SEVEN

But friendship is a nobler thing
When I had money, money, O!

In 5/6, we are said to rescue ourselves, to improve ourselves, to enhance ourselves, to enlighten ourselves, to ennoble ourselves. On the other hand, we must not glide, slide, slip or slurry down the ladder, down the steps of the staircase to fall down to the pit, the abyss, the nadir, the nether. In short, we should try to, we must rise, surge and soar up and up till the peak, the summit, the zenith. In short, we have to make or mar, better or bar our career, our progress. Herein it is stressed that you alone are your friend as much as your enemy. Is it serious, sensible?

Friendship is eulogised eloquently in literature and lore, poetry and parables in all ages, in all societies and all civilisation. Friendship is our propensity and proclivity. William Cowper [1731-1800], the noted Augustan Age English poet says in shipwreck Alexander Selkirk's words,
"Society, Friendship, and Love
Divinely bestow'd upon man,
O, had I the wings of a dove,
How soon would I taste you again!"

Others equally laud friendship in lambast prose and pompous poetry. As Samuel Taylor Coleridge, the Romantic Era English poet [1772-1834] says, "Friendship is a sheltering tree." Aristotle[384-322BC], the Greek philosopher and high priest of scholarship and thoughts, is as spiritual as poetic to say, "A friend is one soul abiding in two bodies." Of buddies, Helen Adams Keller [1880-1968] happens to be profoundly poetic to utter, "I would rather walk with a friend in the dark than walk alone in light." Joseph Addison [1672-1719], English essayist, poet, playwright and politician, adds light and delight to friendship when he announces, "Friendship improves happiness and abates misery, by, the doubling of our joy, and dividing our grief." The great general and first President of the United States of America philosophises friendship by saying, "True friendship is a plant of slow growth."

Ancient authors and thinkers applaud friendship in glowing terms. Marcus Tullius Cicero [106-43 BC], the great Roman thinker said, "A friend is, as it were, second self." Francis Bacon bemoans, "Without friends the world is but wilderness."

The famous poem of the famed poet Henry Austin Dobson [1840-1921], captioned "Fame and Friendship", fantastically compares and contrasts camaraderie, cordial friendship with fame,

"Fame is a food that dead men eat,
I have no stomach for such meat.
In little light and narrow room,
They eat it in the silent tomb,
With no kind voice of comrade near
To bid the banquet be of cheer.

But friendship is a nobler thing.
Of friendship it is good to sing.
For truly, when a man shall end,
He lives in memory of his friend,
Who doth his better part recall,
And of his faults make funeral."

Nota Bene: The author may not be accused of gender bias and sex discrimination in using "man" and its possessive "his" to mean friend and friend's respectively. He means man and woman when he writes "man". *The attribute of a true friend in remembering good attitudes, achievements and attributes* and *"making funeral" of his/her faults, fallacies, frailties and failures is commendable* and *most noble characteristic* of a friend.

There is no dearth of false, feigned, camouflaged, fake friends and friendship. Kings and kingdoms, emperors and empires are steeped in the sacrifices and support of friends and are, at the same time, privy to the treachery and betrayal of ungrateful, roguish, wretched friends. The latter, no doubt, are wolves in sheep's skin, susceptible to shedding crocodile tears, horrible villains in well-clad well-wishers' coats. They are mean, motivated, malicious and malevolent to the maximum degree and dimension. They are a misnomer for friend, though in a friend's garb they are enemies hardcore.

A simple, pastoral tale tells a tell-all on friendship.

In ancient Odisha when the overseas traders and merchants made a mark in the annals of the empire by earning lots of wealth through maritime trading, there was one such maritime merchant [*soudagara*] who amassed fabulous wealth through fair and prudent trade deals, not fortuitous means. His only son was most unlike him, wasting his time, energy and money in the company of bad, vagabond companions. The *sadhava[*soudagara] couple tried hard to persuade their son to mend his ways and mind his father's profession and property. But their efforts were futile. On the contrary, the sadhava junior became more extravagant, wasteful and unmindful of parental advice and admonition. The sadhava apprehended that the boy might one day be apprehended in a gambling den or a bar or a brothel. He might, God forbid, one day commit or accomplice a murder in a fit of rage. While sadhava's savings were dwindling rapidly on the one hand on maintaining family, estates, workers, without incremental income; the fixed assets were diminishing to meet unavoidable expenses on the other hand. The son's lavish but loaferish day to day expenditure rose in inverse proportion to the family fortunes. The son was kind of looting the accumulated wealth to feed his friends wastefully in high parties and mad merry-makings. He bore all the expenses because he was a wealthy and reputed soudagara scion and because he was the emcee of the group and of the merriments.

One day the sadhava called his wife to conspire a prank to teach his straying son a suitable lesson. He called his most loyal servant and made him lie down like dead on the main doorway of the sprawling palace. As his wont for the past many months, the soudagara son returned late night from late-night party, heavily drunken and hopelessly sunken. He tottered inside, at the first instance but ,within minutes, looked back to see his parents sitting sullen, sunk and speechless. He could guess the body lying straight and shrouded to be one of his domestic helps, indubitably the most loyal one, attending to his parents' bidding day in and day out. Any other night, the junior soudagara might have gone his way to his bedroom to sleep and snore, disregarding his awaiting parents. But that night he was taken aback as his father was awake that late, that too at the doorway, and deeply dejected. *A son is a son after all.* He came to his senses too soon and asked his mother what the matter was. The mother remained sitting unmindfully and lamentably. After 2 or 3 persistent queries, his mom gestured feebly to ask his father. More politely, he pleaded with his father to disclose the problem that had perplexed him.

After some time, the father cleared his throat and said, almost sobbing, that for the first time in his long and honourable life he had committed a crime, a gruesome murder. He stopped abruptly, being chocked with dismay and depression. "Murder!" the boy jumped to his feet. He was astonished that his father, a doyen of the soudagaras and an embodiment of all virtues, could ever commit a crime, what to speak of murder.

His mother picked up the thread of the fictious narrative to tell that that evening their best domestic help delayed a little to serve his father's evening cup of milk. As ill luck would have it, the soudagara was enraged out of bounds and hurled a stout lathi nearby at the erring servant. The lathi struck straight on the servant's temple. The mortal blow blew out the servant's life-lamp, who groaned painfully and fell down dead like a housefly. The mother sobbed uncontrollably in perfect dissimulation.

"O, stop crying mom!" the youth consoled. Looking at his father, he asked, "What are we gonna do now, right now?"

The father said succinctly and in a low voice, "For you the whole universe is blank and barren now. I am old enough to mind spending my remnant years behind the bars, languishing in destitution and regretting the unintended single sorrowful crime. Your mom won't live a day without me beside her. The moment I am off to the prison, her life bird would be flown to the far-off blue sky. I am worried a prince like you would lead a pauper's life without a pie in his purse and abuses and insults strewn all his way!"

"Oh, stop dad for heaven's sake! Don't be worried for me if I beg, borrow or burgle to make my both ends meet when you are gone and gone are your prolific properties. I am worried for you. I am out of my wits at your predicament. Come what may, I must save you from the sentence of the crime, from imprisonment!" the junior soudagara spoke in a single breath and in rhythmic emotion.

Soudagara sounded a bit normal to say, "The present task is a bit difficult but achievable with the help of a few confidantes and trusted friends. For some years now I have severed all contacts with my half a dozen friends. Don't know how many of them are alive now…"

The youth interrupted to say, "Don't bother or count your friends! Tell me of the job the friends have gotta perform!"

The old soudagara said, "You know it is a murder and a murderer shall have to be hanged on conviction, if prosecution proved. The flicker of hope here is that the murder was committed in this our sprawling estate. Except for your mother and now you, none else would be in the know of this murder if the dead body removed from here to a long distance overnight and burnt to ashes untraceably.

Our neighbours scarcely know about the inmates of this aristocratic household. The deceased servant was a forlorn from a far-off place, who was picked up by chance but was looked after well as a family member. Nobody would search for him..."

The son interrupted, "Oh, for this small problem, you are unnerved, numb and dumb! The task at hand now is to remove the corpse out of the precincts of our bungalow before the crow caw or the chicken call. By the morrow, the neighbours would see the bungalow as bustling and bright as before without a scratch or trace that a murder was committed inside in the course of the night."

"Yea, that is that. Now it is your friends on whom hinges our fate and our estate. Go and get them in stealth and soon!"

The soudagara scion ran in haste and hoped to get 4 or 5 confidantes and comrades soon enough to get the job done in the nocturnal span with clinical precision so that the daylight lightens his father's misery and his worry. He knocked on one friend's door not because it came first his way but because he was his most cordial and confidential friend.

"Hey, you are here at this unlikeliest hour! What's the matter?" The friend queried in surprise and bother.

"I will tell you all enroute, wouldn't you accompany me as-is- where-is manner?" the soudagara son replied in the hastiest and highly-hopeful manner.

"Don't be stupid and blabber! Shouldn't I know wherefore I am required by the son of soudagara? Is the late-night appearance without rhyme or reason for the usual foolish fun to the whim of the wealthy merchant's son on which we poor fellows have the Hobson's choice?"

The soudagara's son stumbled on the high road of his belief and trust that the friends who feasted fat for fortnights and fortnights were at his beck and call. Keeping quiet a while, he narrated the whole unfortunate affair concerning his highly honourable father.

"Murder! Murder! Coldblooded, unprovoked manslaughter!" the friend exclaimed in terror and tremble.

The sadhava son put his palm on the shouting mouth of the friend to avoid being overheard in the vicinity and pleaded,

"Don't shout for heaven's sake to arouse and awake the asleep neighbours! I seek your help as a friend as you have sworn umpteen times to come to my rescue even at the risk of your life and reputation, haven't you? Did I commit a mistake to approach you in my family's hour of need? Did you say so under booze? What a soudagara's son needs of you people except some aid or advice in time of need that I may require once in a blue moon?" the sadhava son retorted in anguish and annoyance.

All the same, he did not cross his limits of courtesy and decency. The friend, on the other hand, was frank and forthright to denounce the haughty soudagara and the highhanded soudagara's son, and announced emphatically that he would not be a party to the manslaughter of an innocent, hapless fellow by the soudagara father-son duo.

From door to door of 5 friends, soudagara's son ran helter-skelter, ran in a hurry, though each nocturnal knock knocked the last flicker of his hope and belief. Each friend shouted in the worst unfriendly manner about the murder committed by his aristocratic, arrogant father, his fiendish farce to complicit the friends to carry away the corpse, burn the dead body to ashes and to be nabbed by the king's constabulary. The friends minced no words to abuse and offend the soudagara's son with inexpressible expletives for his hypocrisy and heinous dishonesty to send them to jail under the garb of friendship in lieu of some money he spent on them for fun, frolic and feasts.

The sadhava son, on the one hand, was shocked to his bones and unnerved to his brains and bowels at the unexpected tragedy lurking behind his father and the family and at the unimaginably unkind taunt and tirade by the so-called friends at his dire day on the other. Of false, fictitious, fair-weather friends he read, heard a lot, especially from his wise father and soft-spoken mother. But for the first time he saw such friends who sucked his geniality and gentlemanliness without cost or compunction. On the contrary, they belched and blew out poison and venom when sought, nay begged for their help, their hand. The warning words of W H Davis [1871-1940] echoed in his heart,

"When I had money, money, O!
I knew no joy till I went poor;
For many a false man as friend
Came knocking all day at my door."

He sped up fast and furious to reach home early and to report to his father about his miserable failure to find a friend in need. He was sure his witty and enterprising father would find a way out. As he sorrowfully spoke about his sordid, selfish, wolfish friends' reluctance to assist him in their adversity and awaited what his father would say, the senior soudagara sighed and said,

"If your friends on whom you have frittered your father's fortune and your precious time disappointed so dismally, what hope is there in my few, almost-forgotten friends? Nevertheless, like a drowning man catches at straw, we may try our luck with them, mayn't we?"

Then the father directed the son to get running to one of his father's friends living some hundred metres away. The son reached the address, knocked at the door and found an unacquainted frail old man come out and ask politely, "Who are you? Who are you searching for at such odd hour of a bad night?"

The sadhava son said soberly, "I am so and so, son of your old friend. Father had sent for you..."

The old man interrupted, "O, it is no time to listen the whole tragedy in full detail. I know your father pretty well, though for the last 40 years or so we had hardly met or exchanged old pleasantries. He is not prone to err in life, more so to commit a crime, that too manslaughter, Rama, Rama! OK, look up lest we should be late and the job on hand be undone or haphazard!"

On reaching the soudagara's grand palace, the old man patted his sobbing friend and started straight, "I know, I know for certain that you are not the fellow to commit such a cursed crime. It is providence, your providence that has caused it happen to cast a shadow on your unblemished character, untarnished image. OK, rise and lend a hand! We 3 could jolly well lift the corpse, carry it on shoulders and throw it away in a stream or ravine away from your imposing mansion. That too, through the night."

The old sadhava said superfluously, "Let us test him one last time if he is, God forbid, really dead!"

His friend looked askance and added, "God willing, he may be alive!"

As the sadhava pushed the servant a little sideways, he rose as if from some untimely, temporary sleep. The sadhava told his old-time friend the whole farce and the purpose behind it. The old comrade confirmed his unwavering trust in the soudagara who would not kill even a housefly, not even a flea or foul, fat rat, what to speak of a man. He commended the dramaturgical skill of the three characters performing their parts perfectly.

The junior sadhava cried in anguish and remorse for his wayward, wanton, wasteful life with his flattering, false, fair-weather friends despite the repeated persuasion and persistent admonition of his loving parents to desert the good-for-nothing, unworthy friends and their unrighteous, errant ways. "Better late than never", he uttered in relief and swore to abandon his selfish, libertine, exploiting friends then and there, to which his father's uncostly but in-need friend is witness. Needless to say, the soudagara's son acted accordingly thenceforth to become an enterprising, industrious, marine merchant of pervasive repute. Time transformed him to an illustrious son of an illustrious father in place of an errant, arrogant, extravagant adolescent and youth.

SIXTY-EIGHT

The Pardoner's Tale
Go to hell! O they were friends all!

So, we have no friends, no adversaries. We are our friend or foe, none else. Friends can be enemies and vice versa. Friendship is formal, ephemeral, time-space specific, conditional. This is best illustrated in the Pardoner's Tale in Geoffrey Chaucer's [1340-1400] immortal composition, "The Canterbury Tales" [1387].

There were 3 youths indulging infamously in vice, ribaldry, riot, gambling, dicing. They funded their extravagant eating, drinking and enviable lifestyle by robbing people in stews and public houses, feigning as musicians and dancers. One early morning, they sat down to drinking in an ale house and heard a barge. On enquiry, the barboy informed that a friend of theirs in the nearby village breathed his last, last night. Sad, they came out to see a fully wrapped old man. They asked the old fellow why he was alive that long while young men die. The old man told that was Death's discretion. The youths asked him to tell where Death was so that they could accost Him. The old man replied that Death was there under the distant tree. The 3 youths ran fast and were aghast to see 8 bushels of beautiful, glittering gold florins.

Blinded by the glittering gold, they were blind to bothering wherefrom the treasure came there. Robbers and looters that they habitually were, they sat down to hatch a plan to snatch the serendipitously found fortune. First of all, they decided to wait till night to take the treasure home in the town under the cover of darkness lest they should be seen, suspected and apprehended by the village folk. Agreed upon the idea, they rested beneath the tree, hiding the find fully. But soon they felt the pangs of hunger. It was therefore agreed again that one should go to the town to bring bread and bottle. By draw of lot, it was the youngest's lot to go to the town to obtain bread and wine.

While he was off, the foremost wicked who first chanced upon the fortune, parleyed with the other on a perilous proposal to divide the bounty between them two. The other wondered how what could, in all fairness, be partitioned among 3 be halved between them 2. The wickedest first suggested that the third on arrival be invited to a duel with the second. While they were wrestling, the first would stab in the back of the 3rd with his dagger. Since he could not wriggle out of the 2nd's clutch, the 1st would stealthily bring out the 2nd's dagger and stab again. The unprepared third would be done to death by the 2 dagger stabbings inflicted with premeditated planning and precision. The 2nd robber, obviously, succumbed to the lure of gold, to more gold begotten by getting away with the 3rd friend.

The 3rd was younger but no less shrewd or crafty or cruel. While on way to town, the glittering gold goaded him heart and soul. He pondered how to possess more of the booty, how to augment his 1/3rd share with more. He hit upon the idea of eliminating the other two and take home the heist alone. He ran as quickly as he could and first of all approached an apothecary. He asked the apothecary what poison the latter had have that could completely and quickly kill rodents and rats that ravished his granary, a wild cat that caused havoc to his chicken, and also the vermin that vexed him. The druggist assured that the poison he had had must kill the cursed creature within minutes. With the poison purchased, the lustful youngest robber went to the wineshop and purchased 3 bottles of wine. He carefully and skilfully mixed poison in the 2bottles meant for the 2 friends.

The 2 wicked miscreants awaiting the 3rd did not lose time to pounce upon him just on arrival. While the 3rd lay bleeding in a pool of blood and dead, the satanic first suggested to sit and enjoy their drink and food before burying the corpse. Thereafter, they would think of decamping and departing with the plentiful gold. The devilish 2 sat and drank, drank for the last time as the wine mingled with deadly poison did not take a wink's time to make the fallen fellows fall dead.

Greed, avarice and lust are lethal poison to your body, mind and soul. Have not we harped upon,

tri-vidhaṁ narakasyedaṁ dvāraṁ nāśhanam ātmanaḥ
kāmaḥ krodhas tathā lobhas tasmād etat trayaṁ tyajet

[16.21]

SIXTY-NINE

Pittuvani Ammayar and Vaigai flood
A Friend in need: the cool Coolie
Came all the way to Puri to be Witness

But we have our friends, or say, friend, don't we? In the venerable Bhagavat Gita Bhagwan Krishna has announced so succinctly, sufficiently in,

gatir bhartā prabhuḥ sākṣhī nivāsaḥ śharaṇaṁ suhṛit
prabhavaḥ pralayaḥ sthānaṁ nidhānaṁ bījam avyayam
[9.18]

O Arjuna! I am the Destination, the Husband, the Master, the Witness, the Dwelling, the Shelter, the bosom Friend, the Source/Origin, the Deluge, the Container, the Hidden Treasure, the Undecayed Seed.

How is He related to us? God is related to us, among others, as a bosom friend, the most trustworthy, true, fast friend. He is our friend in need and friend in deed. He cares for us, spares no chance or excuse to extend a helping hand, does He? We have spoken supra of saint, poet, bhakta Balarama Das of Puri, Odisha, who accompanied lord Jagannatha to steal jackfruit. While Balarama was beaten black and blue, the Lord bore the bloodstains on His image in the Sree Mandira. In fact, when Balarama was beaten, he felt no pain on his body but the Lord is said to have cried in the sanctum sanctorum of the grand temple.

Something similar occurred in the life of great Shaiva saint and poet Manikkavachakar, the famous 9th century godly person. The medieval Shaiva bhakta quadruplet consisting of Appar, Sundarar, Sambandar and Manikkavacakar are adored and followed by Indians, mainly south Indians, even today. They are as famous Shaiva saints as Jayadeva, Ramadas, Tulsidas, Kavir, Chaitanya, Mirabai are Vaishnava saints.

Born near Madurai, Manikkavacakar was deep Shiva devotee from early childhood. He alone, among his contemporary saints, was credited with miraculous and magic skills. He played pranks with the local king. On one occasion, the king was deftly duped by him in the matter of purchasing speedy, stout and beautiful steeds who fled the kings stable, turning out to heinous hyenas. The enraged king imprisoned him. While he was in jail, unseasonal, fierce floods came in the Vaigai river, breaching banks and inundating Madurai, the capital. King ordered immediate, war-footing repairs and reconstructions to save the town and the townspeople. To meet the instant and enormous labour force needs, the king conscripted engagement of at least one person from each and every house.

One old widow named Pittuvani Ammayar was also required to fill the conscription labour quota by herself or by a hired labourer on her behalf. She earned her living by selling *pittu*, a locally popular sweet cake made of rice powder, jaggery and scant spices and condiments. She was known locally by that cake pittuvani, the pittu maker. She could neither work herself due to old-age incapacity nor hire a local labour in her behalf for want of money to pay wage. Absence from free and forced, compulsory river-repairing work, entailed nothing less than death. She was pious and a staunch devotee of Lord Shiva. Imminent capital punishment terrified her. So, she cried pitiably, "O Lord! What shall I do? Do you want me to die for being poor and incapable of physical labour?"

At this time, a man with a spade slinging from his shoulder appeared serendipitously and called, "Grandma, O grandma! Do you need a coolie?"

"I need one. But I have no money to pay the coolie in wages." The old widow answered in half hope and half frustration.

"Why and where does money come? You are renowned for sweet cakes. You give me some pittu and I will work for you in embankment filling" suggested the strange workman. Then he added, "Why late?"

"No late dear! I am making cakes. Just wait for a few minutes and eat pittu to your heart's content."

The old widow was amazed at the happy turn of events and sat to make cakes. Astonishingly, the cakes were deformed and half-formed despite her widely appreciated expertise, dexterous preparation and cordial care. The Lord incognito ate the half-baked, half-roasted cakes and cheered the "grandma" with wow, wow. The strange labourer ate cakes to his heart's fill, bade goodnight, saying, "Grandma! I am hurrying to Vaigai bank lest I should be late. Fare you well and take care!"

The old woman wondered whether the broken, bits

of the cakes were really tasty or the affectionate handsome youth flattered her to please her despite her unusual failure in cake-making calibre that night. Her astonishment was accentuated to see that the dough did not diminish diminutively even after she made dozens and dozens of cakes.

The coolie in disguise went near the embankment but slept soundly and snored noisily near the spot demarcated for Pittu Ammayar. The king overseeing the work progress himself saw none on the old woman's slot. Irritated, the king queried of the Amma's absence from his servant. The servant gestured at the hired labourer who slept and snored instead of digging soil or bridging breaches on the embankment.

By then, the camouflaged coolie, woken up, was singing a tone. The king thundered, "Bloody beast! Instead of working, you are singing!"

And he started raining harsh lashes on the labourer. Lo and behold! The unusual and amusing scene! Not only all workmen there but even the king writhed in excruciating pain by the canning done by the king. The strange labourer was all smiles as his wont. The king was quick to his wits that the awkward stranger was certainly a god incarnate. But as he looked around to prostrate before the godly labourer, he was utterly disappointed to see him disappear into thin air. No gainsay, soon and rapidly the Vaigai spate subsided to the normal level.

Didn't the hapless old widow have a friend? Instances of the Lord assisting and rendering yeoman's service to the people as bosom friend overflow literature and folklore, fairy tales and telltale legends.

If this is about His friendship, friendly act, what about His becoming Witness?

We have talked of supra, Lord Raghunatha attesting in the court of law as an eye Witness to debt repayment by the rustic poor peasant. Another interesting, intriguing story in this regard will be worth reproducing.

A religious, rich Puri brahmin went on pilgrimage to Vrindavan. In those days, there were no communication means except bullock carts or horseback. Those were costly and inconvenient. Besides, pilgrimage to Vrindavan, Varanasi, Badrinath, Prayag or Gaya demanded taking the long and, at times, hazardous journey on foot. "No pains, no gains" was the maxim of the times, especially in religious affairs. The rich brahmin set out on his long pilgrimage with a servant to assist and attend to him enroute. The faithful helping hand did not fail in his regular, personal service to the brahmin. They reached Vrindavan and paid their humble, honest homage to the gods and goddesses and, of course, the presiding deity Gopal.

They were about to undertake their return journey when, suddenly, the brahmin fell ill. He suffered from dehydration, dysentcry and diarrhoea. The lingering illness compelled the brahmin to overstay some more days. The servant served his master with the best possible care to ensure the master's complete cure. During his illness, the brahmin realised that the young servant served him day and night like a nurse or mother, sans minding he might be contacted with the deadly diarrhoea. So, once the brahmin announced that he would marry off his daughter to the servant in token of gratitude. They set off homewards after the brahmin recovered fully to take the foot journey.

Back home at Puri, the brahmin did not bother marrying his daughter to the servant despite the servant's polite and persistent request. On the contrary, he pooh-poohed the marriage proposal, ridiculing the poor servant's aspiration as sky flower. The servant brought the matter to the king's court not because he was infatuated with the exceedingly beautiful brahmin girl but because he did not take the brahmin's denial lightly. Truth must be honoured at any cost was the popular social prescription of the time. How can a holy and learned brahmin retract his promise, deny the truth? --was what agitated and rankled the servant.

Puri Gajapati called his council. The servant told the tale from A to Z without an inkling of untruth or embellishment. The brahmin admitted the whole narrative except that he never promised his daughter's hand to the unworthy, poor servant. He added that he had handsomely remunerated and rewarded the servant for his service throughout the pilgrimage and the Vrindavan sojourn as well, not neglecting or ignoring the servant's yeoman's service during illness. The counsellors and onlookers were caught between two horns of a dilemma. The faithful servant's report aroused no suspicion except the part the brahmin denied. In social, cultural and economic considerations, the brahmin and the servant were poles apart. No sensible person, not even a senile one, would imagine that the high caste, affluent, pundit brahmin had promised his daughter's hand to a low caste, illiterate, destitute.

The Gajapati could not make head or tail of the matter. After pondering for some time, he asked to the servant, "Who has seen or heard the brahmin promise offering his daughter's hand to you?"

The servant was crestfallen. Who would be there to hear the brahmin uttering giving his daughter's hand in the secluded, deserted lodge when the brahmin was dying daily due to diarrhoea? – he thought to himself. Truthful that he was, deeply pious that he was, convinced that he was that God Gopal of Vrindavan like all gods see and hear all we do and speak, he spoke softly but clearly, "*Manima*! It was in Vrindavan when the brahmin was bedridden and almost dying. I was nursing and nurturing him to the best possible extent without any hope or hesitation but with haste and honesty. Pleased with me for the commendable service, the brahmin promised when we two were alone."

"You may be credible but jurisprudence demands that your statement and summary be attested by witness. Without corroborating evidence, your testimony is unreliable, unacceptable. Think again! Have any witness?", the Gajapati commented.

"There is one witness, *Chhamu*! Only one witness", the servant said soberly.

Everybody looked askance. But the king queried, "Who is he?"

"Lord Gopal! My lord!" the servant quipped.

"Do you mean the Lord of Vrindavan?"

"Yea, Manima! He alone was witness to our dialogue in whispers in far off Vrindavan."

Astonished, the Gajapati asked, "Can he be here to adduce evidence?"

"Why not?" the naïve replied sincerely.

"Then go and get Him! Till then, the adjudication is adjourned."

Hopeful and happy, the servant ran toward Vrindavan in a steed's speed and reached the temple. With tears rolling down his cheeks, he prayed to Gopal silently but from the bottom of his heart, "O Lord! You alone have heard the brahmin swearing to marry off his daughter to me. I did not ask for it in the first place for all my efficient and affectionate personal service to him when he was lying on bed on the daily-dying queue due to diarrhoea. What have I not done? From wiping and washing his faecal excretions on bed to frequent stinking urine that morphed the dingy cell of the solitary lodge a veritable hell. Unsolicited, he proclaimed pairing his daughter with me but presently denies flatly that he had ever sworn anything at Vrindavan. Krishna, Krishna! It is horrible, unholy and since he is a high caste, honourable brahmin, he must go to hell. The wise Gajapati has erred in his judgement by ordering to produce my witness. Will you not go to tender evidence?"

He stopped a while as if awaiting an affirmative answer. He was sobbing, though tears running on his cheeks dried up and glistened.

"Yes, I shall go," he heard Gopal comforting him quickly and clearly. He was overjoyed and turned his back to dash back home but asked in absolute silence, "You are not seen or heard. How can I see you accompanying me to Puri?"

The ethereal voice replied, "I shall follow you close to your heels. You shall be my path-finder. You walk ahead and I follow suit. To make my presence perceptible, I wear a pair of anklets that jingles softly but audibly. But mind it! Once you look behind, the jingling stops and I stop going!"

"Yea," nodded the servant in grateful agreement and exited out of the temple precincts. To his inexplicable delight, he heard sweet, soft anklets' jingling just behind him. He never looked back or around to see Gopal following him lest he should breach the agreement and Gopal be off. As far as Puri, they came together, the anklets' jingling confirming Gopal following. 15 KMs to Puri, the sound was lost for some minutes when the servant was treading on the quicksand Bhargavi river sands. For the first time doubting Gopal's caution, he looked back.

Lovely Gopal whispered, "You breached the agreement to look back. So, I stop proceeding further."

The servant wept bitterly and cursed himself inchoately and incessantly. Sad and sobbing, he reached home. The news of the servant's arrival spread like wild fire in the town. People talked and joked about his witness, that too Gopal. It was incumbent upon him to report to the Gajapati about his fault and failure in adducing Lord Gopal as witness. The night before, Gajapati dreamt about the whole incident. He was counselled to build a temple there to house Lord Gopal permanently. As soon as the royal council assembled and the servant opened his mouth to speak, the Gajapati descended from his throne, embraced the servant with affection and awe. The servant was seated comfortably and respectfully. The Gajapati recounted the dream with celestial excitement. He ordered the brahmin to offer his daughter as wife to the servant as promised. He also took steps to construct a temple on the spot where Lord Gopal turned a statue. Gopal here is deified as Gopinatha.

The small, holy town, the seat of Lord Gopinatha, is called Sakshi Gopal, meaning Gopal, the Witness. The other name of the pilgrim town is Satyavadi, meaning speaker of the truth.

SEVENTY

Kavir and Kamal
father and son- saint or thief?

God, the Lord, Krishna is the Witness, the Eyewitness of everybody, everything, every action, everywhere, every time. If you can witness this with your eye, your wits, and then without eye, without wits, you are the Jnani, the Seer, the Sadhaka, the Sannyasi. Krishna tells Arjuna that He is there everywhere, all the time witnessing everything said and done or unsaid or done. In a very philosophical, paradoxical verse, it is stated thus,

puruṣhaḥ prakṛiti-stho hi bhuṅkte prakṛiti-jān guṇān
kāraṇaṁ guṇa-saṅgo 'sya sad-asad-yoni-janmasu [13.22]

upadraṣhṭānumantā cha bhartā bhoktā maheśhvaraḥ
paramātmeti chāpy ukto dehe 'smin puruṣhaḥ paraḥ [13.23]

O Arjuna! Purusha, the Individual Spirit, coexists in the body with Prakriti, the perishable entity, experiencing good and bad, pleasure and pain due to *gunas*. The gunas factor and affect Purusha due to breeding in higher or lower levels of creation. The Purusha is quizzically separate from Prakriti. It witnesses Prakriti activities and attitudes from too very close quarters, and consents to, concurs in the Prakriti actions and orientations. He is the Nurturer, Sustainer as well Enjoyer, Experiencer of Prakriti effected deeds and demeanours. He is the Maheshwar, great Ishvara. He is called, styled Paramatma. Nonetheless, in the body, He is total stranger, rank outsider.

About God's abode, about God's dwelling inside us, there are plethoric scriptural perceptive. We may like to quote Kavir here to assimilate the truth from the lucid lyric of the saint sui generis, Kavir. The verse runs like this:

Moko kahan dhundhere bande Main to tere paas mein
Na teerth mein, na moorat mein na ekant niwas mein
Na Main jap mein, na Main tap mein na Main barat upaas mein
Na Main kiriya karma mein rehtanahin yog sanyas mein.

O people! Where are you searching for Me? I am near you. I am not there in pilgrimage sites nor in idols nor in solitude. I am not in Japa nor Tapa nor in austere fasting and worshipping. I do not reside in activities nor in yoga nor in sannyasa. Kavir clears one's doubt about God's whereabouts, doesn't he? But we poor fellows searching Him in all unlikely places and practices, don't we?

Of the Lord, God's being witness, we discussed in the preceding section. A little more discussion in this respect is not unwarranted. The story is like this.

A man was exceedingly expert in stealing, thieving, especially at night. He trained his son in the art and technique of thieving to the best possible extent. Like father, like son—the son acquired the methods and manoeuvres of breaking into houses in hush, sneaking into bedrooms even when couples were cracking jokes and whispering amorous rubbish or erotic trifles, and could loot and lift objects and articles even when all inmates of the whole family were debating serious affairs or tasty trivia. So far, of course, the son accompanied the father to witness and appreciate field demonstration of the calibre and competence of his father's thievery.

After some months, the father confided in the son that the latter had excelled in the nitty-gritty, niceties and nuances of thievery and had acquired such fantastic finesse as the former could not master so long. The son was therefore eligible to break into and burgle independently. As one last caution and counsel, the father said, "See that you are not seen or caught by the inmates or neighbours or anybody else for that matter." The son nodded in agreement and broke into a house while the father hid himself in the dark nearby. The son sneaked into the house stealthily, burgled valuables and jewellery while the inmates were fast asleep and was about to come out through the dug-hole he made. Abruptly, he changed his mind, slipped back into the house, put the theft articles in the chests and containers as-is-where-is and exited quietly.

The father who saw things from some distance wondered what made the son to make a successful errand flop. On return and on way home, father asked, "Did anyone notice you break in or burgling?"

"No."

"Did you not get anything?"

"No."

"Did any inmate catch hold of you?"

"No."

"Then why did you return emptyhanded?"

"Because even in the pitch dark when all inmates were fast asleep and I collected all valuables adeptly and there was no noise outside nor were neighbours awake, I realised one did see all I did."

"Who?" the father asked at once and anxiously.

The son indicated upwards to heaven and said, "Father! HE sees everything everywhere even in pitch darkness and, alas! without anybody's knowing or imagining!"

Had the thief's son read Bhagavat Gita, he would have said, "Father, He saw me breaking in, stealing, packing and decamping in the break-in-hole from closest proximity; from the farthest Point Nemo; from North, from South, from East, from West; from up from the apogee as from HD1; from below Tau Tona Mine, farther below Kola Superdeep Borehole; from inside me, from inside my eyes, from my bowels, from my brain, from my being, my whole being..."

The thief father-son duo may be duly disliked, no loathed, though the son was transformed to a saint in course of the thieving act. The father may have followed suit. But there are cases of mindboggling thefts and you are commodiously constrained to hate them a whit.

Here is another instance of thief-turned-saint father-son duo whose legend is told by Maharshi Raman.

The Banaras-based popular poet, superior saint, Kavir was a committed Rama bhakta and spent most of his time chanting Rama Nama or reciting lyrics eulogising and glorifying Rama. He wasted no opportunity to honour and serve participants of Rama Samkirttana and listeners of Rama katha. He considered it the luckiest virtue to feed Rama

Samkirttana congregations. Aware of his Rama Nama mania, people gathered near his house and organised Samkirttana often. Kavir squandered his earnings and savings in feeding the congregations. His son, Kamal, was equally saintly and Rama bhakta to assist and advise his father in these matters.

Daylong Samkirttana breaks for the evening Alati and long rows of participants enjoyed partaking a hearty modest meal before breaking off for the day. Father and son were so immersed in Samkirttana and more so in feeding the people that they did not care for the stock and store of grains and ration. One evening after the day's chanting and eating were over, they were dismayed that the store was depleted to the last grain. They had already borrowed a lot in cash and kind from different sources very much like indulgent, extravagant bhaktas, without thinking over ever about extra income or curtailing the recurring expenditure on this count. The charities that came their way for this purpose purportedly fell far short. They worried that no more borrowing of money or groceries could be possible at short notice to ensure next day's feast of Samkirttana troupe. Since there was no other alternative, they decided to burgle the local grocer's store that very night to procure provisioning for next-day's ensemble eating.

As planned beforehand and threadbare, Kamal hole-breached the wall and entered the grocery granary. He picked and lifted packets and bags of rice, wheat, dal, jaggery, spices, condiments, potatoes etc, and dispatched the bags, packets, pouches, satchels through the hole deftly. Kavir gathered the stolen goods aside safely and systematically with a view to carrying those home when Kamal came out.

The father-son duo completed the theft neatly like

professional thieves and hardened criminals. After pushing out the groceries, Kamal was coming out through the wall-hole when the house-owner awoke and caught hold of Kamal's legs stretching in the dark room. The body from waist upwards was out and rest remained inside the house and in the firm grip of the grocer. Struggling in vain, he could not unfasten or loosen the grocer's vice-like grip. Kavir dragged away son's head and shoulders with all his strength but in vain. Kamal could not edge an inch outward. It was more than certain that the duo be caught thieving red handed.

Kavir was panicked that the loving son be subject to severe punishment for criminal theft. Kamal was pained that father's prestige and popularity be pulverised for this unprofessional misappropriation of grocer's property. Hence, he whispered, "Father, don't delay a whit! Bring the axe there and decapitate my head. Then you run away under the cover of darkness with my severed head and all groceries. Let the grocer keep my torso and do what he likes with it. Nobody with any expertise or ingenuity can identify a person from the torso, more so of mine. Please haste and act accordingly!"

Kavir, dumbfounded at the abrupt striking of unexpected disaster, trembled in the fear of losing his only worthy son in such fateful tragedy on the one hand or being apprehended and punished severely by royal decree for burglary on the other. It was catch-22 predicament. Any procrastination would precipitate the danger and drumbeat the public outcry that would decry his repute and respectability. Kamal was wiser in suggesting escaping the imminent ignominy for good. Since the duo committed the incriminating act for a good cause, they should not regret. And the sacrificing of the son for the pleasure of Rama bhaktas was ostensibly the salvation certitude.

Denuded of his dilemma and depression quickly, Kavir rose to the occasion. He dismembered Kamal's head and decamped with the loot groceries and the dear son's blood-soaked head properly wrapped, stealthily and skilfully. Next day's Samkirttana went on well on the one hand and the Prasada preparation was in full swing on the other. As is the custom, the Samkirttana troupe perambulated the village before eating Prasada and getting dispersed. That evening during perambulation, the serendipitous event occurred.

The grocer there dragged the torso inside and was aghast at the ghastly sight of the torso. He reported the matter to the king who, as usual, proclaimed to the public to identify the torso. People thronged to see the horrible spectacle but none identified nor owned up the torso. Kavir went up his daily chore, ignoring the macabre incident and attendant hullabaloo. The king, bent upon apprehending the culprit[s], devised a way. He directed the grocer to sling the beheaded body from a streetside pole on the intersection of prominent paths of the place with a view to emotionally pressurising relatives of the torso to come forward and claim the corpse for cremation. To his direction, the grocer deployed guards to frighten and flyaway avian carnivores like eagles, ravens and hawks on preying upon the slung cadaver.

When the chanting chorus passed the pole with loud clapping and chanting enthusiastically and excitedly, "Rama, Rama, Jaya Rama, Jaya Rama…" the torso clapped and joined the chorus, chanting and hailing Rama with equal lively and celestial elan. Kamal whose idee fixe was Rama, whose obsession was Rama and who was possessed by Rama from infancy, could not resist chanting Rama Nama with the hilarious humongous crowd crying "Jai Rama, Jai Sriram.."Rama Nama was the agent provocateur to enliven a dead torso. Alternatively, he who sings and chants Rama Nama regularly, religiously cannot die whether you hack his head or chop his hands and feet, liver and limbs. The onlookers and troupers, at first sight, fled in awe and shock at the unnatural happening. They later mustered courage to gather near the pole and chanted encore "Hail Rama, Hail Rama..." more. The torso chimed with the chorus coherently and well. The matter was swiftly reported to the king who arrived at once for on-the-spot assessment. He was bewildered and bothered about who the fellow could be.

All that day long, Kamal was conspicuous by his absence in the Samkirttana. The participants missed him but were neither serious nor in any need of him to bother about his absence. As the chanting continued, first the chorus ensemble and then neighbours and locals, all acquainted with Kamal's voice, whispered that that was Kamal's torso. The buzz reached the king's ears who sent for Kavir. Truthful that he was, Kavir identified Kamal's torso and confessed of the burglary in its entirety. At the king's command, the hewn head was brought out from Kavir's hideout and fixed carefully on top of the torso.

To the amazement and applaud of the curious and praying conglomerate, Kamal clapped hands and hollered "Jai Sriram, Jai Sriram" in unison with the congregation and onlookers. A sorrowful Kavir embraced Kamal with tears streaming from his eyes. Kamal chanted "Rama, Rama..." hilariously with tears of joy glistening on his cheeks. The king, elated with the unprecedented events, exonerated the father-son duo of trespass, burglary, trampling with evidence etc of all criminal charges as a special case that should not be cited as a precedent in future in any similar case.

SEVENTY-ONE

Saga and story of Konark sacrificing son for clan. After you the deluge, Munja?

In the context of sacrificing son for a noble cause, great social cause, the saga of Vishu Maharana comes to mind. The Konark Sun Temple, otherwise and notably called the Black Pagoda, flashes across one's mind. Narasingha Dev I, descendant of the illustrious Eastern Ganga dynasty, ruling Kalinga, the then Odisha, between 1238 AD and 1264 AD, built this massive, majestic temple as a memento of his magnificent, monarchical manoeuvres in military expeditions, public affairs and immortal love story. The architectural, sculptural, masonry marvel that is Konark is a stupendous stone structure on shore sands of Bay of Bengal at a distance of 35 kms from Puri, Odisha. Narasingha Deva I, dashed the Delhi Sultanate's eastward expansionist arrogance by inflicting a crushing defeat on the Turk-Afghan forces in 1243 AD. To perpetuate the Kalingan warriors' valour to posterity, he constructed the Konark temple on the mouth of Chandrabhaga river meeting the sea, in 1250 AD. The flatteringly beautiful spot chosen for the temple is believed to be the site where Shamba, a son of Krishna, seated on Sun-worship and was cured of incurable leprosy. An old shrine dedicated to Sun is said to have stood there in disrepair and dilapidation.

Another legend says that the corpse of princess Maya of upstream Shishupal Gada was found here by monarch Narasingha Deva I. Prince Narasingha in chance encounter with Maya was enamoured instantly and enormously by the latter's captivating grace and mesmerising charms. The youthful prince truthfully swore to marry the princess by persuading his father who, unfortunately, betrothed the prince to the Parmar beauty, Sita Devi, in his absence. Discontented but not disobedient to father, monarch Ananga Bhima Deva III, Narasingha Deva failed in life-partnering princess Maya. On hearing Narasingha Deva's marriage, Maya Devi's health melted down like a candle or pot of butter. She stoutly refused to marry any other prince who were not unobtainable. Narasingha Deva's unexpected, unfortunate though unintended betrayal, told upon her health. And it deteriorated day by day despite all studious and sincere efforts of the Shishupal Gada royal physician and other physicians requisitioned from the kingdom and outside. Narasingha Deva succeeded as Kalinga monarch and was engaged in brisk business of the empire including thwarting annexationist onslaughts by neighbouring kings and monarchs in general and Afghan invaders in particular. Nevertheless, he never forgot Maya, and, at times, was tormented intolerably at heart and mind when Maya appeared like a mirage in vast desolate desert of his mind. As a matter of fact, the momentary Maya mirage was verily a verdant oasis in his mind's Tundra, heart's Sahara desert.

Once he heard about Maya's morbid malaise, he rushed to Shishupal Gada with Sita Devi. The monarch couple spent quite some time there, took best personal care, engaged renowned physicians. Sita Devi even suggested to Maya to become the monarch's queen on the altar and in right regal matrimonial paraphernalia. Maya was moved by Sita Devi's unimaginable magnanimity and cordiality. She was overjoyed with the monarch's endearing and enduring love the lustre of which was not dimmed a dot by then, though he was happily wedded to a deserving princess. Maya was overwhelmed with the couple's care and cordiality, especially when the monarch staked his all to see her recover spectacularly and speedily. She realised for the first time and on facts of her own case that fate, fate alone, finalises the course and discourse of our lives, our ups and downs, our twists and turns, our trials and tribulations. Only because fate did not will so, she was not fettered to Narasingha Deva in wedlock. She would have been happy and honoured to live as Narasingha Deva's paramour or as queen alongside Sita Devi in the Kalinga castle, had fate not snapped her life short. Notwithstanding all odds on the path of her life, Maya devi died the happiest death in the laps of the monarch couple.

The monarch couple mourned her death inconsolably and performed the cemeterial ceremonies and obsequies with all honour and dignity. Sita Devi ensured that Maya was cremated as the deceased queen of the monarch. After the obituary paraphernalia were over, the monarch entrusted Shishupala Gada day to day governance to trusted and capable generals and counsellors and left for his capital. He wrapped Maya's ashes, some of her favourite ornaments in a red cloth and put it in a small wooden casket, and set it afloat on the nearby river so that the remains shall mingle in the holy sea.

Away from Shishupal Gada, the monarch almost unwillingly forgot the whole episode. Once on the coast off Puri near the Chandrabhaga confluence, he was resting after an exhausting hunting outing. A small casket dancing rhythmically to the tide and ebb caught his attention. While opening the box, he at once recalled that it was the same small casket containing Maya's mortal remains and the memorabilia of his undying love. Sita Devi came to know of the serendipitous news and concurred in Narasingha Deva's desire to construct a colossal and captivating temple in honour of, for worship of Bhagawan Suryadev there on the confluence. The couple considered that that would be a glorious and graceful, fitting and fine memorial to the immortal love saga of Maya- Narasingha.

The temple construction began on benign haste with no hindrance or hiatus of any sort and under the meticulous supervision of the capable sculptor, architect and counsellor Shiva Narayana Samanta Raya Mohapatra, popularly known as Shibei Samntara for his stylistic haste and swiftness. He commanded a place of respect and repute in shrine and fort construction craft and art. Narasingha Deva was as addicted to thwarting invading armies as devoted to peace-time temple and castle building. Among his memorable and magnificent structures, mention must be made of the Raibonia Fort in Mayurbhanj district in Odisha; Lord Chandrasekhara temple at Kapilash in Dhenkanal district, Odisha; Varah Laxminarayana temple, Simhachalam, in Andhra Pradesh; Ananta Vasudeva temple near Lord Lingaraja temple,

Bhubaneswar; Kshirachora Gopinatha temple at Remuna, near Balasore in Odisha, among a dozen others. Building a temple on the confluence of perennial Chandrabhaga haunted by humongous seasonal, natural catastrophes like, flood, cyclone, high wind, humidity coupled with soil salinity, high tides and fresh water paucity posed unsurmountable obstacles and inadvertent deadline delays. Shibei Samntara would not budge or grudge the obstructions and the monarch would have none of it.

Konark temple was contemplated to be the magnum opus of Narasingha Deva I's monarchical monuments, epitome of Ganga Dynasty aggrandizement, and epicentre of Kalingan architecture, temple-culture, sculptural grandeur and pilgrims' wonder. In design, dimension, display, it was supposed to surpass existing and prospective temple structures of Bharata. In sheer size and superior exquisite architecture, it must have no comrade or competitor- was what the monarch made up his mind for.

The monarchical ambition was matched by the many a craftsman, sculptor, architect, smith and supervisor minding their job, while unmindful of family, home and their health. The towering temple was 70 metres high with 30 metres high walls. With gates on 3 sides, the temple was walled 264 metres by 160 metres. The sanctum sanctorum was 70 metres high before it collapsed in 1837 AD. The extant Jagamohan is 39 metres tall. Dedicated to the Sun-god, the temple resembled the Sun's diurnal journey in the firmament from East to West, ensconced in a 30-metre-tall chariot consisting 24 wheels each of 3.7 metres in diameter. Each wheel had 8 spokes. Drawn by 7 horses, the chariot seems to emerge from sea on dawn from an inland view. The misty beach dawn of Konark adds mythological halo when the khondalite rock-cut temple-structure basks in the glory of early sunray.

The splendid and stupendous stone structure was not easy to erect. Rome was not built in a day—is what they say. Nor was Konark crafted, sculpted and constructed in a day. Legend is legion that 1200 mason-cum-smiths adept in chiselling and carving sones, sculpting intricate flora and fauna, were employed by the monarch to complete the construction swiftly. Architects and artists assisted the artisans to carve celestial icons, mundane human activities as well as puranic and contemporary wars in live and lovely manner. But the temple building lingered listlessly to complete, though the artisans and stonecutters left no stone unturned to finish the task on time set by the monarch. For the last some weeks, the construction was hamstrung as the spectacular spiral could not be completed. Try as hard and hopefully as they could, they miserably failed to set the kalash [spiral pitcher] atop as it tumbled the moment it was mounted. The monarch did not doubt in the calibre and competence of the craftsmen but was frustrated that the temple could not be finished to consecrate the Sun-god. Lastly, impatient and hopeless, the monarch ordered that all the artisans, smiths, masons, architects, sculptors and artists involved with the project be beheaded en masse next morning if the kalash was not mounted.

Musing and mourning, the workers waited for the mournful morning. And the inevitable, enforced death; mass death, mass death of humans; precious humans and priceless artisans and craftsmen who injected and invoked life into lifeless stone! For having erected a fabulous, fantastic stone structure, they should have been rewarded richly but have, ironically, been awarded death penalty en masse. They found no fault with the monarch's stony, whimsical order for their minor inability to set up the massive spire but found fault, ironically, with their wilful fate that was unwilling to cooperate to complete the holy temple wholly. They were not aware of Henry Wadsworth Longfellow's poem,

> Tell me not in mournful numbers,
> Life is but an empty dream!
> For the soul is dead that slumbers,
> And things are not what they seem.
> Life is real! Life is earnest!
> And the grave is not its goal;
> Dost thou art, to dust returnest,
> Was not spoken of the soul.
> [A Psalm of Life]

They did not doubt in their skill, capacity, competence, dedication or honesty. Their failure was fated to become fatal. Not 1, 2, 3… the whole lot of 1200 smiths and artisans who worked on, talked to, joked with, dreamt of stone, stone… all days from dawn to dusk with their chisel and hammer in winter and summer, forgetting family, friends far or near, would die, die diabolically. No leave nor truancy, no dereliction nor dishonesty, yet death, death like dice cast! Death paradoxical and preposterous! Only work, work with sweat and blood for 12 years, not a day less, not a day lost. Yet, the "Goal of their life" is grave! Sandy, deserted shore grave, unknown, unmoaned, unhonoured, unsung, ignominious grave! They dreamt of riches, reward, reputation after the Sun Temple was erected but it was all kaput! Their life was "an empty dream". Their motto was, "Act—act in the living Present! Heart within, and God ov'rhead." But neglected, ignored, indecent was their end!

Who put the brake in this gigantic temple completion and turned the path of their splendorous fame to stupendous shame?

God! Who else? They were not atheist nor agnostics. They did not shower their angst or anguish, anger or despair on God. It was not their wont. Firm believers in God's fair deal, they believed that a miracle may happen to help the hapless, hopeless humans out of the mass melancholy and manslaughter. They expected that a curative cue would soon come through to settle the spire solidly so that it would never topple! It so happened and soon.

Viswanatha Maharana, nicknamed "Vishu" was best known for his admirable aptitude and inimitable attitude to stone cutting, image carving and shrine building. He was iconic in lionising, enlivening and iconising images and events. He was crafty but thrifty in stonecutting and cutting hard, obstinate, orthodox stones to size. With commendable camaraderie, he was iconic and adorable in the smith and sculptors' fraternity.

He left for the Konark assignment when his lovely wife was a week or so into pregnancy. In his impregnable tight schedule of temple work, more tightened as the construction progressed toward finishing line, he scarcely got a minute to think about his wife, her pregnancy, abortion or miscarriage, or birth of live child, stillbirth or infant mortality. 12 years have elapsed! Meantime, a boy was born to him, who was brought up well and sent to school. His classmates and playmates queried and were worried who his father was who was never seen or heard in the locality.

Dharmapada, Dharama as they called him in short and in colloquial vernacular, was comforted by his mother, telling fluently and mellifluent about the remarkable skill and achievements of his artisan father. The mates and friends were not satisfied by Dharama's exhaustive explanation on his father and his absence. They teased and taunted him often, over and over again. The last nail was struck the day a classmate called him bastard. Dharama was angry, could have hit that friend hard to teach the vulgar a lesson. But the whole class burst into thunderous laughter at Dharama's ignominious sobriquet. The mostly malicious, occasionally mischievous, moniker demoralised and depressed him. He kept his cool and came back from school the very instant.

At home, he demanded of his mother to speak the truth about his father's whereabouts. Only 12 years old though he was, he doubted the chastity of his mother for in rural Odisha adulterous offsprings were not a rarity. His absentee father fuelled his suspicion whether he had a real, respectable father at all. His mother was disheartened by the hardened heart of his tender-hearted son. She was desperate to see or hear his husband at least once in 12 years. But that was not to be. Since Dharama was already 12 and a male child of muscular masculinity, he could go seeking his father- thought the mother in yielding to Dharama's earnest wish to meet with his father. Mother acceded to son's stubborn determination to see his father and son was extremely ingratiated to the dearest, loveliest mother of the world in acquiescing to his risky, explorative mission.

All that is well that ends well. Yet, unexpectedly

the duo was obstructed in smooth implementation of the grandiose scheme. The high tide of their excitement was indignantly ebbed. How can father and son who have never seen each other identify each other? That was the million-dollar question. Neither mother nor son was able to steer the question clear of. It was the Aegean stables sort. In the absence of any identifying individual or indication, seeking the father was a herculean task for Dharama, wasn't it?

The mother looked around painfully and pensively to locate an identifying mark or material. All on a sudden, she saw the old jujube tree standing stately, ripe-fruit-laden. Their jujube is as profusely juicy as Gulab Jamun and tasty likewise. In fact, Vishu was popular in the locality as owner of this unique, sweet jujube nut tree as both husband and wife were never miserly in letting boys and girls, teens and adolescents, adults and elderly people pluck and pocket ripe nuts to enough and spare in fruiting winter. The ripe jujube nuts were terrific identification material object for father to identify the son- the mother thought romantically, merrily.

Dharama started off with a well-wrapped pouch of ripe jujube on the unknown, uncharted road on the assumed, approximate direction and distance indicated by his mother. He walked for some days, furthering his knowledge of the Konark location fortified by travellers and strangers, shopkeepers and cow grazers, innkeepers and innocent roadside-dwellers' advice and assistance. The long and arduous journey was physically exhausting and frustrating at times but mostly a jovial joyride. Who will tire traversing the distance to meet his father for the first time, for the first time in life, especially when his father fathers the gigantic and gorgeous stone edifice called Konark?Finally, he saw the massive, majestic temple splendidly silhouetted in the bushy green landscape of Konark seashore. "Déjà vu, eureka..!" he cried in delight and delirium. Profuse pride electrified his body to think that his father is an architect and artisan of this magnificent, marvellous edifice.

By sunset, Dharama reached the workmen's colony. Unlike other evenings, that evening was darker and gloomier in the artisan's colony. The sunset usually halts construction and tingling and twitching of tools yields to restful jokes and joys with evening tea and snacks. That evening was shrouded in cemeterylike silence and small whispers and sighs occasionally caused ripples in the deadened, desolate atmosphere. Dharama sneaked into the rows of seemingly dehumanised tents. After some time, some artisans peeped out of their tents to witness a tender boy looking out for someone. The boy was buoyed to see so many souls emerging out of their noiseless tents. Swiftly the news spread like forest fire that Vishu's son is on the scene.

Vishu soon joined the collective and was taken aback at the slender-bodied tender son radiating a glow of grace and greatness on his whole being. When Dharama identified himself with their backyard jujube packet, Vishu was bewildered with alternate spells of happiness and hopelessness. Father and son retired to their cabin and sat for dinner. Vishu dissimulated contentment while eating to ensure that the hungry and tired son ate to his heart's content for the first time in his father's company. Nonetheless, the rebellious, obstinate tears welled up in his big black eyes to trickle down the cheeks. The discerning son who construed the tears to be tears of joy soon tore the delusion that his father was struck with a recent tragedy or an upcoming upheaval. Vishu tried to fool Dharama but his bluff was called off by the smart and sensitive lad. So, the cat was out of bag.

In exacerbated distress, Vishu embraced Dharama and cried inconsolably for the inevitable catastrophe hovering over the artisans' colony and his miragelike meeting with the son. Some other craftsmen collected to console the wailing Vishu and disturbed Dharama.

They departing, Dharama prevailed upon his fondly father to see the temple next morning not for fun but to see why and how the spiral kalasha skids off the spherical dome of the temple, deluding the deft and diligent sculptors and architects. Born to the smiths and sculptors' clan, brought in the neighbourhood of stonecutters, sculptors, architects and artisans, like his friends, schoolmates and playmates, he too learnt temple art, sculpture and stone-craft playfully but a bit more enthusiastically, intuitively because his absentee father's bread and butter, fame and treasure sprung from that. And he had heard people say that stone sculpture and temple architecture was his father's heart and soul, life and goal; in short, the be all and end all of his all-honoured, well-honoured, widely-honoured father. Dharmapada learnt the basics, ethics, physics and mystics of shrine structures and temple towers from palm-leaf manuscripts, village elders' discourse and dialogues with concentration and contemplative imagination. And he learnt his lessons mindfully, not leisurely. Imaginative that he was, he imagined following his father, being taught and instructed theories and theorems of temple craft by his father with ample field demonstrations. Sons are usually unwilling pupils to teaching fathers but become the most disciplined, obedient and eager learners when father is absent; because mother filters the fine faculties of father and infiltrates them into son's mind, heart and soul, his whole being.

To oblige his son, Vishu accompanied with a coterie of trustworthy and noteworthy craftsmen left for the temple site by dawn. The rising sunray cast a captivating charm on and around the temple. Dharama felt wandering in a thrilling troposphere with the sky-scrapping temple tearing into the stratosphere and upwards. Descending down to the earthy reality, he climbed the temple in tow with his father and half a dozen veteran artisans. By then, bright sunshine basked Konark was enchanting, enticing. Dharama looked at the huge circular dome topping upper part of the temple. The kalasha has to sit atop with the help of a dozen iron hooks. Somehow or other the skilled and expert architects failed to set the spiral right and tight. Some angular hooks hoodwinked the hardworking, honest artisans. Unless all the dozen angles hooked at one go, the spiral was doomed to fall down to pieces. Intuitively and intelligently, Dharama saw the discrepancy as the first man. He straightened the two slightly slanted iron angles and set the spiral in place and properly. To the utter amazement of the assisting artisans, the spiral sat and sat like a lame duck, silent but steadfast. The job thereafter was child's play to the renowned artisans who fixed the flag-post and finished the temple building for good.

By breakfast time, the incredible, apparently impossible job was done. Vishu gleamed with pride for his young son's fantastic feat. His coworkers applauded the boy's accomplishment joyously and profusely. The entire migrant artisans' temporary sheds and tents celebrated the occasion and Dharama and Vishu were the cause celebre. But by evening, things were not what they seemed. Deeper and direr distress stressed the smiths and sculptors to their bones and being. They thought and thought rightly out of their vast experience that the monarch would, no doubt, marvel at the feat achieved and finesse displayed by a young boy. On the other hand, he would ascribe the inordinate delay in fixing the spiral as much to the laggard, haphazard work culture and nonapplication of mind of the mischievous smiths and sculptors as to the superfluous supervisors and senior artisans. As such, he may honour Dharama with riches, estates, jewellery and titles but would hang the 1200 workmen.

What should they do to save their skins? How could their happy heads remain out of harm's way? Some shrewd, crafty craftsmen suggested a heinous, hideous idea that if Dharama died, 1200 smiths would live; if he lived, the 1200 artisans must be hanged. To find a way out, someone said that except for the craftsmen community there, none else knew that Dharama fixed the problem. If he was out of sight and we consequently convince the monarch that luck smiled on us at last to set the elusive kalasha, the monarch would not smell fish nor read between the lines to uncover our malicious design. But the ball lies in Vishu's court. The axe is in Vishu's hand. He wields the magic wand to kill or heal his clan of craftsmen. Will he ever sacrifice his single dear tender son in lieu of lives of his brethren? Will he opt for the 1200 artisans' lives, their wives, children's happiness in place of a part of his heart? The choice is his was the chorus. He was in no obligation to rescue the 1200 artisans from sure, staring death. But if he did, he would be a legend, lionised in the annals of culture, architecture. He is iconic as such. Henceforth, he would be an ideal, an idol to be worshipped and revered; an immortal to be eulogised.

All afternoon, the colony was agog with whispers and hush-hush discussions on the unimaginable achievement of Vishu's 12-year-old son on the one hand and the upcoming enmasse hanging of the 1200 smiths and sculptors on the other. The consensus of the community of artisans was either Dharama or the 1200 workmen were destined to die; both cannot live side by side by any stretch of imagination. Their costly, cruel query to Vishu was: Which do you care for -son's life or 1200 artisans' life? Nightfall brought curtain-fall to the debates and deliberations. Vishu and Dharama had their dinner without the hypocrisy of eating well.

Before going to bed, Dharama blew off the lid,

"Father! They are right. The monarch would not mind felling heads of 1200 craftsmen on their failure to fix the spiral of the temple on the presumption of conspiratorial lethargy, when a 12-year-old lad fixed the spiral in minutes. Is it worth dying for the community of competent and honest artisans who had sweated for 12 long years to complete the temple? As ill luck would have it, their impeccable craftsmanship was mired in a minor nettle to let them fix the spiral. The temple completion must not be credited to me, but to my clan whose blood runs in my veins and bones. I must die so they may live, a long, live long glorious lives."

"I work with, live with, dream of and love stones so I could be stony hearted but how can you? For the first time I see you in 12 years and you are the pupil of our eyes. How can I sacrifice you like a goat or goose? How can I show my face to your mother who would be waiting for both of us eagerly?

Shall I justify your absence by saying that I sacrificed you for the unpardonable sin of completing the Konark temple with your uncanny ingenuity and intelligence? Don't say so, my dear son!" said Vishu in grief-choked, heart-broken voice.

Dharama continued in a consoling tone, "Father, you have read the verse that boy Bhoja wrote to monarch Munja on mortality, haven't you?"

' mandhata cha mahipatih krutayugalankara bhooto gatah
Seturyena mahadadhou virachitam kwasou dashasyantakah
Anyechapi yudhisthirah prabhrutayoh yata divam bhoopate
Naikenapi samam samam gata Vasumati munjam twaya yasyati'

[Bhoja Pravandha: a book on king Bhoja]

Dharama narrated:Sindhu raja, the king of Dhara, in central India reigned about 200 years ago. His might and manners were exemplary and inimitable. Scholarly and considerate that he was, he was the cynosure of the subjects' eye. He grew old but his son and successor named Bhoja was only 12 years old. He could have anointed Bhoja as his successor monarch before death as his generals and ministers were eminently loyal to keep the minor monarch safe from palace intrigue or external intrusion or invasion. Bhoja was a child prodigy to handle statecraft and warfare effectively. With committed and commendably efficient commanders and counsellors at his beck and call, he could not be vulnerable to internal or external strife. But the wise and farsighted Sindhu raja anointed his younger brother Munja as king with Bhoja as crown prince.

Munja managed family and kingdom matters eminently

well and treated Bhoja better than his own son. In course of time, things changed and changed for the worse. He became autocratic and atrocious and dreamt of perpetuating his line on Dhara throne by anointing his son king. Things became the worst when he hatched a plot to kill Bhoja in secret to stymie any problem or rebellion from him when Munja's son ascended the throne.

In stealth and secrecy, he sent Bhoja on a pleasure trip to nearby dense forest escorted by 3 or 4 strong and stout sentries to ostensibly save Bhoja from wild animal or disguised enemies' attack. But the sentries were instructed confidentially to slaughter Bhoja away in the wilderness and show Munja blood bottles of the slain prince. The initially unwilling sentries were allured to the loathsome act with bountiful riches and prestigious royal posts. Innocent but intelligent Bhoja took Munja's advice of hunting trip lightly and delightfully. The escorts' unhappiness in leading him to uncharted, un-surveyed forests was writ large on their countenance. Bhoja was a lovely and loveable prince with a convivial contour of body and behaviour well known to subjects and soldiers. In the jungle, he smelt something fishy and asked why the escorts were vexed and dejected. At the affable prince's query and concern, they burst out crying and divulged details of the devilish assignment they had been entrusted with in lieu of the gorgeous gold coins they would gain on accurate execution of the heinous scheme.

Prodigious and studious, Bhoja assuaged them to discard sorrow and act as secretly as they were directed to. But he begged them to take a letter written by him and hand over the same to the king on returning to the capital. The kingdom's seniormost and sagacious minister who was excessively loyal to Sindhu raja and was sidelined by Munja in execution of nefarious designs, somehow scented hints of the heinous attempt on Bhoja's life. He sent 2 or 3 capable and confidant soldiers in disguise to the forest to somehow or other hijack boy Bhoja to safe hiding. Sturdy and trustworthy soldiers that they were, their loyalty to Sindhu raja was unquestionable. They were good at espionage. At the nick of time, they arrived at the jungle junction where Bhoja was to be eliminated. The minister's soldiers prevailed upon Munja's men to set Bhoja free, kill a big bird instead, and report Bhoja's slaughter with the pouch of avian blood as evidence. Bhoja would be hijacked and hidden in well-secured forest hideout under proper care and upkeep. As Bhoja desired, a letter with his thigh-blood as ink, broad Sal leaf as paper and porcupine spike as pen, be written and given to the king. The king's soldiers were only too willing to cooperate in carrying out the conspiratorial scheme. Bhoja's last letter was delivered to king Munja.

Munja went through the letter since Bhoja death-wished that it should be read by king Munja himself, by none else by any chance. Munja read the latter silently, slowly, and was heartbroken instantly. He wailed loud and nonstop and blamed him, cursed him, sinned him deliriously. What Bhoja wrote meant,

'Mandhata, the grand monarch who established him as the crown jewel of Satya Yuga is gone; so is Rama who bridged the gulf to Lanka and did destroy the 10-headed monster. So is no more Yudhishthira who stands out as a king divine. The earth did not move nor mourn the exit of such extraordinary, iconic, pious, popular, epoch-making, ever memorable monarchs. Will the earth accompany you crying the day you expire?' Munja read and understood the contents and he read between the lines philosophising the truth that kings, monarchs, emperors, however powerful, popular and piteous, virtuous, sinless had to die and had died. Nothing is permanent in this world except the earth that endures for eons and epochs. The mighty, majestic and memorable monarchs left the world emptyhanded as they descended emptyhanded from mother's embryo. You had so vulgarly, savagely betrayed your fatherlike, fathomlessly famous elder brother in killing his son as if you would be immortal and enjoy the mean, mundane, material earthly possessions and acquisitions ad infinitum till the universe ends.

The wise, old, loyal minister consoled the grieving king and took some time to find out whether the Sindhu raja scion was really slaughtered. Needless to say, Bhoja was traced from the jungle fleeing as per the last act, last scene of the well-played-out theatrical. On attaining majority, he was enthroned with his cousin, Munja's son, accorded deserving and due royalty.

On recounting the story of Kaling's neighbouring empire, Dhara, Dharama asked his father to agree to the unpalatable, unagreeable but unavoidable suggestion made by his cronies and comrades, professional kins and admirable artisans. Dharama said,

"I have done what I was destined to and have lived as long as my destiny has demarcated. Life is not how long one lives in minutes, hours, days and decades but the deeds he has done and how long his deeds live after him. Deeds, great and noble, selfless and societally suitable, are the golden scales to weigh worth of human life. Sacrificing one's life for the benefit of the community, society or kingdom is definitely the most virtuous and venerable life lived by a human being. And a father sacrificing his only young son to save the lives of 1200 of his fellow craftsmen, brothers, members of his clan, coworkers is definitely the most memorable, notable, enviable but inimitable act by a human being. Father! Bid me adieu gladly without further waste of time."

Vishu heard his son speak with rapt attention and it rang in his ears like the rapture of a celestial singer or minstrel. It was unsurprising that Dharama inherited the artisanry trade-secrets and expertise from generations and generations of smiths and sculptors, who lived and loved rock-cutting, temple building by wielding chisels and hammers. But which school or learning tool sharpened his mental skill? Thought Vishu. He smiled to himself despite the heavy load of sorrow-burden in his heart that Dharmapada, his dear Dharama, was akin to Abhimanyu to have learnt the lessons in sculpture and architecture while growing in his mother's uterus. He was undoubtedly caught between Scylla and Charybdis, caught in a catch-22 situation. He cannot sacrifice his lone son on the altar of premature death to protect the dying 1200 smiths on the one hand. He cannot leave his 1200 colleagues in the lurch in lieu of his son on the other hand. Vishu wondered and was woefully worried how he can cross the Rubicon.

Dharama added further, "Father! All must die today or tomorrow, young or old, in war or from illness. It is common, as-of-other-creatures' death; you can say it is cowardice, a coward's death. Manly death, manhood-befitting death is to die for others, for others' welfare, for others' survival, for others' life, for welfare of others' family and friends. Father!

The noblest deed, the supreme virtue, the pinnacle of pious action is to die happily to let others live happily. And you bid me farewell to embrace this ennobling death for the cause of 1200 smiths and sculptors who have raised the massive, mindboggling Konark on the seashore sands to leave their footprints on the sands of time."

Vishu did not wish to lengthen the daylong lingering discussion between father and son, between Vishu and his companion craftsmen. Do father and son debate long and inconclusive? Doesn't even elsewhere unyielding father yield meekly to son's arguments and advice in the end to end the duel decisively in favour of the son? Vishu was hypnotised, mesmerised by the softspoken, heart-touching, mind-churning sensible, sagacious statements of his son. Dharama spoke out eternal truths innocently, intimately, carefully guarding his father's ethos and emotions vis-a- vis ethical, spiritual intricacies. Finally, father agreed to with heavy heart but lofty thoughts that he must opt for fellow craftsmen to his only son. Son was no less emotional though highly elevated by the rare, noble self-sacrifice to save 1200 artisans of articulate artistic skill and tremendous talent.

Night still reigned supreme in Vishu's tent. Thoroughly thoughtful and deeply disturbed, he could not sleep after father-son dialogue ended. Dharama was excited exceedingly to sacrifice his life for the survival of 1200 talented artisans. When his father slept toward predawn, Dharama slipped silently and sneaked toward the deserted seashore. Dawn was breaking on the eastern horizon and the loveliest baby rays of the young, orange sun were scattered serene over Konark spiral.

Dharama climbed the tall, stately temple in hush

hush haste to reach the flag-post faultlessly. Atop the temple, he bowed to the sun-god and the galaxy of gods that figure in puranas and epics; offered his prayers to his pedigree of precious artisanry, masonry, artistry, sculpture and architectural elegance. His eyes welled up for his loving parents. Then he turned around seaward and jumped off the spiral before it was too late.

With a violent splash on the ebbing Chandrabhaga water, Dharmapada plunged under the waves, water and surf. Minor ripples that erupted by his immersion under water were not seen or heard by anyone except shoals of little silver fishes, bales of turtles and other named and unnamed tiny marine creature clubs that worked or played that early. The sound of the splash mingled with chirping and chattering of seashore birds, cry of parliaments of crows in distant hamlets.

When morning waked up all artisan inmates of the colony, all eyes were fixed upon Vishwanath's tent from which emerged Vishu as usual. But his cheerful countenance meticulously hid his mourning heart. 1200 smiths and sculptors took the credit of finally finishing the fabulous shrine and were honoured and rewarded by Narasingha deva I who was crowned and called "Gajapati" the lord of pachyderms for the first time. The saga of Konark completion, whodunit remained shrouded.

SEVENTY-TWO

Who does HE like?
Who is not afraid of nor fearful.

The world is not full of thieves and thugs, looters and plunders; of dishonest, harmful and hypocrites who turn annus memorabilia into annus horribilis. It is beautiful and full of beautiful creatures. There are many a man and woman who are distinguished and deity-like. They outshine others with their outstanding virtues and services. They stand out for their nobility, humility, simplicity, serenity, civility, charity. Who are they? How to distinguish them?

They are not hard to find. You do not have to run hither and thither to locate their habitat and locale. They are among us. They are some of us or several of us. The omniscient Lord, God had defined and delineated them. For a start, some of them are,

> adveṣhṭā sarva-bhūtānāṁ maitraḥ karuṇa eva cha
> nirmamo nirahankāraḥ sama-duḥkha-sukhaḥ kṣhamī [12.13]

> yasmān nodvijate loko lokān nodvijate cha yaḥ
> harṣhāmarṣha-bhayodvegair mukto yaḥ sa cha me priyaḥ
> [12.15]

anapekṣhaḥ śhuchir dakṣha udāsīno gata-vyathaḥ
sarvārambha-parityāgī yo mad-bhaktaḥ sa me priyaḥ [12.16]

O Arjuna! They endear Me who harbour no adversarial attitude to all creatures, rather entertain camaraderie and compassion; not passionate nor arrogant, weigh pleasure and pain in the same scale, and are lenient.

O Arjuna! He who is not fearful nor is afraid of other people, is devoid of delight, intolerance, fear and anxiety, is dearer to Me.

O Partha! I am fond of them who are unexpectant, clean, adept, indifferent, unostentatious, unmindful of pain and suffering, unindulgent in rat race of acquisitions.

"O, wonder!
How many goodly creatures are there here!
How beauteous mankind is! O brave new world,
That has such people in't!"

O my God I have wandered from Bhagavat Gita to the wonderland of William Shakespeare's popular play, "The Tempest" wherein Miranda exclaims so in Act I, Scene V, on her first sight of human beings other than her father.

SEVENTY-THREE

Shun all isms to be shorn of sins
The path of surrender strewn with suffering.
Set the mind and be Brahma!

By now we have acceded to the Gita precept that life is action and action is life. Inversely speaking, inaction is death and death alone is the end of action. The only secret that is unintelligible to the extremely intelligent is why there is so much difference between people and people, between their lives, between their action or inaction. The Gita guidance is to act without aiming at the result, hoping for a result. To follow that or not to follow that is the crux of the matter, is the cream and butter. It is not difficult or bitter to follow the Gita guidelines; it is plain and simple. To follow Gita principles of action without attachment, passion, you have to submit, surrender. To whom?

Mohandas Karamchand Gandhi, the respectable Mahatma, whose interest in the quest of truth, the paramountcy of truth, is a modern creed, a twentieth century philosophy, says, "Add to this fact that at three distinct places, the Gita goes even further and exhorts us to leave all alone all "isms" and take refuse in the Lord alone...." [From Speeches of

Mahatma Gandhi at Banaras and Kanpur]. The Mahatma means,

sarva-dharmān parityajya mām ekaṁ śharaṇaṁ vraja
ahaṁ tvāṁ sarva-pāpebhyo mokṣhayiṣhyāmi mā śhuchaḥ
[18.66]

O Partha! Give up all religions and surrender to me. I shall free you from all sins. Never doubt.

The literal meaning is not complete or comprehensible. Preachers and teachers in general limit the meaning to Krishna assuring Arjuna to shun all religions and seek shelter in Him. Through Arjuna, we are advised, assured to not bother about the past or prevalent religious paraphernalia, philosophy, but to submit to Krishna. Instead of individualising God as Krishna, Gandhi has called the Lord as the only and ultimate asylum. In place of religions, he has alluded to "isms" that have to be shunned. These isms are as much Shaivism, Vaishnavism as different schools and sects; and religions as we know of, speak of or follow. This verse, the very essence of Bhagavat Gita, is definitely not discriminatory. It does not discriminate the protagonist Krishna against other gods, religious heads nor does it eulogise Hinduism the followers of which adore Krishna. It simplifies the fact that while alive and active, you are likely to be eluded by the preachers and promoters of different narrow, sectarian schools. Those obstruct your quest and commitment to Truth, to the ultimate Spirit, the cosmic Spirit. So, you needs must abjure various tendentious, tempting teachings, isms, faiths and fictions.

This sloka hints that you are not alone in this vast universe nor will you be saved or assisted by the galaxy of gods. The religious precepts and practices- pure and plain- promote you, propel you, prop up you but the extravagant, vandalised practices, pompous, ostentatious, ornate, elaborate paraphernalia downs you, drowns you. In society and family, with friends and followers, you seem full and fully protected, but, in reality, you are alone from Birth to Death. You are alone in action or inaction. But you are not lonely, isolated, a hapless shipwreck in a hostile, inhospitable, unhabitable dreary desert. There is the Lord overhead who stands by you in difficulties and distress, troubles and temptations, doubts and dilemma. When you are in the worst of it, just seek His help, just rest in Him. And the LORD! Where is He?

The answer to the question supra could be found in a lot of slokas of the Bhagavat Gita. Interestingly, temples and shrines, monasteries and god-houses, sanctum sanctorum and serene scenes are not the abode of the Lord, of God. In a Bhagavatam sloka, Krishna says to Narada,

Naham tisthami vaikunthe, yoginam hrudaye na cha
Madbhaktah jatra gayanti tatra tisthami Narada.

O Narada! I do not dwell in Vaikuntha nor in the hearts of the Yogis. I stay there where my devotees chant my name.

So, we can assume that God resides in places where His followers sing prayers in His praise. It would then be understood that God goes from place to place, from time to time. He has no permanent, fixed address. Gita differs from such view and decodes God's abode as,

īshvaraḥ sarva-bhūtānāṁ hṛid-deśhe 'rjuna tiṣhṭhati
bhrāmayan sarva-bhūtāni yantrārūḍhāni māyayā [18.61]

O Arjuna! Ishvara, God resides in the heart of all

creatures. But the creatures are ignorant of this as the ignoramuses atop the carousel of Maya are deluded. [This is exactly echoed in Kavir's verse quoted supra.] Krishna exhorts to Arjuna to seek shelter in that Ishvara in entirety, in all respects to acquire permanent peace. And peace, no doubt, is the be all and end all of all creatures in general and of humans in particular.

On total, complete surrender to GOD, the two slokas quoted below identically indicate the same,

man-manā bhava mad-bhakto mad-yājī māṁ namaskuru
mām evaiṣhyasi yuktvaivam ātmānaṁ mat-parāyaṇaḥ [9.34]

man-manā bhava mad-bhakto mad-yājī māṁ namaskuru
mām evaiṣhyasi satyaṁ te pratijāne priyo 'si me [18.65]

In both verses, Krishna tells Arjuna to mind, meditate on Him [Krishna], to worship Him, to bow before Him, stick his [Arjuna's] being, person with Krishna. It means Arjuna must always, attentively think of Krishna, worship and submit to Krishna, behave Krishna-like to attain Him, attain peace. This is first said in 34/9. Almost repeated in 65/18, Krishna confirms His affirmation and adds that He has divulged this to Arjuna as the latter is the dearest to the former.

It is therefore pertinent, important that you submit to the Lord totally, wholly and whole-heartedly. You need not bother about the thread-bare annotations, explanations by knowledgeable preachers or proficient pundits on the nuances and niceties, nitty-gritties of Bhagavat Gita to be near your God. Know and you needs must know the bare, basics of Gita that sings the serenity and supremacy of your near, dear Lord.

It is easier said than adhered to, adopted by us, by humans. It is extremely difficult and is exacerbated once one sets on that path. Krishna says so in,

kleśho 'dhikataras teṣhām avyaktāsakta-chetasām
avyaktā hi gatir duḥkhaṁ dehavadbhir avāpyate [12.5]

O Arjuna! They who set off on the path of the Unknown suffer from untold trials and tribulations. The creatures with body experience exceeding affliction before attaining, arriving at the Unknown, for the simple reason that the path to the Unknown is strewn with suffering, affliction.

Those who set out on the path of surrender, total submission; those who seek refuse in GOD, who seek asylum in the LORD, are affected by, afflicted with innumerable, untold, indescribable pain and suffering. The case of Prahalad flashes in our mind at once, when we speak of submission. How much suffering and torture Prahalad has to bear when he was bent upon surrendering to the Lord. His tormentor, his persecutor was none other than his father who should ordinarily be Prahalad's protector, saviour, rescuer. Finally, of course, Prahalad surmounted all hindrances and handicaps unleashed by his heinous father Hiranyakashipu to reach and rest in Vishnu, didn't he? Harishchandra, the great and glorious monarch of the Sun dynasty underwent trials and tribulations, suffering and sacrifices to reach and take refuge in the Lord. As a matter of fact, surrender is not an armchair affair. On the contrary, surrender to the Lord is full of, filled with suffering and affliction. The path to, the path of surrender bustles with, is strewn with thorns. There is no way to get rid of the thorns and pains strewn on the way to surrender. That is why surrender to the Lord said of towards the end of Bhagavat Gita.

But humans can surrender to the Lord, God, when and if they insist on because they are blessed with, bequeathed with mind, the most notable, marvellous, powerful faculty. If you set your mind on something, you achieve it, get it, don't you?

It will not be inappropriate to tell a story told by Maharshi Raman.

One poor but pious brahmin was issueless. He prayed God to be blessed with sons. Since he was sinless, serene, saintly, God was pleased with him to bless him with 10 sons. The sons followed in their father's footsteps to be learned and lenient. After some years, both of their parents passed away in quick succession. The orphaned sons were inexplicably sad on the sudden, sorrowful demise of their loving parents. They spent time in grieving for quite some months. Thereafter, one day the eldest brother asked his younger siblings,

"How long shall we waste time uselessly like this? You know our parents have left little savings or fixed assets. The generous neighbours have shown sufficient charity to feed and clothe us. It is time that we do something."

"What shall we do?" asked one eagerly.

"Money, money, brighter than sunshine, sweeter than honey. We should earn money enough to feed and clothe ourselves, and to give some to the starving and needy," said one in earnest.

"Hey, what bogus stuff! Sons of scholarly and saintly

brahmin parents will amass wealth like tom, dick and harry?" rubbished another.

"Yea, that is right. Besides, the people compete with one another to get richer and sooner. I do not think it behoves us to join the mad rat race to acquire adequate wealth to make both ends meet and to be contented," added still another.

Another interrupted to say, "In whatever we do and achieve, we must outshine others in remembrance of our illustrious father who stood out as sui generis."

Then the debate went on, on what they should do and do summa cum laude. Intelligent that they were, they explored options of acquisition of knowledge, social service, charity, Tapasya, sannyasa and the like but stopped short of consensual conclusion that in each and every such arena they would obviously lag behind someone else.

"What should we do then?" asked one in irritation.

Looking at the composed eldest son, another asked, "Why are keeping mum? You are supposed to support us, guide us being not only the eldest but the wisest."

The eldest who looked thoughtful but kept his cool, said coolly, "There are peers and predecessors who might exceed us in our endeavours, enterprises. We can scarcely reach the acme of success in comparison with others because Brahma, the Creator, had made them so that they strive hard and break records. If one reaches the zenith, soon another dislodges, displaces him. It may so happen that he is pulled down to apocalypse through the cut-throat competition and calumnious conspiracy encountered."

Another son mused for minutes to remark, "If Brahma sets standards, lay out norms and nemesis, it is only Him

Who is unreachable, unsurpassable and invulnerable to manoeuvrability. Pooh! It is like chasing unicorns."

"Cannot we be Brahma?" queried another.

"Bogus!" cried another.

Others looked at the eldest and repeated the question if they could become Brahma or it was beyond bounds of human imagination, intellect, innovation and industry. The eldest who was intimately involved in the heated discussion and debate of the siblings inadvertently hit upon the notion "Why not be Brahma."

Aloud to the sibling assembly, "Becoming Brahma is not impossible but entails enormous toil, trials and tribulations."

"You play a prank upon us or kidding, or else you are diverting and digressing from the focal point to impossible probability or improbable possibility. Isn't it crying in the wilderness or indulging in wild geese chase?" quipped one.

Another sought details of the modus operandi in a softened tone,

"We must be, how laborious or parlous, arduous or chronophagous the process or the pursuit might be. We raring to go."

The eldest elaborated, "The universe exists and affronts its apocalypse in our Mind. Our Mind determines the deleterious or the ingenious aspects and attainments in the interstellar space and time. We direct and escort our Mind that way, we become Brahma."

"Hurrah! Haste before we are a minute late. "'Better three hours too soon than a minute too late' is not a comedian's joke," said a sibling in excitement.

"Brother, eureka! Please spell out the concrete, how-to-do-yourself step by step formula for facility, shorn of supercilious and ostentatious details," said another.

The eldest elaborated, "It is neither unattainably impossible nor a child's tamasha. The talisman to man *"mana"* is to discard all our other thoughts and concentrate on Brahma. Remember, we have to give up our material belongings and all their appurtenant at one go or gradually. Identically, we shun our mental possessions and their appurtenances like hunger, thirst, anger, envy, avarice, love, loathing, longing, sense of belonging, sense of being one by one or by one fell stroke. When we contemplate completely and comprehensively on Brahma, we lose sight of the body and the body along with its bones, veins, millions of neurons. Then the body embodying the inexpressible noumenon is impalpably lost. Then we are…"

"Brahma!" cried out another in juvenile jubilation.

The brothers sat erect, cross-legged, hands resting on thigh-joints in lotus-shaped posture. As they sat closing their eyes, they closed their mind to the outside and inside happenings. Shut out from the whole worldly hullabaloo, they were thinking of Brahma, Brahma only in uniform manner and intensity. Nobody counted the months and years they spent in such painstaking and pathbreaking penance. With the passage of time, their bodies fell off to the ground like snake sloughs or tree barks and they were ant and termite mounds. Finally, and infallibly, they all became Brahma and created worlds and universes of their choice and curiosity but strictly in accordance with the Creator's design and decorum. None on earth or in the infinite firmament found any flaw in their creation.

One fine morning Brahma perceived to his wonder

that, apart from the one His creation, 10 more Suns shone the firmament. 10 more moons and 10s and 10s more solar systems, billions and billions of bright stars twinkled in 10s of skies.He called for one of the Suns to ascertain what had happened. The Sun soberly recounted the deceased, wise brahmin's 10 sons' feat and fiat. Astonished at their incredible accomplishment but to assuage them, he called for the sons who reported forthwith and were overjoyed to perceive Brahma in person.

They had no need of anything now and said so contentedly. In fact, their Tapasya was concrete and complete. They realised and exhibited what Tapasya could do. Tapasya is not the means only; it is the end as well. The finishing-line, the end of Tapasya is cul-de-sac.

Bemused Vedapati commanded their housing in one corner of the perennial pleasure playground popularly called paradise, where they were the monarch of all they surveyed and where there was none to dispute their right.

SEVENTY-FOUR

Who are ferried across the ocean of Death?

In the preceding section, we referred to chapter 12, verse 5, to emphasize that reaching Him, seeking refuge in the Lord, getting asylum in God is goddam difficult and painful. It is painful and full of suffering on account of the fact God is the other name of trials and tribulations. Some may find fault with the importance attached to this sloka that apparently sounds pessimistic and negative. As a matter of fact, whether with the sloka chapter 2, verse 47 or this one, some westernised, narrow-minded, conservative critics call the Bhagavat Gita defeatist, discouraging, negativistic. For you and me, Gita is the graceful guide to success, superiority, sublimity.

ye tu sarvāṇi karmāṇi mayi sannyasya mat-paraḥ
ananyenaiva yogena māṁ dhyāyanta upāsate

Jetu Sarvani karmani mayi sannyasya matparah
Ananyenaiva yogen ma dhayanta upasate......[12/6]

teṣhām ahaṁ samuddhartā mṛityu-saṁsāra-sāgarāt
bhavāmi na chirāt pārtha mayy āveśhita-chetasām

Teshamaham samurddhartta mrutyusamsarasagarat...
Bhavami nachiratpartha mayaveshitachetasam[12/7]

O Arjuna! Those who entrust their actions and obligations to Me in entirety and worship and pray Me in unwavering contemplation and meditation are the ones I shall rescue quickly from and row across the ocean of painful worldly life of death.

There is, therefore, no occasion to infer that you suffer for Him and He watches and laughs at your suffering and affliction. He is not sadistic or schadenfreude. On the other hand, He is kind, compassionate and curative. He discharges your assignments without grudge or grumbling and tries His best to get you out of the worldly morass and morbidity once for all, for good. The only prerequisite is that you entrust your actions and affairs to God wholesale and wholeheartedly on the one hand and spend your time in wholehearted admiration and adoration of Him without delay, dilemma or diversion.

It is evident from two slokas following sloka 12/5 that God is not only overhead, observing and obviating your pain and suffering, He comes running to rescue you quickly. And to row you across the ocean of painful worldly life, samsara, comprising innumerable lives and deaths. Of course, He waits, maybe for a long time, to satisfy Himself that you have, first of all, entrusted all your activities to Him with full and unfaltering faith that He will discharge your duties immaculately, impeccably. While entrusting your actions to Him, you are not supposed to while away your time in inaction and inertia. On the contrary, you have to be engrossed in yogic contemplation and meditation of the unique, unthinkable kind, enkindling your consciousness. They say there is no royal road to success. The modern management gurus and motivational speakers say so in sugar coated tongue and alluring tone. Millennia before, the Gita Purusha, the Primus Inter Pares, spoke of this. So long you arrogate your activities to yourself, you arrogate the means and modus operandi to yourself and you arrogate the outcomes, consequences to yourself, you struggle and, God forbid, fail. The day, the moment you realise the saying, the sermon in the two foregoing slokas, you work, you work with pleasure, with leisure.

This is further and better expounded in chapter V, slokas,

> yoga-yukto viśhuddhātmā vijitātmā jitendriyaḥ
> sarva-bhūtātma-bhūtātmā kurvann api na lipyate

Yogayukto vishuddhatatma vijitatma jitendriyah
Sarvabhutatmabhutatma kurvarnnapi na lipyate[5/7]
Naiva kinchit karomiti yukto manyate tattvavit

naiva kiñchit karomīti yukto manyeta tattva-vit paśhyañ
śhriṇvan spṛiśhañjighrann aśhnangachchhan svapañśhvasan
pralapan visṛijan gṛihṇann unmiṣhan nimiṣhann api
indriyāṇīndriyārtheṣhu vartanta iti dhārayan

Pashyanchshrunvan sprushnjighrannasnan gachhan
swapnanjshwasan [5/8]
pralapan visrjan gṛhṇann unmiṣan nimiṣann
api indriyāṇīndriyārtheṣu vartanta iti dhārayan

Praklapan visrujan gruhannunnshannimishnnapi
Indriyanindriyartheshu varttanta iti dharayan [5/9]

brahmaṇyādhāya karmāṇi saṅgaṁ tyaktvā karoti yaḥ
lipyate na sa pāpena padma-patram ivāmbhasā

Brahmanyadhaya karmani sangam tyaktwa karoti yah
Lipyate na sa papen padmapatramibambhasa[5/10]

kāyena manasā buddhyā kevalair indriyair api
yoginaḥ karma kurvanti saṅgaṁ tyaktvātma-śhuddhaye

Kayen manasa buddhya kevalairindriyairapi
Yoginahkarmakurvantisangamtyaktwatmashuddhaya[5/11]

O Arjuna! He who is yogic, who has purified soul, who has controlled soul, who has reigned his indriyas, and who treats all creatures the very same way as he treats himself is the one who does everything but is not attached to, bound by anything [5/7].

O Arjuna! The wise work with the preconception that "I am not doing anything." They see, hear, touch, smell, eat, walk, sleep, breathe, speak, discard, receive, open and shut eyes as activities of indriyas with the belief that they do not do these organic activities [5/ 8 & 5/9].

O Arjuna! He who dedicates his/her actions to the Lord and does not bother about the consequences, he/she commits no sin in whatever he/she does. As water stands on lotus leaves without being part of the leaf, so do these people perform their duties without being involved in their actions [5/10].

O Arjuna! The yogis go on their daily physical, mental and intellectual chores with the help of indriyas [very much as all ordinary people do]. But their soul is purified and they are not at all conscious of the outcome of their doings [5/11]. Those who have an inkling of contents and creams of Bhagavat Gita scream that the gist of Gita is ironical, paradoxical. At the first sight, it would seem so. The beginner may stumble and fumble that Gita blows hot and cold at the same breath. It is not ordinary perception. Gita is the dialogue between Krishna and Arjuna on this perception, this perplexity. That exactly is not so. Gita is not full of ironies or paradoxes. Gita is clear and coherent. Gita is cognate and concrete. Gita is logical, not liturgical. In pure and plain parlance, Bhagavat Gita counsels us to work, to work well and all the time. *There is no scope or reason to refrain from working. The only problem arises when we aver, assert that "I" work, that "I" am working, that "I" shall not work etc. So long you refrain from referring to "I" in, with, about your work, your action, it is well. do And you are well done in whatever you do or do not do.*

How could that be? I am writing or typing. Should I not say I am writing, typing, dictating? You are reading. Should you not say that you are reading this book? If you don't say so, what would be your reply when your friend asks on phone what you are doing? Obviously, I shall say I am typing on computer. You should say you are reading. There is nothing to hide or chide. It is simple earthly activities by literate individuals. Maybe intellectual hobby or habit by either or both of us. Maybe a superior, sensible pastime or pursuit. But the Gita prescription in chapter V, slokas 8 & 9 is that I must not be involved intensely or intimately in writing nor you be engrossed grossly or gorgeously in reading. In other words, I must be devoted diligently to writing but not declare, assert or arrogate that "I am" writing. So shall you read the treatise as sincerely and truthfully as a classic or classy exposition but never aver, announce and affirm that "I am" reading.

The sum and substance of the precepts supra, especially slokas 8 & 9 are that our indriyas, our senses, our sensory organs must be deployed, employed to perform, not go perfunctory. But they should be under leash, not at large. For instance, when you eat, you resort to the *root bhook, hit bhook, mit bhook* principle propounded by Bana Bhatta. On the contrary, if your stomach, tongue, mouth and teeth eat to the dictation and direction of your mind, then you eat exuberantly and announce emphatically and to the whole world that you have eaten this and that dish in this or that feast or hotel at the cost of this or that person on this or that occasion. If you just eat, simply eat; you simply forget what, when you ate and just ignore to tell what your lunch today or dinner tonight was.

Modern management mandarins and motivational masterminds harp on total, complete involvement on the job at hand. They exhort you to develop a sense of belonging, involvement to your organisation, to your corporation, to your employer. Track record, target and achievement are their catchwords, catchy phrases. What does Gita, the slokas supra precisely, say? Does Gita speak of easy-going, leisurely, pensionary or sinecure performance or practice? Does Gita induce you to indulge in betrayal, backbiting, sabotaging, stabbing to your organisation, employer? No, never. On the contrary, Gita advises total, complete dedication, loyalty to employer. What Gita does not approve of is cutthroat competition, mischievous manipulation and morbid manoeuvre to achieve results. Intentional, ill-meaning machinations and manoeuvres are "papa," sin. You should, need to work sincerely, not sinfully. You must perform to flourish, not perish. Yet, you must not sin, commit a sin, while working, when discharging your duties.

The metaphor in chapter V, sloka 10 quoted above is apt and eloquent. The water drop on the slippery, oily lotus leaf maintains status quo. The drop of water is not affected by the lotus leaf. It maintains its distinct identity despite its long and seemingly intimate association with the lotus leaf. After a long time when the droplets dissociates itself from the leaf, it is as crystal clear as before, not borrowing a minuscule of greenery from the leaf nor does it leave a trace of its purity, crystallinity on the leaf. Notwithstanding waterdrop's long association with the lotus leaf, the former is not influenced, affected by the latter. In other words, the droplet commits no sin from its association with the leaf. In our case, our actions, activities and the indriyas should be like water droplet on lotus leaf. To stretch the metaphor further, when there is slight shaking or moving, the droplet falls of the leaf instantly, unhesitatingly, leaving no trace of its attributes, affiliation. When we look at something for some time, it is okay we look at different aspects and attributes of the object or individual. Once we close our eyes, divert our eyes from that object or creature, we should ignore them, forget them. The object or creature should be verily like the lotus leaf, while our sight is the crystal-clear droplet.

The inference in chapter V, sloka 11 is the eye-opener. You employ your sensory and motor organs to their full potential and ensure 100 per cent capacity utilisation. But never bother about the outcome, consequences. While acting, activating, accelerating, expediting, monitoring, managing, marshalling, organising, leading, brooding; be yogic i.e. of pure-souled, of purified soul, not *jougic* i.e. complex minded, complicated-souled.

SEVENTY-FIVE

Does God give *papa* to people?

na kartṛitvaṁ na karmāṇi lokasya sṛijati prabhuḥ
na karma-phala-saṅyogaṁ svabhāvas tu pravartate

nādatte kasyachit pāpaṁ na chaiva sukṛitaṁ vibhuḥ
ajñānenāvṛitaṁ jñānaṁ tena muhyanti jantavaḥ

O Partha! The all-powerful Lord has not invested authority or competency in creature in this universe nor does he reward remuneration/returns to any action/ activity. Owing to their own nature, inherent nature some are super active/ hyper active and some reap handsome/golden dividends on their efforts/enterprises [5/14].

O Kounteya! The Lord has not created a sinner nor has He created a virtuous being. The creatures, living beings clouded with ignorance and lacking in consciousness consider/think that God has given some sinful attitudes/ traits and some others pious/virtuous buddhi and behaviour [5/15].

We were about to close our discussions on vintage verses of Bhagavat Gita. Nevertheless, the unending course of Gita forced us to wink at chapter V, sloka 10 discussed in the foregoing section. Herein, it is stated that if you surrender/ submit your actions to God, forget/ ignore about the results/ ramifications of your doing, then you are not attached to your actions nor do you commit a sin. Sin, impiety, *papa* is not plentifully referred to in the Gita because Gita is not pessimistic, negative, sadistic, satanic. It dislikes/discards discussion on *papa*. Nonetheless, *papa* pushes into Gita, nay, gushes into Bhagavat Gita. For instance, impious, inelegant, indecent, *papa* finds its place here 5/10 as in 18/66.

sarva-dharmān parityajya mām ekaṁ śharaṇaṁ vraja
ahaṁ tvāṁ sarva-pāpebhyo mokṣhayiṣhyāmi mā śhuchaḥ

Krishna exhorts Arjuna "to give up all [religions] and take refuge in Me. I shall rescue you from all *papa, papas;* do not bother."

In narrow, literal sense, Krishna advises Arjuna to shun all religions and seek asylum in Him. Since He will save Arjuna from all sins, the latter need not ponder or bother. Religion and sin should not be read in narrow, literal sense. On the contrary, these two words need be understood in a broader, deeper, philosophical, spiritual sense. Religion includes the traditional religious practices, paraphernalia as much as the various socio-cultural viewpoints. Sin includes the innocent, unintentional mischiefs and wrongdoings as much as the gross, grotesque, gruesome crimes and commissions. And sin includes your failings and dealings in compassion, donation, assistance, adherence and acceptance. The Lord protects you from all your sins, if you surrender to Him totally, not tentatively; for all time to come; not ad hoc, not pro tempore.

brahmaṇyādhāya karmāṇi saṅgaṁ tyaktvā karoti yaḥ
lipyate na sa pāpena padma-patram ivāmbhasā

Krishna counsels Arjuna that those who entrust, invest their actions in the Lord and do not bother about results are not attached to their actions and do commit no sin.

Here sin means the traditional offences and crimes that the doer commits. But the doer is acquitted of, exonerated of sins because he has not bothered about the consequences and has dedicated the deed to the Lord in the first place.

Why are some sinful and some others sinless? We in general and the gurus in particular believe that God makes us commit sins or remain sinless. It is He alone Who prompts, pampers, compels us to commit a sin, indulge in sinful doings. On the other hand, God, God alone, stops us, prevents us, forbids us from doing, indulging in sinful activities and atrocities, attributes and avocations.

This is well exemplified in Mahabharata. Duryodhana is lying half-dead, heart-broken, thighs-smashed on the banks of Vyasa Sarovar [Vyasa' Pond], the secure and sublime Sarovar, the abode of venerable Vyasa. Towards the end of the Kurukshetra battle, when Duryodhana lost his able and invincible generals like Bhishma, Drona, Karna etc to the infallible arrows of Arjuna and his 98 brothers including Dushasana to the mortal mace of Bhima, Duryodhana fled the field to hide in depths of the Pond in the laps of Laxmi, his godly mother. Krishna, the omniscient, led the Pandavas to the hideout and incited Bhima to dare Duryodhana to come out to fight or surrender. Bhima insulted Duryodhana by calling him coward, an insult to Kshatriya blood, and an unworthy Kshatriya who had fled the fighting field for fear of death.Conceited to the core for which he is called *Abhimani Managovinda*, Duryodhana rushed out of Laxmi's laps and shouted back to the Pandavas in general and Bhima in particular. Krishna counselled Bhima from heaping further insults on Duryodhana. He then in sympathetic tone and ever enigmatic smile said,

Krishna- What a bad, unfortunate state of affair for the Kaurava scion Duryodhana who had fled the fighting field to hide in a woman's sanctuary! Had you heeded to my truce proposal and parted with only five *padas [hamlets, revenue-earning villages, zamindaris]*, things would not have come to this pass.

Duryodhana- Yes Krishna! Not only your sinister smiles but also intentions, actions and inactions for that matter are intriguing, enigmatic. And cursing! Destructive too! You instigated Yudhisthira to play dice with Shakuni, knowing fully well that the former would lose miserably. You alone incited me to take possession of dear Pandava cousins in stake and drag Draupadi to the Kaurava plenary.

You excited Karna to say Draupadi was my *dasi* [maid servant]. It is you who prevailed upon Draupadi in her *swayambar* to call Karna *shutaputra* and unworthy archer. It is your machination that Draupadi said of me 'As is father, so is the son blind' to enrage me and arouse in me vengeful dislike for her. Who turned down the truce offer in Hastina royal court? You came as the Pandava emissary and spoke like their advocate. Knowing fully well that a little flattery, a small platitude would please me, make me agreeable to everything you say, you did not do that. On the other hand, you infuriated me. You silenced my superiors in the Hastina court and, to cap it all, you lunched paltry eatables at Vidura's place, snubbing my lavish royal party. You are the cause of this calamity. You cursed and smashed our Kuru clan. Who after the Pandava five? None. You conspired to kill Abhimanyu, your loving nephew, son of Subhadra. You airlifted the Pandavas to Dwaraka to save them from Ashwatthama's lethal missile, leaving the five pretty young Draupadi sons in the lurch, to the death-must arrow of Ashwatthama, didn't you? When I was on my way to meet my blindfold mother, fully naked as advised by my mother so that she sees me for the first time in life and empowers me with invincibility, who instigated me to cover my thighs? It is those vulnerable thighs that Bhima struck, shattered and defeated me. Who broke my thighs and paralysed me- Bhima or you?Your actions, advice, advocacy, assistance, admonition, admiration, abatements, abetments .... all are black. Your attitude is as black as your skin. You are shrewd and sophisticated. You are cruel and complicated, though you are called a jewel. Your sins and wrongs, your offences and overbearingness are always and well ambushed, well masked, well masqueraded. Your sins are soon whitewashed. You commit a mistake but others are accused of, cursed of those wrongdoings, those mistakes. And you commit sins but others are punished, penalised as in my case....

Duryodhana's outbursts, outpourings, pleadings appears appropriate, acceptable. But Krishna denies this in the Bhagavat Gita. On pain of pardonable repetition, let us quote,

Na karttrutwam na karmani lokasya srujati prabhuh
Na karmaphalasamyogam swabhavastu pravarttate[5/14]

na kartṛitvaṁ na karmāṇi lokasya sṛijati prabhuḥ
na karma-phala-sanyogaṁ svabhāvas tu pravartate

nādatte kasyachit pāpaṁ na chaiva sukṛitaṁ vibhuḥ
ajñānenāvṛitaṁ jñānaṁ tena muhyanti jantavaḥ

O Arjuna! Prabhu does not allot action/karma to anyone nor does He influence/ interfere in any action's outcomes. Owing to their inherent nature, people opt for their activities and hanker after their result [5/14].
O Partha! Vibhu does not give anybody sin nor anyone virtue. The people blinded by ignorance think so [5/15].

These 2 slokas cited as prologue proclaims our accountability, our responsibility to our actions/inactions, our calling/ course of action, our fortune/misfortune, our success/failures. As you sow, so you reap. It is pertinent to note that it is you who decides whether to hanker after good, lucrative outcomes or to leave things to themselves after you have discharged your duty, performed your assignment. "Prabhu" as said here is of paramount importance. Prabhu is equivalent to Lord, God or any other paramount godhead you mean, like to insert, and is still more, higher, senior, superior. So is "Vibhu". These two words synonymous with the Lord, God, travel beyond, above. Keep it in mind and do not sink in the shallow waters of your religion, sect, school, philosophy to say that your god, your lord.

The pleading and rhetoric of Duryodhana fails, vanishes, evaporates in view of these two verses. What is your view?

No eulogy, No elegy
Let us close, happily, freely

As you begin, so you end. Every beginning has an end except the One Who has no beginning nor end, nor middle.

Before finishing, I should like to say and the reader may expect to know what Gita speaks about *Happiness* that we all so sincerely seek all our life. Similarly, Liberation, *moksha,* that dominates all spiritual treatise and discussions should be briefly touched upon before we close. While Happiness is enunciated in chapter V, verse 23, Liberation is deliberated upon in chapter V, verse 28. Let us look at these two slokas.

Shaknotihaiva yah sodhum prakshariravimokshanat Kamakrodhodbhavam vegam sa yuktah sukhi narah[5/23]
śhaknotīhaiva yaḥ soḍhuṁ prāk śharīra-vimokṣhaṇāt kāma-krodhodbhavaṁ vegaṁ sa yuktaḥ sa sukhī naraḥ

O Arjuna! That person who is able to bear/tolerate the velocity/momentum arising/ erupting out of desire and anger before death is yogi/renunciate, is happy.

To be happy is perhaps not as difficult or complicated as one would be made to believe. Here important things are simplified. First of all, you should be able to bear with, not forbear, the tempo of desire and anger. In other words, you should be humps/speed-breakers on the high road of desire and anger. The time is before death, before you give up this body. If you are able to break, control the speed of desire and anger, you become renunciate, ascetic. And then happy.

Two things seem important. Desire, lust, hankering and anger are excessively bad, negative, destructive.You may have lived all your life with these two evils. You might never ever do without these two villains even towards the end, close of your life. Nonetheless, you need put a brake on the ferocious velocity of these two evils when you are about to die, going to die, going to discard this mortal frame like a worn-out apparel.

Happiness, therefore, is the ability to calm desire and anger. Happiness, in essence, is the competence to cope with lust and anger. You may or may not have lived a happy life, but will you not like to die a happy death?

You may be curious to know how can one know when he/she is going to die? You may question the wisdom of this sloka, the practicality of this sloka. It is not impracticable or utopian. It is plain and simple. Though before-death is the case here in the literal sense, it extends to the whole life. Because no one knows when one will die and because not happy death but happy life is our goal. It is easy and practicable as you have put a brake on your speedy longing, speedy anger.

How to cool, calm, subside longing, anger may raise questions. In Odia, there is a rural, popular saying, 'raise your hand but do not beat; chase the offender but do not catch hold of the fleeing fellow'. The saying is simple but sublime, superbly sensible. As men and women of flesh and blood, we are prone to provocation. And we are very likely to respond and respond swiftly and vehemently, maybe violently. Yet if we pause for a moment, stop for a while, our reaction to the provocation will be stifled, stunted, subdued. As a result, our reaction will be less violent, even non-violent or nil violent.

For example, a child throws dust or stone at me out of fun, of childish mischief. It derives childlike pleasure out of my unease, discomfiture. The more I dissuade it to refrain from its naughty play, the more it indulges with more glee and giggling. To debar it from the mischievous play, I collect a stick and run after it. Initially, the child takes it as fun. But as I articulate anger and run after it, it runs. Soon I catch hold of it and beats it in anger. The child cries and there is a commotion. Neighbours gather and chide me for being bad and cruel to a child which did what it did out of simple childish mischief.

After some time, I am offended. I regret beating the nice little child of the neighbourhood for its innocent age-worthy mischief. What should I have done to debar the child from throwing dust and boulders at me? I counselled it to stop, it is OK. I collected a stick to threaten it with beating, OK. It did not run away. I chased it, OK. I caught hold of it, OK. Then I beat it. It is not okay; it is wrong, inappropriate, inhuman, immoral. I should have feigned running after the child. It must have run out fear and have hidden itself in the safety of its home to get rid of my wrath[feigned]. That should have been the end of the matter. Alternatively, I should have made such a sham chase that I could not catch hold of it. It should have run and gone inside its home. That should have been happy end of the chapter.

To cool, calm, control, contain lust, anger, what do you need to do? You act and/or react childishly, foolishly, farcically, artificially, insincerely, idiotically; not really, sincerely, earnestly, zealously, diligently, intelligently.

How to get moksha, the true and worthy objective humans, the intelligent, conscious, conscionable creatures on earth?

Yatendriyamanorbuddhirmunirmokshaparayanah
Bigatechhabhayakrodhao yah sada mukta eva sah[5/28]

yatendriya-mano-buddhir munir mokṣa-parāyaṇaḥ
vigatecchā-bhaya-krodho yaḥ sadā mukta eva saḥ

O Arjuna! He who has controlled/reined his indriyas/ senses, mind and intellect, keeps mum like a sage minding moksha [from samsara, this life], has given up desire/ ambitions/aspirations, fear and anger, is always Mukta, freed, liberated.

Happiness is not the venue; it is the avenue. Happiness is not destination, destiny; it is the distance to travel, the road to tread upon, the highway to traverse. Happiness is not the end; it is the means. Happiness is not acquisitive or possessive, nor causative; it is positive, creative. Happiness is not material, mundane, mechanical; it is mental, psychological, intellectual. Happiness consists in being, not getting, having. Happiness is infinite, immeasurable, illimitable, indefinite, ever-lasting. We say, "She is happy". If we stop there, then it is okay. If we say she is happy because she topped the Indian combined civil services recruitment examinations, 2024, then the happiness is limited, temporary, tangible, changeable, surreal and may evaporate sooner or later. And that conditional, circumstantial, immediate, measurable happiness may turn to failure, disaster sooner or later.

Real happiness comes from nothing, comes with nothing, consists of nothing, contained in nothing. In fact, it does not come or go. It is and it stays put. It will be pertinent to reproduce the poem "The Enchanted Shirt" by John Hay [1838-1905] to have an inkling of happiness. The poem quoted ad verbatim,

"THE King was sick. His cheek was red
And his eye clear and bright;

He ate and drank with a kingly zest,
And peacefully snored at night.
But he said he was sick, and a king should know,
And doctors came by the score.
They did not cure him. He cut off their heads
And sent to the schools for more.
At last two famous doctors came,
And one was as poor as a rat, --
He had passed his life in studious toil,
And never found time to grow fat.
The other had never looked in a book;
His patients gave him no trouble,
If they recovered they paid him well,
If they died their heirs paid double.
Together they looked at the royal tongue,
As the King on his couch reclined;
In succession they thumped his august chest,
But no trace of disease could find.
The old sage said, 'You're as sound as a nut.'
'Hang him up' roared the King in a gale, --
In a ten-knot gale of royal rage;
The other leech grew a shade pale;
But he pensively rubbed his sagacious nose, -
And thus his prescription ran, --
The King will be well, if he sleeps one night
In the Shirt of a Happy Man.
Wide o'er the realm the couriers rode,
And fast their horses ran,
And many they saw, and to many they spoke,
But they found no Happy Man.
They found poor men who would fain be rich,

And rich who thought they were poor;
And men who twisted their waists in stays,
And women that short hose wore.
They saw two men by the roadside sit,
And both bemoaned their lot;
For one had buried his wife, he said,
And the other one had not.
At last as they came to the village gate,
A beggar lay whistling there;
He whistled and sang in the soft June air.
The weary couriers paused and looked
At the scamp so blithe and gay;
And one of them said, 'Heaven save you friend!
You seem to be happy to-day.'
'Oh, yes, fair sirs,' the rascal laughed,
And his voice rang free and glad,
'An idle man has much to do
That he has no time to be sad.'
'This is our man,' the courier said;
'Our luck has led us aright.
I will give you a hundred ducats, friend,
For the loan of your shirt to-night.'
The merry blackguard lay back
on the grass,
And laughed till his face was black;
'I would do it, God wot,' and he
roared with the fun,
'But I haven't a shirt to my back.'
Each day to the King the reports came in
Of his unsuccessful spies,
And the sad panorama human woes

Passed daily under his eyes.
And he grew ashamed of his useless life,
And his maladies hatched in gloom;
He opened his windows and let the air
Of the free heaven into his room.
And out he went to the world and toiled
In his own appointed way;
And the people blessed him, the land was glad,
And the King was well and gay.

It is evident from the story that the king was hale and hearty, was well physically. But he was mentally, intellectually unwell, feeling unease and sickly. This may have been due to his indifference and apathy to his kingly duties on the one hand and due to his excessive, inordinate sensual pleasure on the other. Steeped in sensuous, indulgent extremity, he felt sick. He became really sick; not feigned sickness for the fun of it, for the heck of it. The sham sickness, the escapable sickness became real, melancholic, morbid, mad disease when he called scores of physicians to cure him. The well-versed physicians were supposed to fail when the king was not physically unwell. How can they cure the incurable mental malaise that the king suffered from owing to his indolence, sloth and sensual indulgence?

The bluff doctor that saw plights of studious, serious medical practitioners called the king's bluff by prescribing an unavailable, utopian drug. The poet has italicised the prescription and has started the important words, "happy", "man" and "shirt" with capital letters. This suggests that there is no happy man and a shirt, the apparel of the man does not make one happy. The couriers searched for the "Happy Man's Shirt" to fail miserably. The one Happy

Man had not a Shirt for his back. We learn the lesson that possessions make one unhappy. The king had everything he wanted, wished at his disposal but was unhappy. The rural beggar, vagabond, tramp, on the other hand, was happy because he had nothing of his own, not even the minimum clothing. The other and more important lesson was the king's indolence and lethargic attitude. He did not bother about the state affairs. He was unconcerned of the weal and woe of his subjects, soldiers and staff nor thought of improvising the status quo.

Happiness and emancipation are interlinked, intertwined. In fact, the two are one; or, at least, two sides of the same coin. As with happiness, so with moksha, you cannot have it, acquire it, possess it, own it. As a matter of fact, both are not objects or concepts, parts or precepts or practices.

From time immemorial, it is stated that the fourfold objects/objectives of human life are—Dharma, Artha, Kama, Moksha. A full, fulfilled life means to have owned all these four. Of the four, Artha and Kama signify material, mundane success and sufficiency. A capable, competent human can have these in this life. Dharma is not material, mundane access or achievement. Dharma is the spiritual, religious achievement, attainment. Available and attainable in earthly life, dharma is mainly meant for after life. Moksha is sought after life. Moksha is the highest, most supreme goal and achievement. Sages, sannyasis, enunciates, ascetics, hermits, mendicants set their eye and attention on moksha.

As it is all people wish moksha along with other earthly successes and assets. The popular Sanskrit sloka runs—

Bina dainyena jivanam

Anayesena maranam
Dehante tava sannidhyam
Dehi mam Parameshwarah.

O Lord! Give me a life without destitution, death without disease and suffering, and your company/custody after death.

This sloka covers the fourfold goals/accomplishments of human life. It compasses Dharma, Artha, Kama, Moksha in simple language.

We do not know how many us would avail of moksha. Even our forehead that contains the destiny mark does not mention of moksha. A story in this respect is enlightening.

A destitute brahmin lived abegging. He has no children nor any property or possession. All he collected during the day was cooked by his wife for the one-meal-dinner-a-day. The brahmin was scholarly and could read even the inscrutable writing on the forehead. One evening while returning from his begging errand, he rested near a cemetery for a while. Casually, he lifted a scull lying nearby and read the writing on the scull's forehead. It ran-

Bhojanam yatrakatra
Shayanam hatamandapam
Maranam Gomatitire
Upare kim bhavisyashi .

The skull told that the owner-person could eat whatever wherever he got. He slept on the village promontory [as he had no home]. He died on the bank of Gomati. What would happen there after?

The wise brahmin wondered about the poor fellow's fate, who could not get two square meals a day, had no hearth and home so had to sleep on the village promontory which was noisy and free for all. Finally, he died on the bank of Gomati and was cremated by do-gooders. Except for the skull, no trace of the destitute could be seen. What would happen next to the hapless fellow?

To see the poor fellow's future, the brahmin took the skull and hid it in his thatch without knowledge of his wife. He went abegging as usual and back home, looked at the concealed skull stealthily. It remained so for days, months. Initially, the brahmin wife had no inkling of it. After some days, she observed the brahmin's queer behaviour in looking at something unfailingly. To her query, the brahmin lied. But she was not satisfied with the false reply of the brahmin. For some days, she was disturbed that the brahmin had hid something suspicious and kept the secret to his chest. During these days, their economic condition was deteriorating day by day. The brahmin wife suspected that the brahmin was practicing tantra as a result of which they were unwell in body, mind and day to day living.

One day, during the brahmin's absence, she made a thorough search to find the frightening, ugly skull concealed in the thatch. She thought for a while and inferred that their misfortune had worsened since the skull was lodged in their hut. She guessed that the brahmin was practicing tantra at the dead of night without her knowledge. But his tantra was failing as a result Kali is enraged and causing them all harms. Infuriated, she pounded the skull to fine powder and threw it in the village cemetery.

For some days, the brahmin did not look at the hidden skull, believing fully well that it was intact. Say, after a month one evening, he looked the concealed skull and suspected its disappearance. From all sides and all angles, he looked but found no trace of the skull. His wife saw his discomfiture and asked,

    Brahmini- What are you looking for so sheepishly?
    Brahmin- Nothing
    Brahmini- Strange! You are looking at, searching for something and hiding it from me. If you say what it is, I shall help you locate the lost valuable, shan't I?.
    Brahmin- Hey, no valuable! Useless, trash!
    Brahmini- Then why worry and search so vigorously? Certainly something precious and prized but you think I shall divulge the secret out for which you will be punished, condemned or criticized. Ah! We are man and wife, together for all our life. I am with you through thick and thin, through sun and rain and you take care of me in good time and misfortune. What secret it is that you will not disclose to me?"

After a bit bickering and mutual accusing, the brahmin was compelled to disclose his well-kept secret. The *brahmini [brahmana's wife] was* convinced of the credible explanation. Now it was brahmin's turn to inquire what happened to the scull. Initially afraid of her fault of smashing and powdering the scull, the brahmini floated a few false narratives. Later, ready to confess and bear with the brahmin's ire and recrimination, she vented the truth out. The brahmin kept his cool and went toward the cemetery. His wife followed to show where exactly she flung the scull powder. By then, no trace or track of the scull could be found. The brahmin looked skyward and sighed vacantly.

    That was the finality of the pitiable wretch that did

not have a good meal to eat, a comfortable bed to sleep all his life, and died a poor death on the bank of Gomati. The wretched fellow got nothing of the sort cited in the sloka supra, "Bina dainyena.........dehi ma Parameshwarah."

Moksha as mentioned in 5/28, Bhagavat Gita, is earthy, earthly; achievable, obtainable in this life, in the samsara and amid the din and bustle of worldly affair. You do not have to work for it. On the contrary, you have to be. Moksha is not an act or achievement, a precept or practice, a philosophy or prayer. It is a state, a condition of being, of your being. Moksha is not what; moksha is who.

We have read/heard of jivanmukta to mean sages like Vyasa, Janak, Shuka, Shankar and so on. It is contradictory or misleading to say jivanmukta, though useful to instil the concept in the naïve or novice, beginner or foreigner. When Mukta, one is not conscious of living or dying. To him life and death is the one and the same. To him, life and death are illusion, unreal, phantom. To him living is dying and vice versa. To him, there is no distinction between vice and virtue.

Who is jivanmukta? He/she who has reined, controlled, leashed, subjugated, subjected, manned, mangled, mastered, marshalled his/her senses, sense and motor organs, mind and intellect; is interested in/ inclined to moksha, quiet and silent like a sage; is devoid of ambition/aspiration, fear and anger, is jivanmukta, Mukta, moksha. He/she is freed, liberated, emancipated. He/she is free, frank, fearless, full, filled, still, stilled.

END

Black Eagle Books

www.blackeaglebooks.org
info@blackeaglebooks.org

Black Eagle Books, an independent publisher, was founded as a nonprofit organization in April, 2019. It is our mission to connect and engage the Indian diaspora and the world at large with the best of works of world literature published on a collaborative platform, with special emphasis on foregrounding Contemporary Classics and New Writing.

www.ingramcontent.com/pod-product-compliance
Lightning Source LLC
Chambersburg PA
CBHW060546080526
44585CB00013B/464